A Problem-Solving Revolution

MAKING CHANGE HAPPEN IN STATE COURTS

EDITED BY GREG BERMAN, AUBREY FOX
AND ROBERT V. WOLF

CENTER FOR COURT INNOVATION
NEW YORK, NEW YORK

Published by the Center for Court Innovation. Printed in the United States of America

First Edition

Library of Congress Control Number: 2004111118

ISBN: 0-9759505-0-9

Contents

Acknowledgements

The Center for Court Innovation is the product of a unique public-private partnership between the New York State Unified Court System and the Fund for the City of New York. This partnership would not be possible without the vision, leadership and on-going support of New York State Chief Judge Judith S. Kaye, New York State Chief Administrative Judge Jonathan Lippman and Fund for the City of New York President Mary McCormick.

The essays contained in this collection were underwritten by a range of funding sources including the Bureau of Justice Assistance at the U.S. Department of Justice (Chapters Two, Four, Five and Six), the California Administrative Office of the Courts (Chapter Nine) and the Open Society Institute (Chapter Ten).

The publication of this book was underwritten by the Bureau of Justice Assistance, Office of Justice Programs, U.S. Department of Justice through grants 2002-DD-BX-0046 and 1998-DC-VX-K007. Special thanks to the U.S. Congress and the members of the New York delegation for their support of the Center for Court Innovation's budget request.

Please note that the opinions expressed in this book reflect those of the authors and not necessarily those of the funders.

Introduction

GREG BERMAN

Written by Malcolm Gladwell, *The Tipping Point* is a book about how simple ideas and humble beginnings can sometimes lead to major changes in the world around us. As Gladwell describes it:

> *How does a novel written by an unknown author end up as national bestseller? Why do teens smoke in greater and greater numbers, when every single person in the country knows that cigarettes kill? Why is word-of-mouth so powerful? What makes TV shows like Sesame Street so good at teaching kids how to read? . . . the answer to all those questions is the same. It's that ideas and behavior and messages and products sometimes behave just like outbreaks of infectious disease. They are social epidemics. . . . The virtue of an epidemic . . . is that just a little input is enough to get it started, and it can spread very, very quickly.*[1]

In recent years, state courts have offered up another case study to go along with the ones that Gladwell documents in *The Tipping Point*. It is the story of problem-solving courts.

The story begins back in 1989. Miami, Florida, is the location. A group of frustrated system players—lawyers, judges and administrators—gathers together to discuss drugs and crime. In particular, they are concerned about the problem of drug-fueled recidivism—the fact that the courts seem to be recycling the same offenders through the system over and over again.

In an attempt to address this problem, the group arrives at a novel solution: a specialized "drug court" that will handle exclusively cases involving non-violent, addicted defendants. Defendants will be mandated to receive long-term treatment. Their progress will be closely monitored by a judge through regular appearances in court and frequent drug testing. Success (defined as achieving sobriety and leading a crime-free life) will be rewarded with graduation exercises and the dismissal of criminal charges against the defendant. Failure (repeated relapse, continued criminal behavior) will be punished with graduated sanctions, including jail.

The Miami drug court planners had relatively modest aspirations for their initiative. They did not set out to change the face of American jurisprudence or launch an international movement. They simply sought to respond creatively to a challenging local problem. By almost any measure, they succeeded: researchers documented that the Miami experiment helped reduce both substance abuse and recidivism among participants. Results like these attracted attention not just locally but nationally and internationally as well.

Less than 15 years later, it is possible to trace the remarkable trajectory of the drug court idea. The common-sense approach of combining punishment and help forged by the Miami planners has picked up momentum year after year. Today, there are more than a thousand drug courts in operation in the United States, with hundreds more in the planning stages.[2] The drug court model has also been adopted in England, Guam, Australia, Brazil, Canada, Scotland, Ireland and other countries. The annual conference of the National Association of Drug Court Professionals attracts thousands of participants. And the U.S. Department of Justice—with the active support of Congress—provides tens of millions of dollars to drug courts each year.

As impressive as these accomplishments are, they just begin to scratch the surface. The Miami experiment may have come first, but it is far from the only new model of court administration to emerge over the past two decades. In Miami's wake have come hundreds of other new projects that have sought to address specific problems faced by the courts. These include community courts that seek to improve the quality of life in crime-plagued neighborhoods, domestic violence courts that enhance the delivery of services to victims and mental health courts that link mentally ill offenders to community-based treatment.

While most of these courts deal with the problem of addiction only peripherally if at all, they share something important with the initial drug court: a problem-solving orientation. Each of the new, specialized courts seeks not just to process cases, but to solve the problems facing victims, defendants and communities. They are, in a word, problem-solving courts.

From the foundation provided by the early drug court pioneers, the idea of problem-solving justice has spread quickly. All 50 state court chief justices and state court administrators have formally endorsed the concept. So too has the American Bar Association.

What makes the story of problem-solving innovation truly remarkable is that it has occurred within a branch of government (the judiciary) and a profession (the law) that are not known for embracing change. Far from it. Judges and attorneys tend to see themselves as upholding centuries-old traditions rather than responding creatively to emerging problems. Any effort to promote reform within state courts not only must overcome the usual obstacles to change (limited resources, bureaucratic inertia, etc.), but also the institution's conception of itself. It is a measure of both the persuasiveness of the first generation of problem-solving advocates and the severity of the legal and social challenges facing state courts that problem-solving courts have replicated as quickly as they have.

The battle is far from over, however. While there are more than 2,000 problem-solving courts in operation or planning in the United States, these projects remain, for the most part, at the margins of state court systems. The challenge that now faces advocates of problem-solving justice is not how to create additional drug courts or community courts or mental health courts—they've proven they can do that. Rather, the challenge that increasingly confronts the field is how to spread the principles and practices that have proven successful in problem-solving courts throughout state court systems. It is the challenge of going to scale with reform. It is the challenge of changing the institutional culture of the courts.

Going to scale with an innovative idea or practice in any field is difficult. The social policy literature is littered with isolated success stories: an exemplary inner-city school with high test scores or a cost-effective nurse visitation program that raises infant mortality. The problem is navigating the transition from small to large: from successful experiment to system reform. Unfortunately, most innovative practices fail to make this transition.

While mainstreaming innovation is hard for any bureaucracy, it's particularly hard for state courts. Many judges are elected officials, and thus are not directly answerable to court administrators. Even those who aren't elected typically serve long terms. The American tradition of judicial independence offers perhaps the most significant challenge to changing institutional behavior. Judges rightly view efforts to influence their behavior on or off the bench with skepticism.

And then there is the reality that judges are far from the only players involved. Courts are by their nature collaborative enterprises. System reform inevitably requires the active endorsement of clerks, defense attorneys, prosecutors and other players, each of which have their own professional culture, their own internal politics and their own institutional values.

While the obstacles to lasting change are significant, so too are the potential rewards. After all, problem-solving courts have shown that, when executed properly, they are capable of changing the behavior of offenders, improving victim safety, reducing crime and enhancing public confidence in justice.[3] These are results well worth building upon.

This book is an effort to do just that. *A Problem-Solving Revolution* explores the practical, political and conceptual challenges faced by states as they seek to reform their court systems. Those looking for silver bullets or instant gratification will be disappointed. *A Problem-Solving Revolution* does not contain explicit policy prescriptions or step-by-step models for innovators to follow. Nor does it contain a thorough exploration of the origins, philosophical underpinnings and results of the problem-solving movement (for this, please see *Good Courts: The Case for Problem-Solving Justice* forthcoming in 2005 from The New Press).

What *A Problem-Solving Revolution* does contain is some of the best thinking from the Center for Court Innovation, an independent, non-profit think tank that seeks to improve the performance of state courts. Over the past decade, the Center for Court Innovation has played an active role in promoting problem-solving reform. It has done this in two principal ways. In New York, thanks to the leadership of Chief Judge Judith S. Kaye and Chief Administrative Judge Jonathan Lippman, the Center serves as the independent research and development arm of the state court system. In this capacity, the Center for Court Innovation has helped to plan and implement a wide range of problem-solving experiments, including drug courts, community courts, domestic violence courts, mental health courts, integrated domestic violence courts, family treatment courts, youth courts, reentry courts and others.

The Center plays a role beyond New York's borders as well, seeking to contribute to the national (and international) conversation about justice. It does this by performing original research, convening roundtables that bring together leading thinkers and practitioners and writing for scholarly and professional journals. Samples of all of this work can be found within these pages.

The essays contained in *A Problem-Solving Revolution* were written by a range of authors from the Center for Court Innovation over the course of the past several years. Taken together, they offer an overview of both the opportunities for large-scale problem-solving reform and the challenges that will inevitably confront efforts to achieve this reform. Along the way, *A Problem-Solving Revolution* poses a series of provocative questions: What are the elements of problem-solving courts that are most easily replicable? How might these components be implemented within traditional courts rather than specialized courtrooms? And is it possible for every court to be a problem-solving court? The future of problem-solving justice may well depend on the answers.

Essays

The chapters in this section focus not only on the key ingredients of problem solving, but on how some states are attempting to integrate at least some of these ingredients in their courts in a systematic way. In Chapter One, Greg Berman looks at some of the practices that judges themselves have identified as most transferable from problem-solving courts to conventional courts. He then discusses six strategic investments that advocates of problem solving might want to consider as they seek to influence the culture of state courts over the long haul.

In Chapter Two, Aubrey Fox and Robert V. Wolf analyze efforts in four states to support the development of drug courts. The authors outline what factors have played a role in the growth of drug courts to date and what steps are being taken to promote successful integration of the drug court model into statewide systems. They conclude with a look at the lessons gleaned so far from the institutionalization experiment.

In Chapter Three, John Feinblatt, Berman and Fox take a detailed look at New York Chief Judge Judith S. Kaye's plan to adopt drug court principles in courthouses across the state. The authors, writing in 2000, look at both the challenges and opportunities that confronted Kaye's ambitious plan shortly after it was announced.

CHAPTER ONE

The Hardest Sell? Problem-Solving Justice and the Challenges of Statewide Implementation

GREG BERMAN

Visitors to the Red Hook Community Justice Center in Brooklyn, New York, are often overwhelmed by what they find there. That's not surprising—after all, the Justice Center is designed to be a state-of-the-art experiment in problem-solving justice.

Located in the heart of a low-income, predominantly minority neighborhood, the Justice Center is the nation's first multi-jurisdictional community court. An official branch of the New York State Unified Court System, the Justice Center handles criminal, civil and family cases that would otherwise be addressed in multiple courthouses. Operating out of a refurbished parochial school, a single judge hears cases involving drugs, quality-of-life crime, delinquent youth, domestic violence and landlord-tenant disputes. Offenders are linked to a wide range of on-site services (e.g., drug treatment, job training, GED classes) and are mandated to pay back the neighborhood through visible community restitution projects (e.g., painting over graffiti, cleaning local parks, fixing broken windows). Compliance with these alternative sanctions is rigorously monitored—the judge requires offenders to return to court regularly to report on their progress.

Like the other first-generation problem-solving courts—which include drug courts, domestic violence courts, mental health courts and family treatment courts—the Red Hook Community Justice Center seeks to achieve several goals simultaneously. First and foremost, it is designed to make a difference in Red Hook, improving public safety and bolstering public confidence in justice. But the project has broader ambitions as well. The Justice Center is intended to be a conversation-starter, encouraging practitioners around the country to re-think business as usual in the courts and to test new approaches to cases where legal issues and social problems are inextricably intertwined.

Unfortunately, it is not uncommon for visitors' first reaction to Red Hook to be: "We can't do this in ________ [pick your city]." That's an understandable response to the new technology, architecture, on-site services and staffing resources at Red Hook, but it is not exactly the reaction that the project is intended to provoke.

It may be unrealistic—for reasons of philosophy or resources or political will—for most jurisdictions to replicate the Red Hook Community Justice Center model wholesale, but that doesn't mean that other places can't adopt some of the problem-solving principles and practices that Red Hook has tested. All of which begs the question: What are the elements of a problem-solving court like Red Hook that are most easily replicable? And how might these components be implemented within conventional state courts rather than specialized, stand-alone courtrooms?

More and more, these are the kinds of questions that are occupying our thinking at the Center for Court Innovation. We are far from alone in grappling with these issues, however. Given the increasingly well-documented results of problem-solving courts, court systems across the country are also trying to come to grips with the problem-solving phenomenon and how it fits within the regular administration of justice.

One such court system is California's, which has made a significant investment in what is known locally as "collaborative justice." Several years ago, the California Administrative Office of the Courts established a Collaborative Justice Courts Advisory Committee, which was charged with, among other things, looking at the application of problem-solving approaches on a statewide basis.

Focus Groups

Recognizing a shared interest in "going to scale" with court innovation, in 2003 the California Administrative Office of the Courts and the Center for Court Innovation embarked upon a unique partnership designed to gather more information about how some of the practices associated with specialized, problem-solving courts might be applied within regular state courts.

Together, we convened a series of focus groups in both New York and California with judges who had presided over problem-solving courts. All told, 35 judges from drug courts, domestic violence courts, mental health courts and other specialized, problem-solving courtrooms participated in the study. While all of the judges had experience in problem-solving courts, all had since gone on to sit in "regular" criminal courts.

Each of the focus groups featured broad-ranging conversation. At the most basic level, the underlying question driving the discussions was: Is it possible to uncouple problem solving from specialization? That is, is it possible to practice problem solving outside of the specialized courtroom setting? Encouragingly, the answer to this question appears to be "yes." Participants identified a number of practices that could be transferred from problem-solving courts to conventional courts, including:

Problem-Solving Orientation

Problem-solving courts require a significant shift in judicial orientation, demanding that judges measure their success in new ways. The operative question in most criminal courts is fairly straightforward: guilty or not guilty? By contrast, in a problem-solving court, judges are encouraged to ask an expanded array of questions: How can we improve public safety given the facts of this case? How do we address the harm to victims? What are the underlying problems of the defendant and how can we address them? The focus group participants suggested that this kind of problem-solving orientation could be adopted by judges in a variety of court settings.

Social Service Integration

Problem-solving courts have sought to expand the menu of sanctioning options available to judges by creating new links with community-based social service providers (drug treatment, job training, adult education, anger management, etc). The focus group judges suggested that improving access to, and coordination of, social services was crucial to doing problem-solving within conventional courts.

Interaction with Defendants

Rather than rely on prosecutors and defenders for all of their information, problem-solving judges often directly engage defendants as part of their effort to encourage behavior modification. The focus group judges regarded this as one of the easiest practices to transfer to other types of court calendars.

Judicial Monitoring

Problem-solving courts rely on ongoing judicial supervision to help ensure the compliance of offenders with community-based sanctions. While acknowledging the time limitations of practicing judges, focus group participants thought that judges in conventional state courts could be encouraged to promote greater accountability in alternative sanctions by requiring offenders to return to court to report on their progress.

Redefining Adversarialism

Problem-solving courts have asked whether it is possible to achieve better outcomes in selected cases by reducing the adversarial nature of the courtroom and encouraging prosecutors and defenders to craft mutually agreeable case resolutions. There was a fair amount of conversation about this subject in the focus groups, with the consensus being that Family Court offered a particularly ripe area to promote increased collaboration among courtroom advocates.

Obstacles

So what's the bad news? Participants in the focus group identified a number of significant obstacles to the spread of problem-solving justice. Generally, they can be grouped into two major categories. The first is resources. Effective problem solving takes both time and money. Who is going to pay for the kinds of tools—technology, staffing, social service provision—that problem solving requires?

The second major hurdle is philosophical. Problem solving in the courts requires the active engagement of attorneys and judges, many of them deeply invested in the traditional approach to case processing. How do we convince them that problem solving isn't antithetical to American legal values, that courts can perform their traditional roles—weighing the merits of each case, safeguarding the rights of individual citizens and ensuring that laws are obeyed—while also attempting to address the problems of individuals and communities?

As the focus groups make clear, courts are by design the most tradition-oriented of our government institutions. But this is by no means the end of the obstacles. Court systems are also sprawling bureaucracies that do not lend themselves to centralized control. A number of factors—including the fact that many judges are elected, the importance of preserving the independence of the judiciary, and the interdependent nature of court systems, which require the active participation of numerous players (e.g., prosecutors and defenders)—stand in the way of any reform idea, no matter how good, spreading quickly and broadly throughout a state court system.

All of which is a long way around to saying that cultural change within the courts is going to take time—and it won't come easy. Replicating discrete problem-solving courts is one thing. Attempting to spread problem-solving values, principles and approaches throughout a state court system is quite another.

So, is spreading problem solving the judicial equivalent of selling fiscal restraint to George Steinbrenner? Is it, in fact, the hardest of hard sells?

Six Strategic Investments

Recognizing the challenges, we have identified six strategic investments that advocates of problem solving—both those within the courts (judges, attorneys, administrators) and those outside the courts (foundations, think tanks, academics)—might want to consider as they seek to influence the culture of state courts over the long haul:

Information

At the core of the problem-solving approach is a reliance on data to identify problems, improve operations, promote accountability and document results. Institutionalizing problem solving will require a deep commitment to data collection, analysis and dissemination. One of the best ways to promote problem solving is to build effective management information systems and to create a new set of performance measures for courts. This means providing administrators with regular research reports that detail not just how many cases are handled and how quickly, but problem-solving indicators as well:

How many individuals received treatment mandates? How many were linked to community service? What was their compliance? How many have been rearrested for new crimes? By asking these questions on a regular basis, administrators would begin to change the institutional culture of the court system.

Education/Training

Institutionalizing problem solving will require judges, clerks, attorneys, court officers and other court players to change their standard operating practice. You can't ask professionals, many of whom have been in their current jobs for decades, to do this without showing them how—and why. Training is crucial. States should develop standard curricula to introduce all judges to problem solving. These could include the history of problem solving, the underlying philosophy and a detailed exploration of the methods employed by problem-solving judges. Curricula could also include a component on judicial ethics to help define the boundaries of appropriate judicial behavior in this new context. States should invest in training clerks and court administrators in problem solving as well.

Incentives

State court administrators have a particularly important role to play if problem solving is going to spread more broadly. First and foremost, they can use their bully pulpit to explain the value of the problem-solving approach and encourage its practice. Just as importantly, they can reward those who engage in problem solving. A variety of incentives are possible, including salary increases, public recognition, choice assignments/promotion, travel opportunities and prime office space. Using these kinds of levers aggressively will send a strong signal to those within a state court system that problem-solving work is valued.

Ongoing R&D

History tells us that today's innovation is tomorrow's conventional wisdom. To stay at the cutting edge, state court systems must continue to invest in seeking out new ideas, questioning accepted practices and testing new approaches even as they attempt to go to scale with problem-solving innovation. In this way, they can guard against the danger of institutionalization becoming bureaucratization. One of the lessons from statewide implementation efforts in other fields is the value of creating an intermediary authority charged with the responsibility of promoting the idea of change—providing technical assistance, disseminating best practices and serving as an information clearinghouse.

Legal Curriculum

Because today's students are tomorrow's judges and attorneys, law schools are a crucial vehicle for advancing problem solving. Already, problem solving has started to sneak into law schools on an ad-hoc basis thanks to judges and other adjunct faculty. The trick is to figure out how to build on this progress to make problem solving part of the standard legal education across the country.

Communications

The court system doesn't operate in a vacuum. It is affected by a variety of external forces, including policymakers in the executive and legislative branches, the media and public opinion (not to mention the opinions of those who staff the courts). For all of these reasons, it is important to have a communications strategy in place to support the institutionalization of problem solving. This means looking for every possible opportunity—public service announcements, op-eds, public events—to spread the gospel of problem-solving justice.

Over time, these kinds of investments have the potential to achieve a significant shift in the orientation of state courts. It is important to make clear, however, that even if all of these dominoes fall into place, there are limits to how far the problem-solving approach can realistically extend. It is difficult to imagine that every judge in every courtroom across an entire state is going to engage in something that looks like problem-solving justice in every case. It is also difficult to imagine that state courts will want to abandon the idea of specialization entirely—there is likely to be an ongoing need for special approaches to certain kinds of problem cases.

Perhaps the best analogy for how problem solving might spread comes from the world of art history. As law professor Bruce Winick has pointed out, there are interesting parallels between problem-solving courts and the Impressionist movement. The advent of Impressionism—which was widely reviled by critics at the start—didn't result in every painter suddenly producing art that looked exactly like Monet's. Rather, over time, painters began to take certain elements from Impressionism—the use of color, the choice of subject matter, a move away from strict Realism—and apply them to their own work. As the focus groups highlight, there are a range of problem-solving elements that might be spread—and indeed, are already being spread—through the judiciary in a similar fashion.

Judges' Survey

Encouragingly, it is worth noting that the 35 judges who participated in the focus groups are hardly alone in their interest in problem solving. A few years back, we commissioned a survey by the University of Maryland's Survey Research Center. More than 500 criminal court judges, randomly selected, participated in a phone survey. While most were unfamiliar with the term "problem-solving court," they were broadly supportive of a range of problem-solving activities. For example:

- Participants supported treatment as an alternative to incarceration for addicted, nonviolent offenders (77 percent agreed that treatment was more effective than jail).

- Judges overwhelmingly agreed that the bench should be involved in reducing drug abuse among defendants (91 percent).

- Judges cited the need for more information about past violence when deciding bail and sentences in domestic violence cases (90 percent agreed).

- Sixty-three percent of the judges surveyed said they should be more involved with community groups in addressing neighborhood safety and quality-of-life concerns.

All of this runs counter to the popular assumption that judges, concerned with neutrality and independence, are unwilling to engage with communities or address the problems of individual defendants and victims.

Moreover, a 2001 survey by the National Center for State Courts found strong support—particularly among African-American and Hispanic respondents—for common problem-solving strategies, including the hiring of treatment staff and social workers, bringing offenders back to court to report on their progress in treatment, coordinating the work of local treatment agencies to help offenders and bringing in relevant outside experts to help courts make more informed decisions. The report concluded:

> *A solid majority of the public backs new court and judicial roles associated with problem solving. Support for these new roles is strongest among African Americans and Latinos. For example, more than 80 percent of those groups support courts' hiring counselors and social workers. The highly positive response of African Americans to changes that would increase the involvement of the courts in people's lives is a marked contrast with the negative views African Americans generally have of judges and the courts.*[1]

Even taken together, the existing research into public attitudes and judicial attitudes toward problem-solving courts just begins to scratch the surface of what we might learn about this new approach. Going forward, it is worth testing some of the operating assumptions of problem-solving advocates with regard to procedural fairness (how do defendants perceive problem-solving courts?), job satisfaction (are judges and attorneys who practice in problem-solving settings more satisfied with their jobs than those who do not?) and public confidence in justice (how does interacting with a problem-solving court affect citizens' perceptions of courts?).

While there is much work to be done, it is already possible to say with a fair degree of confidence that there is a growing number of people, both inside and outside the court system, who are interested in exploring new approaches to justice. If problem-solving courts don't have judges and citizens on the same page yet, they at least have them reading from the same book. And that's good news indeed.

CHAPTER TWO

The Future of Drug Courts: How States are Mainstreaming the Drug Court Model

AUBREY FOX AND ROBERT V. WOLF

If history could be encapsulated in headlines, the early years of the drug court movement might be summed up as follows:

1989:

"Dade County Experiments with Court Program for Drug Offenders"

1997:

"Drug Courts Proliferate As Jurisdictions Try to Duplicate Florida's Success"

These two imaginary headlines tell as concisely as possible the story of the drug court model. Drug courts, which offered state courts a new way to handle drug-addicted defendants, proliferated rapidly after the first court opened in Miami: from one court in 1989, to 300 courts in 1997, to 1,042 drug courts (and 429 more in the planning stages) by 2003.[1] But the numbers do

This essay was originally published in May 2004 by the Center for Court Innovation as a white paper under the same title. Its publication was supported by the Bureau of Justice Assistance, Office of Justice Programs, U.S. Department of Justice. Points of view and opinions in this chapter do not necessarily represent the official position or policies of the U.S. Department of Justice. In an effort to minimize the use of endnotes, only information obtained from previously published material is cited. Endnotes are not provided for quotations derived from interviews with one or both authors.

not tell the whole story. The headline today would not be: "Drug Courts Continue to Proliferate." Rather, the headline would reflect the fact that drug courts are now entering a new phase. It might go something like this:

2004:

"Drug Courts—Once a Novelty—Now Becoming Business as Usual in Many States"

The phrase "business as usual," of course, connotes bureaucracy and a lack of innovation—precisely the sort of things that drug court practitioners have long labored against. But the reality is that any new idea in any area of social policy that has proven as popular as drug courts eventually confronts such a phase: either it gets absorbed in some way by the existing system or it gets discarded as a passing fad.

Take juvenile courts. The first juvenile court was created in Cook County, Illinois, in 1899; a quarter century later, juvenile courts had spread across the country. Today, with a few notable exceptions, the principle that young people should be treated differently than adults by the criminal justice system still holds.

And yet juvenile courts are the exception to the rule. The social policy literature is littered with isolated successes: an exemplary inner-city school with high test scores or a cost-effective nurse visitation program that lowers infant mortality rates. Unfortunately, these programs appear to work in spite of the systems in which they are located, not because of them. Most fail to navigate the transition from small to large, from successful experiment to system reform.

'Going to Scale' Is Difficult

So why did juvenile courts become so widely adopted while so many other small-scale experiments fade away? The reality is that "going to scale" with an innovative idea or practice in any field is difficult. In writing about the challenges of moving innovations from a small scale to a larger scale, Lisbeth Schorr, an expert on social policy innovations, has noted that there is the tendency for policymakers to "discover one isolated success after another, only to abandon it, dilute it, or dismember it before it can reach more than a few."[2] To Schorr, successful institutionalization takes far more than just copying an innovative practice—what she calls the "McDonald's Model" to connote the simplistic belief that a successful program can be plunked down anywhere. According to Schorr, going to scale requires mastering a series of difficult political and operational challenges—everything from identifying the "active ingredients" of innovation to working to approximate the spirit of creativity and personal commitment that animated the program in its early days.

While institutionalization is hard for any bureaucracy, it's particularly hard for state courts, most of which have highly decentralized decision making. Many judges are elected, and thus not directly answerable to court administrators. Even appointees, however, are independent and typically serve long terms, making it difficult to change institutional behavior. And there are, of course, other actors within the court system, such as prosecutors, defense attorneys and clerks, who hold different professional values and answer to their own institutional hierarchies. Short of major legislative change, getting a new idea implemented throughout a state court system is exceedingly difficult.

There is another reality for state courts, however: Drug courts will not survive for long unless they are institutionalized. Federal funding for drug courts will not last forever. And those states fortunate enough to receive federal grants must deal with the reality that grants usually terminate after a few years, and states will have to cover costs to keep drug courts running. Already some states are faced with a difficult choice: Kentucky, for example, was forced to commit $15 million (in the midst of a $700 million budget deficit) for the state's existing drug courts or watch them disappear.[3]

It seems fair to say that the decisions made by states today could be the difference between success or failure—whether drug courts are seen as a noble but unsustainable experiment or an enduring part of the criminal justice system's response to the problems of drug addiction and crime.

Focusing on a New Phase in Drug Court Development

Much has been written about the first phase of the drug court movement, in which entrepreneurial judges and others, inspired by the Miami model, brought the first drug courts to their disparate states, and the second phase, in which states, boosted by federal dollars, encouraged the proliferation of drug courts.[4] But little has been written about the third, newly emerging institutionalization phase, which is characterized by the creation of new systems, policies and funding to support the absorption of drug courts into the mainstream of judicial operations.[5]

Describing this "institutionalization" phase, and seeing how states are meetings its challenges, is the purpose of this essay. What does the term institutionalization mean? Drug court practitioners around the country have different responses to the term. Brooklyn Treatment Court Judge Jo Ann Ferdinand views institutionalization in terms of legitimacy, turning drug courts from "cute little things" into an "accepted part of the court system." Mike Loeffler, an assistant district attorney in Bristow, Oklahoma, sees it as a matter of scale: making drug court available across the state to all drug addicts picked up on non-violent charges. To Maria Nemec, who oversees treatment staff at the Greater Cleveland Drug Court, institutionalization means "a guaranteed stream of money."

Combining all these notions, one might define institutionalization this way: the process by which individual drug courts evolve from separate experimental entities to a statewide network that is stable, far-reaching, reliably funded and closely monitored.

For some, the notion of institutionalization doesn't stop there. For these practitioners and policymakers, institutionalization means re-orienting entire court and treatment systems according to drug court principles. In their view, drug courts will be institutionalized only when their key elements—intensive judicial monitoring, referrals to treatment, graduated sanctions and rewards—become a part of every state court's approach to drug addiction. "I'd like to see less emphasis on drug courts per se, and more emphasis placed on making treatment a mainstream enterprise by developing partnerships between courts and state agencies that oversee treatment," said Dan Becker, Utah's state court administrator. Speaking at the same roundtable discussion, Adele Harrell of the Urban Institute agreed, saying, "I share the vision of making this a way of doing business across the justice system, and maybe even fading drug courts out of existence as their tenets become embedded in practice."[6]

Clearly, the term institutionalization is a broad umbrella, one large enough to incorporate multiple definitions. One of this chapter's findings, in fact, is that there are many viable ways to go to scale with drug courts. This reality makes studying drug court institutionalization a challenge.

During the institutionalization phase, drug court practitioners and policymakers are no longer grappling simply with the logistics of developing new specialized dockets, but tackling a host of new responsibilities, among them: creating statewide offices and commissions to oversee drug courts, developing best practices to guide drug court operations, lobbying for steady funding from state sources, creating and implementing statewide management information systems and developing collaborative relationships among agencies at the highest levels of state government.

In carrying out these tasks, state leaders face a difficult challenge; the values of statewide institutionalization, which often require uniformity and top-down management, rest uneasily with the founding values of drug courts, which celebrate grassroots innovation, flexibility and local control. Drug courts have always been an alternative to the mainstream judicial system: what happens when they lose that status? Will they survive the transition? Will they lose some of the qualities that made them attractive in the first place?

This essay, in an effort to analyze developments on a national scale, focuses on four states—Louisiana, Missouri, New York and Ohio—all of which have made significant strides toward drug court institutionalization. These states were chosen because of their diversity in geography, politics, resources and approaches to institutionalization. For example, three states gave their electoral college votes to Republican George Bush in 2000 (Louisiana, Missouri and Ohio) and one gave its votes to Democrat Al Gore (New York). Some states, like New York, have abundant treatment resources and others, especially in rural districts, have limited resources. And in some states, the court system has taken the lead, while in others leadership is shared among more than one branch of government. To ensure a complete sampling of the national scene, however, the essay also draws select examples from drug court developments in other states, dozens of mainstream and academic articles about drug courts and over 100 interviews the authors conducted with judges, drug court staff, prosecutors, defense attorneys, treatment providers and government policymakers from around the country.

Drawing on this information, this essay attempts to describe how states are institutionalizing drug courts, focusing on both common challenges states are facing and the various strategies states are employing to meet those challenges.

I. The Early Years of Drug Court

The history of drug courts has been widely reported. It's easy to understand why the drug court story—in particular, the explosive growth of the movement from a lone experiment to a widely promulgated model in the course of a single decade—has been so frequently repeated. For many, the explosive proliferation is a sign that the model works, as if to say, "Drug courts must be doing something right, otherwise why would so many jurisdictions have embraced them?" But beyond that, the story is retold so often simply because it's a good story; it has the same dramatic rags-to-riches qualities that made Horatio Alger stories so compelling.

Because the story has been told elsewhere, this chapter will not tell it again—at least not in the usual way. The fact that drug courts have proliferated so quickly is not, in and of itself, relevant here. The more important question is how the exporting of the drug court idea around the country was successfully carried out. What are the key ingredients that have shaped drug courts as their presence and influence have expanded? How have those key ingredients laid the groundwork for the current phase of drug court development?

While it is difficult to study a phenomenon as large and complex as drug courts with scientific rigor, it is possible to identify some of the key factors that distinguished the first two, pre-institutionalization phases of drug court development. Importantly, the factors fueling drug courts' explosive proliferation continue to play a critical role in the institutionalization phase.

This section will take a look at how four factors—leadership, salesmanship, legislation and federal funding—have impacted the development of drug courts in Louisiana, Missouri, New York and Ohio.

Leadership: Mavericks at the Helm

When describing early drug court leaders, the word "mavericks" is often used. The individuals who got drug courts off the ground were dynamic individuals—judges mostly—who were free-thinking, charismatic and well-connected. To anyone in the drug court world, the names are familiar: Judges Herbert Klein and Stanley Goldstein in Miami, Florida; Prosecutor Claire McCaskill in Kansas City, Missouri; Judge John R. Schwartz in Buffalo, New York.; Judge William Hunter in St. Mary Parish, Louisiana; and Judge Jeff Tauber in Oakland, California. Each can take credit for playing a significant part in bringing drug courts to their states. In some cases, by the sheer force of personality alone, they were able to overcome bureaucratic inertia and skepticism.

The idea that these leaders are mavericks is based, in large part, on their willingness to act independently in experimenting with a new approach to the long-standing problem of drug addiction and crime. Referring to the nation's first drug court and its creator, Judge Herbert Klein, researcher John Goldkamp wrote, "It is easy to overlook how dramatic a departure from prevailing judicial philosophy Miami's drug court represented." He added: "Judge Klein's endorsement of treatment as a court strategy, his advocacy of what was received as—how awkward—rehabilitation, was met with an uncomfortable silence. Many judges believed that rehabilitation had long ago been discredited."[7]

Lessons Learned

There is a second element, as well—the sense that these early advocates were working against the grain and, in some cases, overcoming long odds to create drug courts. This anti-establishment, underdog camaraderie pervaded initial conventions of the National Association of Drug Court Professionals. "[We were] a community," said Oakland Drug Court Judge Jeff Tauber, who helped create the association in 1994. "When [people] came to our conference, they felt they were part of a movement, something larger than themselves. . . . People felt so high after that, they'd go home and slay dragons."

Judge John R. Schwartz, the supervising judge of the Rochester City Court, worked outside the system to open New York's first drug court in 1995. The local supervising judge opposed the creation of the court, but Schwartz persevered. Schwartz looked for funding outside of government, enlisting the support of local foundations. The United Way paid for a drug court coordinator. The American Bar Association provided technical assistance. Treatment providers agreed to post, on a rotating basis, case managers in the court.

Despite the lone wolf nature of its origins, the Rochester Drug Treatment Court quickly earned the admiration of statewide court system leaders, including Chief Judge Judith S. Kaye, and soon drug courts were opening in Buffalo, Brooklyn and other jurisdictions around New York.

Judge William D. Hunter played a similar role in St. Mary Parish, Louisiana, a largely rural jurisdiction of about 50,000 people. In creating the drug court, Hunter and a group of local colleagues had to overcome the traditional, tough-on-crime attitudes that helped give Louisiana the highest rates of incarceration in the nation.[8] "There are certain law-and-order groups in Louisiana who feel that locking people up and throwing away the key is the best way to go," Hunter said. But Louisiana's early drug court advocates—deftly using salesmanship and legislation—were able to turn Louisiana into a leading drug court state.

There are several lessons that can be drawn from the experience of early drug court leaders like Schwartz and Hunter. Perhaps the most obvious lesson is that leadership matters, and that a single person can, with skill and vision, change something as traditionally resistant to reform as the court system.

The other lessons from the experience of the movement's early leaders are more subtle. One such lesson is the importance of partnerships. Local drug court leaders have succeeded only where they've built constructive partnerships with other key players, including the community. For example, in Louisiana Hunter made sure to win the support of the St. Mary Parish sheriff and local prosecutors—crucial allies in the fight to avoid a "soft on crime" label.

Partnerships, only on a much larger scale, are important for those who are currently leading the process of institutionalization. State leaders must cultivate support among different branches of government and among the leaders of different agencies. Even community support, in the form of statewide public opinion, needs to be cultivated effectively—especially in light of the numerous statewide referendums in recent years that could directly affect drug court operations.

The task of building partnerships is, of course, more easily accomplished in a small town than across an entire state. In St. Mary Parish, a web of personal relationships was already in place—Hunter and Bernard E. Boudreaux, the then St. Mary Parish district attorney (and current counsel to Governor Mike Foster Jr.) were good friends; Jimmy Sennette, the assistant district attorney assigned to drug court, and Sheriff David A. Naquin were first cousins. "If we have one outstanding characteristic," Sennette said, "it's that we all know each other."

It also helped that the early leaders were often in positions of authority. Some, like Claire McCaskill, the former elected prosecutor in Jackson County, Missouri, and currently the state auditor, convinced voters to support a quarter-percent sales tax to go towards public safety projects, including Missouri's first drug court. This gave her an enormous amount of authority over project partners. "Frankly I had the money to give out. If the police didn't play nice and the treatment people didn't play nice, I had a great stick: funding for other things that I could hold over their heads," McCaskill said.

Early drug court leaders also had another thing going for them: consummate communication skills. This could be because, as McCaskill points out, judges and prosecutors, as lawyers, are trained persuaders. In addition, many of them run for election, ensuring that they know how to win supporters. McCaskill feels that prosecutors are the best advocates for drug courts precisely because "they're politicians—they have the connections, the skills. Most of them have had their upbringing in a courtroom and think on their feet and are articulate."

A final leadership lesson worth noting is that the early drug court leaders worked effectively to promote change within the existing system. While visionary, they weren't radicals—they were attempting to reform court practice, not overturn it. Drug courts, after all, are still courts. The strategy of working from within the system proved to be critical in both getting drug courts up and running and paving the way for broader acceptance.

Salesmanship: The Art of Selling Drug Courts

The idea of "selling" drug court has been with the model from its inception. That's largely because a drug court depends on the participation of so many partners, including court administrators, treatment providers, prosecutors, defense attorneys, judges, police, probation officers and others. In order to get buy-in from these various groups, advocates of drug courts have had to craft careful arguments demonstrating why the model offers benefits to all institutional partners.

From the early days, advocates have worked on selling the drug court concept on not only a local level, but on state and national levels, too. The National Association of Drug Court Professionals was created in 1994 to advocate for drug courts. In turn, the association encouraged practitioners to form their own state associations to help generate local momentum for drug courts. The Louisiana State Association of Drug Court Professionals, for example, was created in late 1997 to lobby the legislature for more drug court money, to support the development of a management information system and to create statewide best practice standards. The association also began sponsoring a state conference. The first conference, in 1998, was less about substance and more about getting the word out about drug courts, according to organizers. Governor Foster supported the effort by signing a letter of invitation to potential conference participants. For a little-known initiative, the governor's letter sparked enormous interest. "We had 120 people at the first meeting and they didn't even know what drug courts were," said Lars Levy, the administrative director of drug treatment services for St. Mary Parish's five drug courts.

In addition to creating professional associations, drug court advocates looked to other ways to sell the idea of drug court. An event that speaks eloquently for this purpose, of course, is a drug court graduation. Virtually every drug court invites to graduations not only friends and relatives of graduates, but community leaders, elected officials and members of the press. The stories of jaded observers who have been converted by the drama of a graduation are legion.

Judge Schwartz, for example, invited one of New York's main skeptics, Deputy Chief Administrative Judge Joseph J. Traficanti Jr., along with New York's chief judge, Judith S. Kaye, to the Rochester Drug Treatment Court's first graduation. Kaye, who had already demonstrated a commitment to innovative court management, not only accepted the invitation but agreed to speak. From that point forward, Kaye and Traficanti were both drug court supporters, and attended drug court graduations frequently. In fact, under Kaye's management, nearly a dozen drug courts opened in New York over the next two years.

In her "State of the Judiciary" address, delivered in March 1998, Kaye explained: "At our last drug court graduation, Judge Traficanti told me that he would either have to stop attending these events or learn how to cry in front of 200 people. I know the feeling. It is a moving and gratifying experience to attend these graduations and hear long-time substance abusers say 'I wasn't just arrested, I was saved.'"[9]

Other drug courts have been successful at attracting press coverage of drug court graduations—in some cases, so successful that they can't get local newspapers to cover them any more. For example, the local press in Boone County, Missouri, had covered so many graduations that reporters were beginning to balk at going. "Once the governor came and our daily newspaper did not show up," said Judge Christine Carpenter. "Their response was, 'This isn't news, you're just using us for good PR,'" Carpenter said.

Another dimension of good salesmanship involves learning how to respond to critics. For example, some critics have said drug courts are soft on criminals—a so-called "Hug the Thug" program.[10] As Judge Hunter put it: "The issue for me in a conservative southern state is: How do we embrace a program that is [seen as] warm and fuzzy? How do I sell that to law enforcement when Louisiana is number one in per capita incarceration in the U.S?"

A second criticism is almost the opposite of the first: that by imposing tough requirements on defendants, drug courts set up participants for failure and expose them to more jail time than if they had gone through traditional prosecution.

Advocates have responded to these criticisms by articulating a nuanced message about drug courts. As James L. Nolan Jr., a drug court critic himself, writes in his book *Reinventing Justice: The American Drug Court Movement*, the message is: "Drug courts are tough and therapeutic at the same time."[11] Drug court judges, for example, often point out that participants are subject to more intensive supervision than they would be if they were supervised by probation. On the other hand, they also stress that drug courts provide a helping hand to addicted offenders who have hit rock bottom.

The drug court message—saving jail space for violent offenders, turning offenders into productive citizens, reducing recidivism and strengthening supervision of participants in drug treatment—has played well in both liberal and conservative states. Drug courts have made use of research—however provisional—to strengthen this sales pitch and respond to the concerns of critics.[12] John Creuzot, a state district judge in Dallas, Texas, for example, said a favorable recidivism study of his court as well as a cost-benefit analysis that showed how every dollar spent on treatment produced a $9.43 savings helped him garner the support of Texas Governor Rick Perry and other state leaders.[13]

Mastering the ins and outs of state politics has been critical in helping to spread the drug court model. McCaskill, the former Jackson County, Missouri, prosecutor, saw a natural advantage in having judges, prosecutors and police take a lead role in developing drug courts. "Frankly, it's important that the prosecutors and police be in the forefront because it's easy to pigeonhole drug court in the social service sector." To McCaskill, this type of hard-nosed political calculus is critical if drug courts are to successfully go to scale. The lesson for the long term, McCaskill said, is that "the drug court movement needs to become more of a political player."

Legislation: The Role of Statutes in Drug Court Growth

The role legislation plays in relation to drug courts varies from state to state. In some states, there is little or no legislation pertaining to drug courts. In New York, for example, the court system, which is leading the effort to institutionalize drug courts, has not sought enabling legislation; court system leaders argue that legislation is both unnecessary and potentially restrictive. In Deputy Chief Administrative Judge Joseph Traficanti's words, it would be "an invasion of the executive and legislative branches into the judicial branch of government." Ohio has also avoided enabling legislation, fearing it would prove too restrictive, according to Melissa Knopp, program manager of specialized dockets for the Supreme Court.

In many states, however, legislation has been an integral part of the proliferation of drug courts. Mike Loeffler, an assistant district attorney in Bristow, Oklahoma, said counties could have technically created drug courts without legislation, but he added, "I think it makes it more politically palatable if an enabling statute exists, especially for prosecutors."

Similarly, Judge Hunter and then St. Mary Parish D.A. Boudreaux in Louisiana pursued legislation more for political than legal reasons. Basically, they believed that a law authorizing the creation of drug courts was the best tool to get the attention of the Louisiana legal community. A law was not technically required—St. Mary Parish launched its court without one—but Hunter saw Louisiana House Bill 2412 as a tool in the public relations campaign to legitimize drug courts. The law made it clear that court-supervised drug treatment was an officially sanctioned option in every parish. The legislation made participation contingent on a plea of guilty, allowed the court to "impose any conditions reasonably related to the complete rehabilitation of the defendant" and allowed for convictions to be set aside and prosecutions to be dismissed upon successful completion.

The only point of controversy in negotiations over the wording of the bill was the right to determine eligibility. "Everybody wanted to decide who got in," Hunter said. The law gives the district attorney the right to refer defendants to the program but reserved for the judge "the final determination of eligibility."

The language in the law was opaque enough, however, that a turf battle between a handful of judges and New Orleans District Attorney Harry Connick Sr. continued for several years. The judges insisted that they didn't need a referral from the prosecutor to accept a client into the program. But Connick sued, feeling that by providing intensive supervision of defendants, drug court judges were usurping the executive-branch authority of the probation department.[14] The issue made its way to the state Supreme Court, which ruled that "a defendant may only be considered for the program upon the recommendation of the district attorney."[15] This ruling gave prosecutors strong control over drug court operations, ensuring that programs could no longer admit clients without a prosecutor's consent. Hunter called the lawsuit merely a "bump in the road" in the growth of drug courts in Louisiana.

In Missouri, drug court supporters pursued legislation to create a Drug Court Commission, composed of agency heads from courts, corrections, public safety and public health to oversee drug court development at the state level. The legislation also had practical implications, allowing for "a bigger budget and staff" for the commission, said Ann Wilson, the alcohol and drug abuse coordinator with the Office of State Courts Administrator. "The point of the legislation was to create state funding and create new positions, like drug court administrators," Wilson said.

Laws Creating Alternatives to Incarceration

Legislation, of course, does not have to directly mention drug courts to be helpful to their development. While Ohio doesn't have any laws on the books prescribing how drug courts should operate, the legislature has adopted some laws that have supported the work of drug courts. The most significant law is probably the sentencing revision legislation known popularly as Senate Bill 2. The bill, adopted in 1996, rewrote the felony sentencing laws in Ohio and established a presumption that lesser felony offenders (those in the 4th and 5th degrees, except for 4th degree drug offenses) should not go to prison but rather remain in the community under probation. The bill does not require substance-abuse treatment as a condition of probation, but it does urge judges to provide offenders with substance-abuse treatment or some other appropriate intervention before sending them to jail for a violation.

Although the law was originally drafted by the Ohio Criminal Sentencing Commission in 1993—and thus did not have drug courts in mind—it has served to encourage some judges who might otherwise have been reluctant to endorse the drug court concept. "Senate Bill 2 came about more with an eye toward dealing with crowded prisons in a logical enough way to make sure we have enough space for the worst guys," said David Diroll, director of the sentencing commission. An important key to the law's success is that the state made an investment in the mid-1990s in treatment and other services. "It works because the resources are there," Diroll said.

Another important law for Ohio drug courts is Statute 2951.041, known as "Intervention in Lieu of Conviction." The law began its life in slightly different form in the late 1970s, but it was rarely used, Diroll said. The original law said a judge could sentence any low-level offender, including repeat offenders, to residential substance-abuse treatment so long as the offender entered treatment immediately and was not on a waiting list. It made no provision for other forms of treatment, and it also required the judge to send the offender to prison if he or she violated.

"It was a pretty inflexible statute," Diroll said. "It seemed to ratchet you from diversion to prison without steps in between." The sentencing commission proposed changes to the law, which were adopted by the legislature and went into effect in 2000. This time, the subcommittee that worked on the revision had drug courts in mind. In fact, one of its members was Judge Deidre Hair, the state's first drug court judge.

The new law defined intervention broadly to include abstinence from the use of illegal drugs and alcohol, regular testing and "any other treatment terms and conditions similar to community control sanctions that are ordered by the court."

"A lot of judges have told us that that [the legislation] gave them permission to do drug court," said Fritz Rauschenberg, a program administrator at Ohio Department of Alcohol and Drug Addiction Services and former research chief at the Ohio Criminal Sentencing Commission. In fact, some drug courts have based much of their program on the language in the statute.

Laws That Require Jurisdictions to Create Drug Courts

Perhaps the most aggressive use of legislation are laws that actually require jurisdictions to create drug courts. One of the most explicit examples is Texas House Bill 1287, adopted in 2001, which mandated the creation of drug courts by September 1, 2002, in counties with populations of more than 550,000. The legislation also requires drug courts to follow the key components, a program framework promulgated by the Department of Justice.

Texas has seven counties with more than 550,000 residents, and four of them already had or were planning drug courts. As for the remaining three, none had drug courts in place by the statutory deadline. The law threatened to withhold funds for community supervision and corrections departments from non-compliant counties but the executive branch has yet to carry out the threat. (The counties have been non-compliant largely because they lack sufficient funds to pay for treatment, according to the Texas-based Criminal Justice Policy Council.)[16]

Judge John Creuzot, who presides over drug court in Dallas, thinks the law "is great for drug court." He draws a parallel between the coercion that takes place in a drug court and the coercive effect of legislation. "Can you force a drug addict to treatment? The answer is yes. If you force them to do it, will it work? Well, again, the answer is yes. I don't see why that paradigm isn't good here, too," Creuzot said. "I've seen judges in other states assigned to drug court and they come in angry and resentful ... and then after a few months they're wondering why they weren't doing it all along, and I think it's the same thing that can happen to communities [that are ordered by legislation to create a drug court]."

Referendums can also impact drug court, as has been the case with Proposition 36 in California. In November 2000, 61 percent of voters approved the measure, technically known as the Substance Abuse and Crime Prevention Act, which diverted first- and second-time drug offenders into treatment and added $120 million annually for treatment programs statewide.

Proposition 36 has had a mixed impact on drug courts. While drug court advocates actively lobbied against it, the initiative has not turned out to be as bad for drug courts as expected. On the one hand, it greatly restricts judicial discretion, limiting the use of jail as a sanction (which reduces the leverage judges have to compel offenders to seek treatment) and forcing judges to impose a final sentence after only two drug relapses (less leeway than is often provided in drug court). On the other hand, drug court advocates have helped create implementation standards that closely mimic drug court protocols. In areas such as promoting early intervention and creating links between courts and treatment agencies, "the drug court model is being used by the vast majority of courts to implement Proposition 36," said Judge Stephen Manley, the supervising judge of the Santa Clara County Superior Court and a member of a court system-led work group on Proposition 36. In addition, the courts have created a mechanism for Proposition 36 failures to go directly into drug court.

The issue for drug court advocates is whether or not to support Proposition 36-style ballot initiatives in other states. In Ohio, drug court supporters played a key role in turning aside an initiative patterned after Proposition 36, arguing that it would have a destructive impact on drug courts. But this was a costly position, especially in a tough fiscal climate, since it meant foregoing additional funding for drug treatment—specifically, $38 million annually for the next seven years.

Federal Support: Money and Guidance

The most obvious fuel for drug court growth has been the federal government, which since 1996 has provided millions of dollars a year in planning, operating and enhancement grants, along with training and technical assistance, to over a thousand drug courts. Most of the money—up to $50 million a year, in recent years—has come from the Department of Justice, but other agencies, like the federal Center for Substance Abuse Treatment, have also pumped money into operations and research.

Hundreds of drug courts have relied—and many continue to rely—on federal dollars. In New York, court administrators used the federal grant-making process not only to promote the creation of drug courts but to control the process. Jonathan Lippman, the court system's chief administrative judge, required all prospective drug courts to submit grant applications through his office. "We used the grant process to control growth," said Michael Magnani, an administrator in Lippman's office.

Even more importantly, perhaps, the federal grants came with rules and requirements that enforced a level of uniformity and quality control on the new courts. According to Magnani, "By having all grants come through our office, we could hold each court to the grant requirements and, in that way, establish controls and standards. [Through] the feds [we] enforced the 10 key components, the team building, etcetera."

10 Key Components

The 10 key components may, in fact, be the most enduring legacy of federal involvement in the drug court movement. Written by a committee of practitioners assembled by the National Association of Drug Court Professionals in 1996, with funding from the Department of Justice, the 10 key components received the federal government's official stamp of approval when they were published by the Department of Justice as *Defining Drug Courts: The Key Components* in January 1997. The components clearly articulate such principles as prompt placement of clients into treatment, reduced adversarialism and the use of frequent testing to monitor compliance.

Interestingly, the authors of the components acknowledge "that local resources, political, and operational issues will not permit every local adult drug court to adopt all aspects of the guidelines." In fact, they say that the components are intended only to be "inspirational" and not a "certification or regulatory checklist."

The Department of Justice never actually required programs to adhere to the components, although it did begin to require grant recipients to discuss the key components in their applications. Practitioners over time began to treat the components as requirements, and a number of states actually codified the 10 key components into law. In Texas, for example, a "drug court program" is statutorily defined as a program that follows the 10 key components.

In many respects, the 10 key components helped unify the drug court movement by creating a set of universal principles. They allowed practitioners in one state to converse with colleagues across the country without having to first explain to each other what they meant by the term "drug court." They have also allowed states to ensure a level of consistency without being overly restrictive. In Missouri, for example, "each county is free to set their own rules, within the constraints of [the] 10 key components," said Steve Narrow, coordinator of the Jackson City Drug Court.

But as the movement has matured, practitioners have had to grapple with the reality that some courts simply don't have the resources to adhere to all the components. In addition, as research into drug courts expands, evaluators are asking which of the original components are truly essential, raising the possibility that some of the components may be found to have little or no impact on rates of abstinence or recidivism.

All of this means that as the institutionalization of drug courts progresses, many administrators are wondering how to apply the 10 key components to circumstances in their states. Should the components be required? Should they be non-binding guidelines? Should they be modified in some way—and if so, how? Or should new guidelines be developed?

Another legacy is Congress's requirement—part of the 1996 Crime Bill—that grant recipients not accept violent offenders. Some drug court practitioners think the future of drug courts rests in accepting a broader array of participants, including those with a history of more serious crimes. One reason for this is that the serious offender is more likely to be prison-bound, and thus the jurisdiction is more likely to realize substantial savings by sending him into treatment. In addition, the judge has a larger hammer (the threat of a long prison term) to motivate compliance. But in many jurisdictions there is a deep-seated reluctance to move in that direction. Part of that reluctance can presumably be traced to the congressionally mandated ban on working with violent offenders.

II. Going to Scale

By 1999, New York had about 30 drug courts. In a state with 62 counties and 19 million people, that meant that drug courts were available only in a limited number of jurisdictions to a relatively small number of defendants. This situation led Chief Judge Judith S. Kaye to appoint a special commission to answer, among other things, the following questions: If judicially monitored drug treatment offered an effective approach to working with drug-addicted defendants, should the court system ensure its availability in every corner of the state? On the other hand, if such an approach had not proven effective, shouldn't it be scrapped and other approaches explored?

The New York State Commission on Drugs and the Courts, chaired by Robert B. Fiske Jr., assembled a group of judges, prosecutors, defense attorneys, researchers and experts in areas like treatment and probation to study the impact of drug cases on the court system. The resulting report, "Confronting the Cycle of Addiction and Recidivism," which was released in June 2000, strongly endorsed drug courts and the broader concept of judicially ordered and monitored drug treatment for non-violent addicted offenders.[17]

At that time, drug courts in New York had a one-year retention rate of over 60 percent and a one-year re-arrest rate of less than 15 percent—"far below the one-year recidivism rates of drug offenders on probation and drug offenders released from prison, which are generally about 34 to 35 percent," the report found. The report also noted that it cost between $29,000 and $47,000 a year to incarcerate an individual compared to an average cost of $18,400 per year for residential drug treatment and $5,100 for an outpatient program.

Up until that point, however, there had been little organized effort to expand the availability of drug courts and other court-based treatment programs, the commission said. Efforts to date had been "ad hoc" and "patchwork." It was the commission's feeling that "if this type of treatment is to have a true impact, it must be expanded considerably, and in some coordinated way."

The commission then called upon the statewide Office of Court Administration to "take a leadership role in significantly expanding the availability of drug treatment, with the goal of making treatment available to the entire universe of eligible addicted, non-violent offenders in every jurisdiction."

On June 22, 2000, Kaye formally adopted the commission's recommendations, an announcement that resulted in widespread media coverage, including an article on the front page of *The New York Times*. In her State of the Judiciary Address in January 2001, Kaye announced a three-year plan to expand drug courts to all 62 counties in the state. The agenda was perceived, both inside and outside the court system, to be highly ambitious, calling as it did for at least one criminal drug court and one family drug court in all 62 jurisdictions.

"To have drug courts embraced by our chief judge . . . let me know that the initial desire to set up a drug court was not in vain," said Judge Robert Russell, founder of the Buffalo Drug Treatment Court (the state's second drug court), who sat on the Fiske Commission. If there was anything that could be remotely construed as criticism, it was expressed politely by practitioners at drug courts already in existence who were concerned that the court system's assertive embrace of drug courts might impose an unwelcome bureaucracy on what they felt needed to be a flexible operation.

"In the first year, we were cautious," said Jeff Smith, the coordinator for 12 small, pre-existing drug courts in eight upstate counties. "We weren't sure what the state wanted. Are you suggesting you're going to take a grass-roots effort and turn it into a bureaucracy?"

An Operational Challenge

The commission recommended that the court system appoint a "representative who is vested with the authority (and the necessary staff and resources)" to coordinate the expansion of drug courts. In October 2000, Chief Administrative Judge Jonathan Lippman appointed Judge Joseph J. Traficanti Jr., who, by the end of 2003, helped establish 108 drug courts across the state.

The appointment of Traficanti reflected the recognition that launching drug courts on such a wide scale was a significant operational challenge. Traficanti—a Republican and former prosecutor—would not only have to navigate a system that included layers of village, town, county and district courts, but also sell the idea to communities that, left to their own devices, might have little or no interest in the drug court concept. Traficanti, who six years earlier had looked askance at Judge Schwartz's efforts to found the Rochester Treatment Court, noted that the statewide coordinator needed "to be someone who has a sense of New York State's legal culture and who understands court operations as opposed to someone who might know a thing or two in theory but not how things work on the inside."

Traficanti, a judge since 1982, clearly had the knowledge of an insider. As deputy chief administrative judge for courts outside New York City, Traficanti had responsibility for the operations of courts in 57 counties. That fact gave him the leverage he needed to carry out Kaye's mandate.

Different Models

New York's effort is but one example of drug court institutionalization. Like Chief Judge Kaye, leaders in a number of other states are eyeing ways to integrate drug courts into their court and drug treatment systems. In states such as Missouri, Louisiana, Ohio, Utah, Wyoming, California and Virginia, a new set of actors has emerged to manage and oversee drug courts. These actors include administrators like Judge Traficanti in New York, who created the Office of Court Drug Treatment Programs specifically to oversee the implementation of drug courts in every county in the state. They also include new boards like Missouri's Drug Court Commission, which pools funds from various state agencies and issues grants to drug courts.

Drug court institutionalization is, of course, a massive and complicated task. That basic truth makes it not only difficult to carry out, but difficult to describe. States are approaching the task in their own way, with different goals, different resources, different political considerations and different legal and regulatory landscapes.

While each state's approach to drug courts is unique, it's possible to identify three basic models that states are using to pursue institutionalization. These are:

Judicial Branch Model

Both New York and Louisiana's statewide institutionalization efforts are led by the judicial branch. In New York, the court system dedicates close to $12 million annually for drug courts through the Office of Court Drug Treatment Programs. In July 2001, the legislature transferred authority over drug courts from the state's treatment agency to the Supreme Court, which administers $13 million annually in funding.

Executive Branch Model

From the early days, the judicial branch has been an enthusiastic supporter of drug courts in Ohio. However, drug courts' primary funder has been an executive branch agency—the state's drug and alcohol treatment agency. (Wyoming has taken a similar approach.)[18] Currently, the Ohio Department of Alcohol and Drug Addiction Services distributes $2.5 million in grants towards treatment services to 19 drug courts and works to create linkages between the criminal justice and drug treatment systems.

Collaborative Model

Missouri has taken a collaborative approach to drug courts. (Utah is another example.)[19] Rather than filter drug court money through any single agency, Missouri created the Drug Court Commission, which brings together leaders of the court system and three executive branch agencies (Mental Health, Corrections and Public Safety) to coordinate and jointly fund drug courts across the state using a single statewide budget.

New Tools, New Challenges

State leaders have made considerable progress in their efforts to institutionalize drug courts. And yet, considerable challenges lie ahead. Those challenges can be broken down into five key areas:

Centralizing Authority

As states have assumed more financial responsibility for drug courts, they have also begun to take on more policymaking authority in areas such as setting and enforcing best practices, creating statewide management information systems and targeting new populations for drug courts. While some amount of centralized authority seems necessary for drug courts to thrive, questions remain about the dynamic between a "top-down" versus "bubble-up" approach. Which functions should be centralized and which should be left at the local level? How are states balancing the need for quality control and uniformity with the desire to encourage local flexibility? And which state agency or branch of government should lead the drug court effort?

Building Support

To advance institutionalization, who needs to be on board? Which individuals and agencies need to be cultivated? In New York, state court administrators, in order to establish a drug court in every county, need to cultivate the support of judges, prosecutors and defense attorneys at the local level. In Missouri, the challenge has been different—to create alliances among the leaders of the various executive branch agencies that participate in the Drug Court Commission, persuading them to share resources in the name of drug court institutionalization. In each state, drug court advocates have learned to reach beyond the boundaries of a single agency or branch of government in an effort to obtain needed resources and support for institutionalization.

Establishing Best Practices

The question of best practices has been with drug courts since the beginning. The challenge for state leaders is identifying a set of best practices that work in all environments—in big cities and rural counties, in communities with numerous treatment resources and those with limited capacity. Another challenge is updating best practices as new research adds to an understanding about how and in what circumstances drug courts work. And even if a universal set of best practices is identified, the question arises: How should they be disseminated?

Creating Infrastructure

For many administrators, building strong drug courts means building statewide infrastructure—management information systems, research benchmarks and staffing protocols—for all drug courts. What kinds of tools need to be developed to sustain drug courts over the long haul? Drug court leaders in the states profiled have identified a number of key investments that can be made to advance institutionalization.

Increasing Capacity

For drug courts to reach their full potential, they need to reach as many potentially eligible clients as possible. But how is this best achieved? In jurisdictions like Hennepin County, Minnesota, Dade County, Florida, and Brooklyn, New York, drug court leaders have identified a number of different models for reaching a larger population. Some have accepted more serious offenders into drug court, thereby greatly expanding the drug court universe. Others are experimenting with exporting drug court principles to conventional courtrooms in an effort to make judicially supervised drug treatment the new "business as usual" within the courts. A third strategy has been to apply the drug court approach to different non-drug-related cases. Each strategy has its own set of trade-offs, advantages and disadvantages.

What follows is a look at how states are answering these various challenges.

Centralizing Authority

Drug courts bring together in partnership different branches of government and numerous outside partners. As such, it isn't always obvious in any given state who is—or should be—overseeing the process of institutionalization. Further, since drug courts' success has long been attributed largely to leadership at the local level, many drug court practitioners are wary of rules or regulations that are not home-grown. This can put leaders at the state level in a bind as they try to define their role and scope of responsibilities. Which functions should be carried out by a statewide overseer of drug courts and which should be left to individual courts? To what extent is uniformity among drug courts needed or desirable? In one way or another, each state is grappling with these issues.

New York

In New York, the statewide drug court leader has been obvious: the court system. This is the case for a number of reasons. First and foremost, the court system is "unified," meaning that many administrative functions are consolidated, rather than handled on a county-by-county basis, as they are in non-unified systems like Ohio's and Missouri's. This means that court administrators at the state level have a degree of power over judicial assignments and responsibilities and can decide how money is spent across the system. They also have the authority to require courts to adopt certain policies and procedures.

Another crucial factor has been Chief Judge Judith S. Kaye's strong interest in drug courts and other "problem-solving courts." Since the beginning of her tenure as chief judge in 1993, Kaye has made the development of drug courts, domestic violence courts, community courts and other innovative courts a hallmark of her administration. And her authority to launch these new courts is strengthened by the fact that she is appointed by the governor for a term of 14 years, in contrast to other states where judges must run for re-election more frequently (every six years in Louisiana) or where the position of chief judge is rotated among the judges on the state's highest court, as is the case in Missouri (where a judge's tenure as chief is limited to only two years).

Another factor making it easier for the court system to serve as lead agency in New York is the fact that finding funds for treatment in New York is easier than it is in many other states. New York is a relatively treatment-rich state—Medicaid managed-care plans are required by statute to pay for court-ordered treatment, while the state reimburses treatment providers for uninsured clients who can't pay their bills. Because of this, the court system has been able to focus its resources not on paying for treatment but on hiring new court staff, developing new technology and training judges and others in the drug court approach.

The question of how the court system has used its authority is an interesting one. While administrators have declined to issue binding rules about how drug courts should be structured, and have rejected the necessity of legislation to guide their implementation, they have nonetheless taken aggressive steps in support of drug courts. For example, administrators authorized drug courts to hire resource coordinators to serve as a bridge between the courts and off-site treatment programs despite a system-wide hiring freeze. The state court system has also organized a series of trainings for drug court players and non-drug court judges, conducted a statewide evaluation of drug court outcomes and is putting together a set of best practice manuals as a resource for drug courts. Finally, the court system has created a universal management information system for all courts to use to track program outcomes.

Thus it seems that New York has walked the line between top-down governance and local control by making certain tools, such as a universal management information system and trainings, available to all drug courts, but then leaving individual courts to determine their structure (e.g., pre- or post-plea, length of phases, types of sanctions and rewards, etc.) and how they will run on a day-to-day basis.

Ohio

In Ohio, the Department of Alcohol and Drug Addiction Services has been drug courts' primary funder. This has been due largely to the Department's cabinet-level status and the leadership of the Department's director, Luceille Fleming, who headed the agency from its creation in 1989 through her retirement in mid-2003. Fleming made drug courts—and, more generally, linkages between the criminal justice and drug-treatment systems—a priority. The Department of Alcohol and Drug Addiction Services currently subsidizes treatment services for 19 of Ohio's 55 drug courts and funds additional courts through county boards that dispense discretionary funds.

The Supreme Court's role in drug courts is necessarily limited because the court system is not unified and each county has significant latitude in organizing and administering its courts. And yet, the court system, led by Chief Justice Thomas J. Moyer, has also played a role in advancing drug courts. For example, in 1993, the Supreme Court co-sponsored with the Department of Alcohol and Drug Addiction Services a statewide conference on drug courts with about 80 participants. Also, since 1992, the Supreme Court has had staff assigned to support the development of drug courts and, more recently, other problem-solving courts, like domestic violence courts and mental health courts.

Over time, the Supreme Court and the Department of Alcohol and Drug Addiction Services have developed a comfortable working relationship. Officials at both agencies emphasize that there is a strong partnership between the two agencies, which work together regularly to plan conferences and provide technical assistance to local jurisdictions. They also agree that the state's treatment agency is the appropriate locus of authority when it comes to the treatment side of drug courts, and the Supreme Court asks drug courts to use drug treatment counselors certified by the Department of Alcohol and Drug Addiction Services.

This shared authority over drug courts does, at times, present difficulties since local justice and treatment systems do not always see eye to eye. For example, in Fairfield County, Judge Steve O. Williams has refused to use an Addictions Services-certified treatment program and has instead raised money to hire his own counselors for his juvenile drug court. As a result, his court does not receive Department of Alcohol and Drug Addiction Services funding for drug court treatment services. Not surprisingly, Williams feels that the Supreme Court should be more involved in funding drug courts. "The plain fact is that drug courts are courts," Williams said.

Missouri

In Missouri, Supreme Court Judge William Price Jr. in 2001 created—with legislative approval—a multi-agency Drug Court Commission to oversee drug courts around the state.

Prior to the commission, Missouri's drug courts were funded through a patchwork of local, state and federal funds. Individual drug courts were free to pursue federal grants, and many received supplemental funding from local authorities. In addition, the state provided $1.6 million in annual funding to various counties for drug courts through the Department of Corrections, albeit without any specific instructions about how the money was to be used.

For Price, the problem was that no single agency had authority to oversee drug courts effectively. "We had a great program but no control over who gets funding and what they do," he said. While the Department of Corrections had helped get a number of drug courts up and running, they were doing little to track where the money was being spent or what results the new courts were achieving, Price said. Also, by law, the Department of Corrections could establish only adult drug courts—meaning that state dollars could not go to family drug courts.

Price's solution was to seek legislative approval for the Drug Court Commission, composed of representatives from key state agencies that would administer—in a single general fund—a pool of money related to drug courts. "The idea was to have an umbrella organization that will gather data about how drug courts are being funded and [promote] drug court best practices," Price said. The Department of Corrections was reluctant to relinquish control of funding, however, resulting in a "knock-down, drag-out battle" in the legislature, Price said. Ultimately, through legislation—and after a change in administration that resulted in the appointment of a new director of corrections, Gary Kempker, a supporter of drug courts and an active member of the commission—the Department of Corrections money was added to the commission's pot.

In addition to receiving the $1.6 million that had previously been allocated to Corrections, the newly created commission also received $1.1 million in Byrne grant funding from the Department of Public Safety. This was accomplished even though "it's very difficult to pry money away from a law enforcement grant," according to David Brown of the Department of Public Safety and a commission member. The willingness of the Department of Public Safety to re-allocate the dollars was a sign of the commission's ability to win collaborative support. When added to $375,000 in court funding for family drug courts, the new funding brought the commission's total annual budget to $3.1 million.

That still did not mean that the commission was able to identify—let alone control—all the funding that goes into drug courts. For example, the Department of Mental Health estimates that it spends $3 million annually on treatment for drug court clients, but can't track the amount because it does not code for drug court in its billing procedures. Michael Couty, director of the Department of Mental Health and a commission member, plans to start tracking this information. The hope is to "get a sense of the actual demand for services," which can be used as a baseline to determine additional funding needs, Couty said.

With most, if not all, of state drug court funding under its control, the commission's next move was to create a data collection process to evaluate individual drug court performance. The goal was to use data to help make funding recommendations under an annual grant-making process. Beginning in 2003, the commission mandated that a formal application be completed by drug courts seeking state funding. For individual drug courts, the change was noticeable. "What's unique [about the new application]," said Steve Narrow of the Cape Giradeau Drug Court, "is that it's very much about outcomes—[such as] how many people got sober and stayed sober, how quickly you get [individuals] engaged in treatment."

In its first year, the commission received over $6 million in requests for funding, twice as much as it had available in its budget. Faced with excess demand, the commission took a fairly conservative approach—to continue awarding grants to drug courts that had received funding in previous years. "We decided the thing to do this year, until we get smarter about how to allocate money, was to hold people harmless on state funding," Price said.

The challenge for the commission, going forward, will be to create and enforce a set of standards for all drug courts to follow. That conversation has already begun, said commission member David Brown: "Our initial agenda was 'we've got a pot of money, let's divvy it up.' Now the discussion is 'how are we going to hold people accountable for results?'" Still, the commission is committed to allowing a good deal of local flexibility. "We started out with the idea that local judges and prosecutors could run the program any way they wanted to. It would surprise me if [we changed that]," Price said.

Louisiana

In Louisiana, the question of "who's in charge?" was answered by the state legislature in 2001.

Twenty-nine drug courts were up and running in the state by 2000, and several more were in the planning stages. Up until that point, the Office of Addictive Disorders, an executive-branch agency, was the primary backer of drug courts. The Office of

Addictive Disorders was providing about $1.5 million a year to fund a number of the courts, and Louisiana was attracting both planning and implementation grants from the U.S. Department of Justice. The Office of Addictive Disorders had also contracted with programmers at a local university to develop a management information system, but, unhappy with the product, it abandoned the effort, leaving Louisiana's drug courts without a way to collect information on a statewide level.

Concern over the lack of a statewide management information system was just one of several factors that eventually propelled some judges to seek a change in leadership. Another concern was that some courts were calling themselves drug courts—and obtaining drug-court funding—while failing to provide adequate treatment services or rigorous judicial monitoring. But perhaps the biggest concern was financial. Although the Office for Addictive Disorders had funded drug courts since their inception, the other major source of funding—federal grants—was starting to dry up. In addition, the Office for Addictive Disorders had to reapply to the legislature every year for continued funding, leaving the courts vulnerable to potential belt-tightening and political maneuvering.

Drug court advocates, including Bernard E. Boudreaux, former St. Mary Parish district attorney and counsel to Governor Mike Foster Jr., felt that the Supreme Court, as a separate branch of government free from the Legislature's line-item oversight, could provide more secure funding. When asked in 2001 by judges in New Orleans to take over the drug court budget, Supreme Court Justice Catherine D. "Kitty" Kimball, who chairs the court system's Budgetary Control Board, assented.

Kimball said she was convinced drug courts helped reduce recidivism and were therefore good for the long-term health of the state and the court system. When "the Criminal Court in New Orleans came to us and said their federal funding is drying up,"

Kimball said she felt that the Supreme Court had no other choice but to step up to the plate. "As it turned out, courts were having the same problem all over the state. I said, 'If we're going to do it in one court, let's do it for the whole state.'"

Officials from both the Office for Addictive Disorders and the Supreme Court met with the legislature and House Appropriations and Senate Finance Committee chairs to discuss the transition of control over drug courts from the Office for Addictive Disorders to the Supreme Court. The Supreme Court officially took over in July 2001. At the same time, legislators allocated $13 million for drug courts, including $8 million from the state budget and $5 million from the state's welfare block grant.

Although the transfer understandably caused some tense moments between the Office for Addictive Disorders and the Supreme Court, it was supported by most key players across the state. Members of the drug court community, like Lars Levy, the administrative director of drug treatment services for St. Mary Parish's five drug courts, welcomed the move because they felt the Supreme Court budget was more secure and the Supreme Court would have more authority over judges to enforce standards. Even Jake Hadley, who in 1997 was the first director of the Office of Addictive Disorders to take an interest in funding drug courts, now agrees that the move was the right one, saying that "a judge or a D.A. is going to react differently if the Supreme Court says, 'let's do something'" than if the Office of Addictive Disorders makes the suggestion.

The current head of the Office for Addictive Disorders, Michael Duffy, indicated that it is his agency's primary mission to maintain the integrity of treatment. "It's a precarious position," Duffy stated. "The problem is that this arrangement could place the judiciary in the position of having to make clinical decisions rather than legal decisions based upon clinical experience and sound clinical opinion. My only concern is that when you blur the line between clinical and judiciary, the clinical component does not suffer."

After assuming responsibility for drug courts, the Supreme Court created a new department, the Drug Court Office, which oversees the Supreme Court's $13 million drug court budget. Cary Heck, who was hired to serve as the director of the office, has worked to increase the courts' capacity to oversee treatment, hiring Sandi Record, the former director of treatment for the Office of Addictive Disorders, to travel around the state and confer with courts about their treatment practices. Record said her goal is to strengthen courts' links to treatment. "I think there needs to be oversight of treatment," Record said. "Treatment needs to be happening, and I'm not sure that's always the emphasis with the courts."

Building Support

If drug courts are to survive the transition from a series of isolated experiments to an institutionalized feature of a state's criminal justice and drug-treatment systems, they need to maintain and even expand the support—financial, logistical, political—that they've so carefully cultivated over the years. The question becomes, of course, whose support is needed? And the answer depends on the individual state's approach to institutionalization.

New York

In New York, Judge Kaye's plan to create at least one criminal and one family drug court in all 62 counties has required the cultivation of support on the local level. One of Deputy Chief Judge Joseph J. Traficanti Jr.'s first actions as director of Court Drug Treatment Programs was to convene a meeting of administrative judges who oversee the state's 12 judicial districts. The support of the administrative judges was crucial if drug courts were to be absorbed fully by the system, said Traficanti, since the administrative judges retained ultimate responsibility for day-to-day operations. "I didn't know how it would be received, but, to a person, they committed themselves to me," Traficanti said. "I was calling in some chits I'd earned over the years. That personal commitment by the administrative judges was important, because ultimately, around the state, the commitment isn't to me, it's to the administrative judges, to whom everyone in each district looks for guidance and leadership."

Traficanti also reached out to other state officials to foster cross-agency collaboration. His office has worked closely with officials from the Office of Alcoholism and Substance Abuse Services, which funds and certifies treatment providers; the Department of Children and Family Services, which oversees agencies working with parents in Family Court; and the New York State Association of Directors of Probation, since many counties rely on probation officers as drug court caseworkers. Traficanti said the early outreach consisted largely of assuring the various agencies that the court system did not want to step on anyone's toes nor was it seeking to "compete" in any way.

The Office of Alcoholism and Substance Abuse Services, for one, has welcomed the expansion of drug courts because the courts are channeling more people into treatment and improving rates of retention, said Howard Schwartz, the office's director of criminal justice services. Today court officials and Alcoholism and Substance Abuse officials meet regularly to resolve conflicts that arise in particular jurisdictions. "We try to resolve the problem, then we go to the jurisdiction as a unified body to address it," Schwartz said.

Within his office, Traficanti created a team of three project managers, assigning each one a different region of the state. The three project managers spent a good deal of time traveling around their regions trying to set the planning process in motion for drug courts at the county level. That process often began with a meeting of court staff and potential project partners. "Sometimes it takes two or three trips to get people to the point where they start planning," said Kathi Chaplin, project manager for central and western portions of the state. Chaplin provided attendees with an outline that included examples of actions that New York's existing drug courts had taken to get their programs up and running. She also helped them apply for federal planning grants and signed them up for team trainings coordinated by Traficanti's office and the Center for Court Innovation, which serves as the state court system's independent research and development arm. It usually takes from eight to 12 months after a drug court team is assembled for a new court to open, Chaplin said.

Traficanti and his staff say that, for the most part, judges and community partners, including district attorneys and the defense bar, have been eager to participate. The key, however, is the court system's willingness to be flexible. "Each community in New York State is like a fingerprint and has different needs," Traficanti said. As such, "We let each drug court be self-developed. We let the whole thing come from the bottom," said Mizzi Diamond, Traficanti's executive assistant. As a selling point, the court system has offered each drug court not only assistance in planning and training, but money to hire a resource coordinator, pay for drug testing and buy computers and software.

In the end, "Working with the judges has been easier than I thought," Traficanti said. "There have only been two who refused to do it, and I'll get to them eventually." The support of judges who are not in drug court is also important because it is these judges who are often tapped to back up regular drug court judges when they are sick or on vacation. Some drug courts also depend on those judges for referrals. In Rochester, for instance, the number of clients has been limited by other judges' resistance to sending their cases to drug court. "Some judges still believe probation is better," said Rochester's supervising judge, John Schwartz. "They still have the discretion to keep the case. That is the flaw in the system, a big flaw."

Court clerks are sometimes the least interested in drug court, said Chaplin, a clerk herself for 25 years. "Clerks hate this—their initial attitude, with some exceptions, is 'You know what? Having to do more with less is getting old.'" Chaplin says it helps that, because of her years of experience as a clerk, she can "talk their language. . . . I can show them how it can be done and how it can make their lives easier. I tell them how this will become the most rewarding part of their career. In 25 years, I never felt really good about what I did until I did drug courts."

Ohio

Drug court leaders around the country have found that growing more drug courts in their states gets harder as time goes on since the only counties without drug courts are usually ones that have steadfastly refused to create them.

In Ohio, this phenomenon is exacerbated by the state's home-rule tradition: elected judges in each county have considerable authority over how their courts are run on a day-to-day basis.

In such a setting, the drug court sales pitch has required persistence. For instance, drug court leaders, like Luceille Fleming, long targeted Franklin County, home of Columbus, the state's capital, but to no avail. "We trained and trained and trained folks from Franklin County. We've invited them to the [annual Ohio Association of Drug Court Professionals] conference and offered scholarships, and brought judges and teams to Franklin County to share their experience with drug court," says Joani Moore, coordinator of drug courts for the Department of Alcohol and Drug Addiction Services.

One reason Franklin County was less interested in drug courts was because, unlike many other Ohio counties, it wasn't facing a shortage of jail space. "It's a wealthy county. It's one of the few in the state that has never been under a federal court order that would restrict the housing of sentenced inmates," Moore says. Because of this, it has been under less pressure to innovate.

In addition, the judicial philosophy in Franklin County has been "against specialized dockets," said Melissa Knopp, program manager of specialized dockets for the Supreme Court. It wasn't until 2003 that the 16 judges on the Court of Common Pleas finally agreed to start a drug court. This was largely due largely to the work of a new judge, Jennifer Brunner, who was elected to the bench in 2000 and worked on the initiative for a year with a task force that grew to over 60 criminal justice and treatment representatives. Brunner worked with people outside the court who demonstrated strong support for a drug court. The initiative was also aided by Evelyn Lundberg-Stratton, a former Franklin County judge who sits on the Ohio Supreme Court, who started taking an interest in specialized dockets and urged her former peers in Franklin County to start one.

Brunner said it took her many months to develop several models and submit them to a large focus group and then to the 15 other judges for their sign-off on the plan. "I was allowed to pursue this specialty docket, as long as it would not cost the court any money—I had to find outside funds for the effort, which came from the Ohio Department of Alcohol and Drug Addiction Services through our local drug and mental health treatment funding board," Brunner said. She agreed to add drug court to her own caseload. "We carry more cases per judge than any other county in this state. In fact, our county has looked to the legislature to give us two new judges. I had difficulty convincing my colleagues that drug courts will actually reduce caseloads. They agreed to a pilot program of 50 participants. When one judge criticized the effort, saying that what the court needed was a judge whose docket was solely drug court cases, I told the judge that he was asking for a bulldozer to solve our county's drug-related crime problem, but that we couldn't afford a bulldozer. I told the judge that all I was asking for was a little ice pick like Tim Robbins had in the movie *The Shawshank Redemption*. The judges thereafter agreed to start a pilot program."

Brunner believes that as more new judges join the bench, especially since the drug court is now under way, resistance to problem-solving courts in Franklin County will wane, and drug courts will be accepted as part of the court's landscape. "There's a new generation of judges getting elected to the bench, judges who see a role for restorative or therapeutic justice and the unique contribution the judiciary can make in this way to the well being of the community. When I go out into the community, people ask me, 'What are you going to do besides show up to work and go home?' When I talk about SAMI (substance abuse, mental illness) courts in the community, ordinary people nod their heads. They get it," Brunner said.

In Ohio, drug court advocates also grappled with a referendum that could have dramatically affected the way drug courts operate. "Issue 1" would have amended the state constitution to require courts to suspend criminal proceedings and provide treatment for any offender charged with or convicted of illegal possession or use of a controlled substance who asks for treatment.[20]

The campaign in favor of the referendum was supported by the three billionaires—financier George Soros, University of Phoenix founder John Sperling and Ohio insurance executive Peter B. Lewis—who had bankrolled successful campaigns to adopt similar referendums in California and Arizona. As the campaigns for and against Issue 1 built momentum from June to November, the debate became increasingly bitter and divisive. Among the opponents, led by Ohio First Lady Hope Taft and Toledo Mayor Jack Ford, were drug court practitioners and a long list of law enforcement, judicial and criminal justice organizations, as well as coalitions of treatment providers, businesses, labor and dozens of newspapers who editorialized against it.

The main concerns animating opponents were that the amendment would reduce the discretion of judges and take away jail as a potential sanction. Some also thought that amending the state constitution was not the best way to reform sentencing laws. Drug court practitioners were particularly vocal in opposing the amendment, predicting a dire future for drug courts if judges were forced to accept all comers and lost the ability to threaten recalcitrant participants with prison. "It was dangerous and detrimental to [the] whole fabric of what we built," Fleming said.

In the end, Issue 1 was resoundingly defeated, 67 percent to 33 percent. The referendum lost in all 88 Ohio counties. The reason voters voted "no" is not clear—many, including opponents of the measure, feel voters were not reacting to the measure's policy implications but to ballot language that referred to the amendment's $247 million cost.

The successful campaign against Issue 1 gave drug court practitioners the chance to galvanize support for drug courts and educate the public about how they work. Drug court advocates like Fleming and Judge John Durkin, president of the Ohio Association of Drug Court Professionals, lobbied heavily against the measure, writing opinion pieces in local newspapers and participating in radio debates. "Issue 1 didn't create momentum for drug courts—we already had that," Durkin said. "What we accomplished was to educate local leaders, commissioners and senators that drug courts save lives and money." Fleming noted that since the defeat of Issue 1, "Fifteen more drug courts have opened. Many more people understand it now."

On the other hand, the fight to oppose Issue 1 was not without its costs for drug courts. For one thing, Issue 1 would have greatly increased the amount of money available for treatment.

Michael Stringer, the chief of justice services for the Department of Alcohol and Drug Addiction Services until mid-2003, said that if the proponents of Issue 1 had been willing to collaborate with drug court advocates, the outcome might have been different. "But [Issue 1 proponents] just couldn't accept the idea of coercion," Stringer said.

Missouri

In Missouri, like New York, drug courts have benefitted from a strong push from court leadership. During Judge William Price's two-year term as the state's chief judge, he moved drug courts to the top of the agenda and organized a judicial conference on addiction in 1996. "We invited judges from around the state. We only had about 45 out of 305, but the facilitators were impressed with the turnout," said Ann Wilson, a Drug Court Commission staff member who serves as the alcohol and drug abuse coordinator with the Office of State Courts Administrator. "The conference was a preliminary to talking about drug court because there was such adamant opposition to having judges care about substance abuse. I've seen a 180 degree turnaround in our judges' attitudes since then."

In addition to offering training, Price created a task force on drug courts. Its 48 members included judges, prosecutors, defense attorneys and representatives from probation and parole, drug treatment, job training and educational programs. The task force helped draft legislation that established state funding for drug courts and created new positions, like drug court administrators, to support drug court functions.

The legislation also created the Drug Court Commission, which consists of four judges and the heads of the departments of Social Services, Mental Health, Public Safety and Corrections. The commission helps to ensure open communication between all the agencies that have a role to play in drug court development. David Brown of the Department of Public Safety, who lobbied his boss for an appointment to the commission, said that the level of cooperation has been unusual. "Everyone here is a true believer," said Brown.

Judge Lawrence Mooney, a commission member who sits on Missouri's Court of Appeals, noted that the "degree of support" among state policymakers for drug courts was very high, noting that "we had a [drug court] conference a few years ago and the governor showed up." He also believed that Price's leadership on the commission "helps give [drug courts] credibility within the judiciary." In Missouri, then, support from high-level executives sent a strong and consistent signal to local jurisdictions that drug courts were a priority for the state.

Establishing Best Practices

Almost from the very start, the drug court movement has relied on research to inform practice—to identify what works and what doesn't. As states grapple with the challenges of institutionalization, many have sought to articulate best practices for drug courts culled from both experience and research. Disseminating best practices is viewed as a way to ensure a minimum level of quality throughout a state's varied drug courts.

States are attempting to promote best practices in various ways. Some enforce best practices as a condition of receiving grant funding. Others have promoted a set of voluntary practice guidelines for drug courts to follow. And some are using trainings and certification programs to educate practitioners about best practices.

Louisiana

In Louisiana, the first entity to actively pursue the establishment of best practices was the Louisiana Association of Drug Court Professionals, created in 1997. The association formed a best practices committee, which, after several years, produced a document modeled closely after the 10 key components but with Louisiana-specific detail.

The best practices specified eligibility criteria, testing requirements and minimum treatment standards for drug courts. They were, of course, non-binding, since they were issued by the Louisiana Association of Drug Court Professionals (although developed in cooperation with the state court system and Office for Addictive Disorders), which has no official authority over the state's drug courts.

Nonetheless, board members of the association were hopeful that the Supreme Court would use the best practices as a basis for establishing statewide standards. Cary Heck, who was hired to administer the Supreme Court's $13 million drug court budget, initially declared that the best practices set the bar too high, and that not all drug courts around the state had the resources to meet the guidelines. "I had to allow for rural courts and small courts," Heck said. "We have courts that serve three parish regions and the judge commutes and serves in different parishes each week. They can't be held to the same standards as [a larger, better funded] court, which has its own inpatient facility. It wouldn't be fair."

It was Heck who suggested that the association call its guidelines "best practices" while Heck's office promulgated "minimum standards." "I said, 'You guys keep working on best practices, and I'll work on minimum standards, and maybe one day, they'll meet.'"

Heck also thought it was counterproductive to establish standards that were too rigid. "Being a small government kind of guy, I love that drug courts are locally initiated programs with their own character," Heck said. His goal was to establish a basic level of uniformity among Louisiana's drug courts without forcing local drug courts out of business.

Louisiana Supreme Court Justice Catherine Kimball said the

standards are loose enough to support the diversity many feel has been a strength of the drug court movement. "Communities in Louisiana are so different that they have to have freedom to set up programs that work in those communities," Kimball said. "To me, institutionalization doesn't mean making identical the way each court operates. Institutionalization is about the larger concept. On a conceptual level, all the courts are the same, but in the details they can be different."

Still, Heck's statewide drug court program standards—released in the summer of 2003—ended up looking like the state association's best practice guidelines. In some areas, they even exceeded them: For example, Heck's standards specifically outline the membership of drug court teams, while the guidelines do not. Like the guidelines, the standards also require testing at least twice a week during the first two phases of drug court and spell out minimum treatment standards for each phase—for example, "treatment should consist of a minimum of six hours of therapeutic contact per week for adults [down from nine hours in the guidelines] and three hours for juveniles" during Phase I. Additionally, Phase I should "last at least two months." Heck's standards also spell out a new monitoring regime for drug courts, requiring them to file monthly reports and submit to bi-annual field reviews.

To enforce the minimum standards, Heck requires all courts receiving drug court funds to sign an annual contract. "We hold the purse strings, and if they agree to these standards and sign off on them, and they don't comply—I'm not expecting that at all—then we would have a reason to modify behavior through that money," Heck said. He also hired Sandi Record, who formerly worked on drug courts for the state's treatment agency, to conduct bi-annual reviews of each drug court.

Minimum standards are not the only way the Supreme Court intends to promote best practices. Heck is working with two colleges to develop a voluntary certification program for drug court professionals "that will cover everything from ethics to case management." The program would promote best practices and a baseline of knowledge throughout the state, Heck said.

New York

New York has taken a different approach. The court system does not plan on setting specific drug court standards, although it is working to create a best practices manual for adult drug courts. The guide is intended to serve as a "kind of constitution, some kind of structure or skeleton" that expresses "core values," according to Judge Joseph Traficanti. But the manual will only be advisory, underscoring drug court principles without binding practitioners to a pre-determined plan of action.

Traficanti, working with the Center for Court Innovation, has convened a committee to create the best practice guide. Supported by a grant from the U.S. Department of Justice, the guide is expected to address three main areas: planning a court, treatment issues and post-discharge services. Tom Kubiniec, a prosecutor in Erie County who sits on the best practice committee, said the committee is trying to identify "the ingredients of a successful drug court, and those ingredients should be adhered to as best as possible."

The Center for Court Innovation is also working on a separate but similar guide for family treatment courts. Both guides will be "tools for setting acceptable standards to guide drug courts," said Valerie Raine, director of drug treatment programs at the Center for Court Innovation. "In my opinion, we should steer away as far as we can from absolute rules and standards."

In fact, when court administrators in New York issued an over-arching policy regarding one aspect of drug courts, the response was resoundingly negative. In that instance, top administrators issued a rule that every drug court contract needed blanket language about ex parte communication that would have the effect of allowing drug courts to hold case conferences without a defense attorney present. When defense attorneys balked, however, administrators rescinded the mandate and created a subcommittee to review the issue. On the recommendation of the subcommittee, court administrators now plan to advise drug courts to address ex parte communication on an as-needed basis, obtaining client's specific consent for specific instances of ex parte communication when necessary, rather than use a blanket consent.

And yet while New York does not plan to enforce rigid standards, it has nonetheless invested in research through the Center for Court Innovation and its 10-member research team. Research conducted by the Center, for example, played an important role in the development of the Brooklyn Treatment Court, one of New York's first drug courts. A full-time researcher used data to inform policy, leading the judge and court staff, in one example, to send heroin addicts to residential treatment as soon as they entered the court. "The rationale was, 'Why wait if we know there's a high probability they'll end up in residential treatment down the road?'" said Michael Rempel, director of research at the Center. In another example, the researcher established that there was a high rate of no-shows in the first 30 days after admission to the treatment court; in response, the court developed preplacement groups to keep clients engaged with the court while they were waiting for admission to a substance abuse program.

In addition to helping shape practice at individual drug courts, research has also helped build knowledge about drug courts across the state. In November 2003, the court system and the Center for Court Innovation jointly released a study that demonstrated consistent and meaningful reductions in recidivism across a large number of drug courts.[21] Among other things, the study identified participant characteristics and programmatic features that increased the likelihood of successful drug court outcomes. It underscored, for example, the importance of immediacy and early engagement. It showed a high relapse rate among participants, thus reaffirming the importance of giving offenders multiple chances. The study also pointed out populations that may require new approaches. Addicted offenders who were not charged with a drug offense, for example, did not do as well as those facing a drug charge.

New York has also sponsored more than a dozen trainings throughout the state, lasting anywhere from one to five days. Planning teams of eight to 10 people (generally including judges, attorneys, court staff, probation officers and treatment providers) are invited to participate. These training sessions give participants the opportunity to learn about drug courts, get acquainted with one another and come to rough agreements about program elements—important factors given that so many drug court components (e.g., a non-adversarial approach, partnerships between drug courts and other agencies and a coordinated strategy) are collaborative in nature.

Most practitioners seem to actively embrace the team approach, and many insist it is crucial. "I've had phone calls from other defenders, and I tell them, 'Unless you're part of the planning process, you shouldn't support drug courts,'" said Ed Nowak, a public defender in Monroe County. In addition, researchers often make an appearance at these trainings, providing participants with the latest research-based knowledge about best practices.

Interestingly, New York has also provided drug court training for non-drug court judges. In May 2003, 20 New York City criminal and family court judges attended a day-long training on drug courts at New York's Judicial Institute. Topics included a discussion of how judges in non-drug court parts could employ drug court best practices in conventional courtrooms.

Ohio

Ohio uses the grant process to enforce standards. The effect is limited, however, since the Ohio Department of Alcohol and Drug Addiction Services provides direct grants to only 19 of the state's 55 courts. Grant recipients are required to use department-certified treatment providers, which are in turn compelled to follow the department's protocols outlining appropriate levels of care. "If someone is assessed to be in need of short-term outpatient counseling, the treatment agency can't put him in a residential program because the court thinks he's dangerous," said Joani Moore, the department's drug court coordinator.

The department's grants also cannot be used for defendants facing driving-under-the-influence charges. "In this state we have very stiff DUI laws. There's a mandatory three days in jail for first offense. The second gets 10 to 90 days. If we allowed drug courts to include DUI offenders, jurisdictions would do nothing but work with [them], and we wouldn't be serving [other] criminal offenders," Moore said. In addition, DUI impacts the county jail population while the department's goal is to reduce the statewide prison population. "We want to work with criminal offenders who would otherwise burden the state jail population—that's why the legislature gives us money," Moore said.

Grant recipients are also prohibited from accepting the severely mentally ill. "These are not mental health courts," Moore said. "If you're [severely] mentally ill, these aren't the places for you. The mentally ill don't get much from [the drug court program], and they hurt the program a lot. If they're too fragile to incarcerate, it makes the other drug court participants frustrated because the court's not consistent."

Creating Infrastructure

What kinds of tools need to be developed and implemented to sustain the statewide institutionalization of drug court principles? In New York, for example, the court system has created new civil service positions for drug court staff. Although this may not seem noteworthy, it has had the effect of allowing non-traditional, drug court-related staff to become a regular court presence.

Another investment states interested in drug court development are making is in the creation of management information systems. These computerized systems, which are crucial for evaluating drug court performance, require a great deal of statewide coordination. To work well, all drug courts within a state must use the same terms, input the same information and measure the same outcomes—a considerable implementation challenge, considering that many drug courts prefer to use their own homegrown information systems and assessment tools.

Here is a closer look at some infrastructure investments:

Staffing and Purchasing

In addition to creating new civil service positions to reflect the responsibilities of drug court case managers and resource coordinators, the New York State Unified Court System has sought to achieve economies of scale when it comes to purchasing and negotiating with statewide partners. Judge John Schwartz of the Rochester Treatment Court recalled "practically stealing urine cups" to make drug court happen. Those days are long gone. Court administrators are now more sophisticated about drug court's unique needs. "We're used to ordering pens and paper. Now we're asking 'What drug tests do you order?' Some courts will have a heavy cocaine problem and they'll want one kind of test, and others will have a different problem and need a different kind of test," said Diane Lundin, law clerk to the 9th district administrative judge.

Management Information Systems

A statewide management information system can make it easier for state leaders to collect standardized data about court outcomes, but building the system itself is no easy task.

As early as November 1997, an Office of Addictive Disorders-led working group on drug courts identified the development of a computerized system for collecting drug court statistics as a key priority for Louisiana. Accordingly, the office signed a contract with a local university to develop the system. After several years of trying, however, the agency abandoned the original effort. But in January of 2004, nearly seven years after the first contract was signed, the Supreme Court successfully launched a statewide system that established a uniform data collection system for every drug court in the state.

Although some of the obstacles Louisiana has encountered in developing a management information system are technical, others relate to the difficulty of getting each drug court to agree on uniform terminology. "[Courts] couldn't agree on definitions. They couldn't even establish what admission meant," said Cary Heck, Louisiana's drug court coordinator. In the end, Heck decided what terms to use. "I just told them that I was going to make the decisions. If they really want to be institutionalized and sustain their courts I need to be able to say an apple is an apple."

Louisiana is hardly the exception when it comes to technology development. One consequence of the home-rule structure in Ohio is that there are over 300 different computer systems in use, according to Melissa Knopp, program manager of specialized dockets for the Supreme Court of Ohio. Still, the Ohio Supreme Court is asking all courts within the state to develop new management information systems according to pre-determined statewide standards. Because of home rule, jurisdictions will have the authority to contract with different companies to develop the new management information system, but the goal is that, in the end, they will all be able to communicate with each other more easily than they can using the current hodge-podge of systems, Knopp said.

In New York, state officials have spent the last six years working on a computer program, known as the Universal Treatment Application, that captures all the information about a drug court case. The Universal Treatment Application, which was piloted in the Brooklyn Treatment Court, facilitates case management as well as data collection. Treatment providers and probation departments access the database via a secure "intranet" connection; this allows them to update client records (including information about attendance and drug tests) easily, without having to fax progress reports or exchange phone calls with court staff. The right to review files is restricted and access to the database is password protected. It took several years to work out kinks, but by the end of 2003, the technology was being used by drug courts throughout the state.

By requiring all drug courts to use the treatment application, court officials in New York hope to enforce uniformity in both practice and data collection. For instance, the application includes the psycho-social interview used to screen clients for treatment eligibility. That means drug courts around the state are asking the same questions of clients and using the same diagnostic tools to determine whether a client is drug addicted and what treatment modality is most appropriate.

Research

States have also invested in research into drug court effectiveness. Research into drug courts has two potential benefits—positive results can bolster support for the model, while research findings can also be used to improve operations.

Building a management information system is a critical first step towards obtaining high-quality research about drug courts because it can ensure that consistent information about outcomes is being collected across the state.

But in order for the information system to be effective, researchers need to play a role in its development. In addition, states need help interpreting the raw data provided by local jurisdictions. Some states, like Ohio, have asked local universities to produce statewide evaluations. Other states, like Louisiana and New York, have worked to create an in-house research capacity that allows state agencies to produce their own research reports.

One recent report issued jointly by the New York state court system and the Center for Court Innovation examined six drug courts in New York and found an average 29 percent reduction in re-arrests for participants over a three-year period when compared to a matched set of offenders not in drug court. Even after leaving drug court, benefits persisted: one-year post-program recidivism rates dropped 32 percent.[22]

Well-executed research can not only help build a case for drug courts (the report was covered widely by local and national press), but can also be used to help identify characteristics of drug courts that promote program success. For example, a consensus has emerged among researchers nationally that enrolling offenders into treatment quickly, imposing sanctions and rewards swiftly and appropriately, bringing high-risk offenders back before the judge regularly and ensuring that drug court participants feel they are being treated respectfully by the judge and are being listened to in the courtroom are critical to successful drug court implementation.

Screening and Assessment Tools

Another significant investment states can make is in improving screening and assessment tools to ensure that all drug-addicted offenders are identified and evaluated for drug court eligibility.

New York is piloting a universal screening process to identify and assess all potential drug court clients in a county. Currently, in most drug courts around the state, only non-violent defendants charged with a drug crime are screened for eligibility. The universal screening process would expand the pool of potential participants by identifying all non-violent defendants who are drug-addicted—whether they are charged with a drug-related crime or not. Implementing this process, however, requires a major investment. Staff with assessment skills need to be hired or borrowed from a partner agency. Courthouse intake needs to be restructured. The daunting size of the task has led the court system to pursue this goal slowly.

The first step has been to create a pilot screening project in Brooklyn. "We are attempting to screen every single person arrested and charged by the district attorney," said Justin Barry, the New York City drug court coordinator. The court system began the Brooklyn pilot in January 2003. As part of the procedure, the court system has created three treatment courts for the borough. Each court is designed to capture a different offender population: the Brooklyn Treatment Court works mainly with felony offenders; another court deals only with misdemeanants; and a third works with participants in the D.A.-run Drug Treatment Altnerative-to-Prison program, as well as with offenders between the ages of 16 and 18.

The screening process works like this: All defendants are screened prior to arraignment by a clerk who determines if a defendant is drug-court eligible (based mainly on the severity of the charge and history of violence). The judge handling the arraignment then places the case on the calendar of one of Brooklyn's three treatment courts for the next business day. When the defendant appears the next day, a case manager administers a complete psycho-social assessment, which is recorded in the Universal Treatment Application. Clients deemed appropriate for treatment are offered admission to the court.

Jim Imperatrice, the chief clerk of Brooklyn Supreme Court, said the new system is less prone to error than past practice. "Screening of potential clients used to happen at arraignment in criminal court, which is open seven days a week, two to three shifts a day," Imperatrice said. "With all the different shifts, different judges, D.A.s and court staff, people would fall through the cracks. The new system is a lot simpler. Everything goes before a single clerk and then gets reviewed by the arraigning judge."

Increasing Capacity

Expanding the reach of drug courts is one of the key goals of many within the drug court movement. Marilyn Roberts, the former head of the U.S. Department of Justice's drug court office, often said that one of her goals was not to open more drug courts, but to get more participants into drug court.[23]

One of the powerful arguments advanced by proponents of Issue 1 in Ohio was the idea that drug courts served only a fraction of the population. "[They] said, 'We don't serve enough people.' That's a good criticism," said Judge Steve Williams, a juvenile court judge. This critique has been echoed by drug policy scholars like Marc Kleiman of UCLA, who has written that drug courts are too expensive and too reliant on a flawed treatment system to implement on a widespread basis.[24]

What strategies are available to states that want to increase drug court capacity? One is to loosen the restrictions on the types of cases that are eligible for drug courts. This, of course, can be politically difficult. "The feds say no to violent offenders," said Michael Stringer, the former chief of justice services for the Ohio Department of Alcohol and Drug Addiction Services, "and we also said we won't take violent offenders in the courts we fund, but that is starting to change. . . . Where courts have said they were comfortable, we've shifted to say that they can deal with the offenders that your court and your judge is comfortable with in your community."

Stringer said two groups should be the focus on any expansion in drug court eligibility: those who would otherwise be headed to prison and those who are coming out of prison. Accordingly, the Ohio Department of Alcohol and Drug Addiction Services has approached the governor's office with the idea of creating legislation that would mandate treatment for 5th-degree felons. The department is also trying to build more bridges between drug courts and in-prison treatment programs. "We're working on a pilot where the court after repeated failures will use the in-prison treatment program for 90 days and then the offender will come out under judicial release," Stringer said. "That's the kind of continuum we're trying to put in place."

There are, undoubtedly, numerous ways to expand capacity. What follows is a look at two interesting approaches taken by courts in Minnesota and Florida that offer lessons for others.

Hennepin County, Minnesota

In Hennepin County, Minnesota, all drug offenders in the county are admitted into drug court, regardless of their arrest history. "We are already at scale," said Chief Judge Kevin Burke, who created the drug court in 1997.

Today, according to coordinator Dennis Miller, the Hennepin County Drug Court has over 4,000 participants at any one time—about a third of the county's total criminal court caseload. Because of its large size, the drug court has a number of dedicated staff—three judges, seven prosecutors, seven defense attorneys, over 20 probation officers, six "chemical health assessors," job training specialists and an adult educator. The court also has relationships with 20 community-based treatment providers. All told, the drug court costs $2 million more than “business as usual,” paid largely through local tax dollars.

The “take all comers” approach of the Hennepin County Drug Court has had some interesting programmatic implications. For example, because the drug court takes all drug offenders, there is no “opt out” option to the traditional court system. Defendants are given their full trial rights, meaning that drug court judges conduct close to 35 trials a year. Hundreds of pre-trial hearings over issues like search and seizure are also conducted. As a result, close to 20 percent of all drug court cases are dismissed or result in acquittals. An additional 10 percent of cases—generally involving high-risk offenders with multiple priors—are sent to prison right away.

All told, the percentage of drug offenders in Hennepin County going into treatment has steadily increased from 45 percent in the first year of the drug court to 74 percent in 2002.

The drug court has also become a major player in shaping the treatment marketplace in Hennepin County. “There’s not a lot of mystery to treatment any more,” said Miller. “We know a lot more about what effective treatment should look like.” Miller said he looks for treatment programs that “treat the whole person” and offer a rich set of ancillary services. Accordingly, the bulk of the court’s caseload goes to the six (out of 20) treatment programs in the county with a similar treatment philosophy.

Dade County, Florida

Dade County, Florida—the birthplace of drug courts—has taken a very different approach to the issue of increasing drug court capacity. Court administrators have long been frustrated by their inability to reach agreement with prosecutors and the public defender’s office over a post-plea program. As a result, Miami’s drug court, while large (around 1,500 cases annually), is a pre-plea drug court largely limited to low-level offenses.

More out of desperation than design, Drug Court Administrator Robert Koch decided to hitch the drug court approach to an existing probation sentencing option as a means of getting around the restriction on post-plea cases. The idea was to add judicial monitoring to probation sentences and require offenders to come back to court regularly to report on their progress in treatment. Dade County Chief Judge Joseph P. Farina signed off on the plan—provided that judges supported it. "He told me, 'If you get five judges to agree to this, we'll go ahead,'" recalled Koch.

Much to his surprise, all 19 judges agreed to the proposal. "In every [new program], there are moments when things happen that blow you away," Koch said. "We had a skeptical judge say, 'I've been a judge for 20 years, and this is the greatest thing I've ever heard of.' Her support brought on board another five or six people." As a result, the chief judge issued an administrative order authorizing each felony division judge to make use of a "Judicial Monitoring Program" in partnership with probation.

Together, Koch and Farina designed a set of protocols for judicial monitoring and a sanctions-and-rewards scheme for judges to follow. They also educated judges about drug court. "A lot of judges didn't know anything about drug courts," Koch said. "We had to teach them about relapse and substance abuse itself." The minimum period of supervision in the Judicial Monitoring Program is 18 months, though early termination is possible as a reward for program compliance. Probation officers are responsible for enrolling program participants into treatment and conducting drug tests, while judges are free to set their own monitoring schedules.

Not surprisingly, implementation varies widely. As of July 2003, there were 473 offenders enrolled in the Judicial Monitoring Program, but one judge had 108 active cases, another 85 and a few had only four or five cases. Judges also differ in the types of sanctions and rewards they impose and the frequency of court appearances, though court administrators believe they have successfully introduced the idea of intermediate sanctioning and have increased judicial tolerance for drug relapses.

In addition, the Judicial Monitoring Program does not include all of the 10 key components of drug courts. Most notably, there is no "team" approach—prosecutors and public defenders still spar with one another in an adversarial environment. With three prosecutors and three public defenders assigned to each of the county's 19 courts, it was impossible, according to Koch, to get "everyone to embrace a non-adversarial process." Court administrators are trying to educate prosecutors and defense attorneys about the drug court approach, but the work of winning hearts and minds is slow.

Lessons from Dade and Hennepin Counties

The Dade County approach suggests that creating more "drug courts" per se is not the only strategy available to state leaders attempting to increase the court's capacity to link addicted offenders to judicially supervised treatment. As Koch put it, the key question is "Do we need to create more drug courts, or does the concept of drug court need to become an inherent way of dealing with these types of cases in every criminal division?"

The Dade County model also suggests that modest changes in courtroom structure might result in courts getting most (if not all) of the way towards the drug court ideal. "Instead of trying to change the jurisprudential process," Koch said, "we just embraced the additional use of treatment and judicial monitoring in a typical courtroom model."

The contrasts between Hennepin County and Dade County are also instructive. Hennepin County essentially carved a drug court bureau out of a much larger court system: only three out of a total of 57 judges are involved in drug court at any one time.

This approach appears to have two major benefits: according to Dennis Miller, it greatly reduces court costs through economies of scale, and it allows for judicial specialization. Its main drawback appears to be the potential for marginalization: while drug court has resulted in "tremendous relief for the [overall] system," according to Miller, it has not come close to receiving a proportionate share of court resources. At the same time, the court has had trouble gaining the support of other system players, like police and prosecutors, to broaden its scope to include cases like shoplifting and welfare fraud that may be driven by addiction.

Alternatively, Dade County's model only requires modest changes to current court procedures, and does not require advocates on either side to abandon adversarial practice. Because of this, it has taken place without a great deal of controversy or additional resources. The drawback, however, is its widely divergent implementation and essentially voluntary nature for judges—Koch believes that only about 10 percent of eligible cases are being referred for enhanced judicial monitoring.

A final strategy for states seeking to reach new clients involves taking the drug court approach and applying it to different kinds of cases. In New York, for example, Judge Kaye has launched a number of "community courts" (neighborhood-based courts that use community resources to respond to low-level offending and other local problems in creative ways), as well as a pilot mental health court, domestic violence courts and family treatment courts throughout the state. All these efforts point in a similar direction, toward a court system in which the principles of strict judicial supervision, collaboration with non-court partners and new measures of success (such as higher rates of sobriety, increased victim safety and lower rates of recidivism) become commonplace.

Nor is New York alone in these efforts. In Louisiana, for example, a judge in St. Mary Parish has created his own "mini-drug court" for persistent drunken-driving offenders. In Richland County, Ohio, there are not only regular drug courts, but also a separate court for drunken drivers and the state's first re-entry drug court, which provides parolees with strict judicial supervision. And in Missouri, judges and prosecutors are creating drug court-like experiments dealing with problems such as driver's license revocations and child support. "Our judges are much more amenable to sending people into treatment," said Ann Wilson, a staff member on the Missouri Drug Court Commission. "Even judges that don't have drug court are assessing [offenders] and [requiring] them to come back to court frequently."[25]

These three capacity-building strategies—creating a drug court large enough to take all drug offenders (Hennepin County), encouraging all judges to adopt select drug court principles (Dade County) or applying problem-solving court principles to different kinds of cases (New York)—are options for state leaders to consider as they attempt to take drug courts, or a drug court approach, to scale.

III. Lessons of Institutionalization

After just a few short years, drug courts are poised to achieve a dramatic transformation, moving from a set of marginal experiments to becoming an accepted part of the courts' response to the problem of drug addiction and crime.

It's no longer possible to argue that drug courts' "continued popularity is a testament to . . . the irrational commitment of a handful of true believers."[26] Today, among the first rank of drug court advocates are governors, state chief judges, legislative leaders and heads of state agencies. In fact, as scholar John Goldkamp notes, the debate about drug courts has changed. "No longer are state supreme court justices arguing about whether drug courts are appropriate," writes Goldkamp. "Instead . . . the chiefs now debate how [drug courts] should be integrated into the overall judicial function."[27]

The questions ahead for state leaders is not whether to support drug courts, but how to create drug court systems that are cost-effective, sustainable and reach all potentially eligible offenders. Toward that end, this final section seeks to answer the question: What lessons can be drawn from the experience of states that are currently attempting to "go to scale" with drug courts?

Leadership matters

In each state—and at each stage of their development—drug courts have relied on the energy, enthusiasm and creativity of a small group of leaders. In the early, pre-institutionalization stages, drug courts were propelled by entrepreneurial leaders—judges, district attorneys and treatment advocates—willing to experiment with a new approach to the problem of drug addiction and crime. With the help of powerful patrons in the federal government, these local leaders were able to spread drug courts far and wide.

While the accomplishments of early drug court practitioners are legion, in some respects their most important success was in attracting the support of a new group of leaders—including state chief judges, the heads of executive branch agencies and elected officials—positioned to take drug courts to the next level. Without the support of these statewide leaders, drug courts would probably not have progressed very far beyond the demonstration phase. In creating statewide offices and commissions to guide drug court operations, developing collaborative relationships between agencies at the highest level of state governments and assuming financial responsibility over drug courts, these state leaders have fueled the movement of drug courts towards institutionalization.

Equally important has been the willingness of top state leaders to champion drug courts. These leaders have sent signals throughout their states that drug courts are a priority. The importance of the "bully pulpit" cannot be overestimated, particularly within bureaucracies like courts, which are traditionally slow to change.

An encouraging corollary of the lesson that "leadership matters" is the idea that leadership can come from a variety of places among the judicial, executive and legislative branches. In New York, the leadership of the chief judge was the decisive factor; in Ohio, leadership from the state's treatment agency was important; in Louisiana, the legislature played a key role; and a collaborative approach carried the day in Missouri.

A variety of tools can advance drug court institutionalization

There is no magic wand that state leaders can wave to go to scale with drug courts. Even an individual drug court can't open without the support of a variety of players from different agencies. Building a statewide drug court system is even more difficult.

The good news for state leaders, however, is that they have a range of tools at their disposal to guide drug court growth. These include:

Building Infrastructure

The states profiled in this paper have focused on creating resources—best practice standards, management information systems, screening and assessment tools, research capacity—that everyone across the state can share. Infrastructure can also encourage new thinking; for example, a management information system that solicits information about treatment modalities and sobriety communicates to its users that this kind of data—and not just conventional data about case processing—is important.

Providing Training and Technical Assistance

States have also provided training, technical assistance and money to local jurisdictions to encourage them to start their own drug courts and to offer support and guidance.

Providing Funding

In the way that the federal government has used grants to ensure adherence to key drug court principles, state governments are using the grant-making process to encourage conformity with statewide policies.

Using Legislation

Many state legislatures have created new resources, such as a line item in the budget for drug courts; new tools, such as statutory authority to send offenders to treatment in lieu of incarceration; and new statewide bodies to oversee drug court development and operations.

Creating New Titles/Positions

By establishing new positions, such as a drug court resource coordinator, state governments can begin to change long-established ways of doing business.

Setting Benchmarks

By promoting new benchmarks of success, administrators can begin to change thinking about the role of courts. For instance, by using new measures—the number of offenders referred to drug treatment, compliance and re-arrest rates—rather than simply conventional measures, like tallying how many cases are processed and how quickly, court leaders begin to nurture attitudes that support drug court institutionalization.

> Rallying the Troops
>
> Through speeches, interviews and press coverage, state leaders like chief judges and governors can have a significant impact on the attitudes of staff and the public, sending a message that institutionalization is doable and worth the effort.

At the end of the day, the key task for state leaders is creating an environment in which drug courts can flourish. This means providing a set of incentives for local jurisdictions—through training, new money and encouragement from above—to adopt a new approach.

Successful institutionalization means mastering state politics

Much of this paper has focused on internal system issues faced by state leaders in their efforts to institutionalize drug courts—everything from designing management information systems to creating new positions within the bureaucracy.

However, institutionalization also presents a host of thorny political issues. Among those is determining which state agency is responsible for drug courts (a contentious issue in Louisiana, where the state's drug agency and judiciary competed for control), promoting drug courts in the face of alternative drug policy approaches (as Ohio's drug court advocates did in the face of Issue 1) and convincing state legislatures to continue funding drug courts in the midst of a fiscal downturn.

Fortunately for drug courts, the message of tightly monitored treatment for addicted offenders continues to be appealing, popular with both sides of the political spectrum. The ability of drug courts to recruit a diverse group of allies is particularly important in tough fiscal times. This fact was recently demonstrated by the Philadelphia Treatment Court. After being cut out of the Pennsylvania state budget, funding for the drug court was restored when the district attorney and the local drug court judge successfully lobbied the legislature to reverse its decision.[28]

As drug courts grow, so does the demand for accountability

Along with increasing state control over drug courts has come added pressure to show results. For Louisiana Drug Court Coordinator Cary Heck—who oversees an annual $13 million appropriation for drug courts from the state legislature—a top priority is "developing a system for fiscal responsibility" that would allow him to collect and report information about drug court effectiveness to the legislature.

Heck, upon starting his job, revived what had become a moribund effort to build a management information system in Louisiana, using his authority to resolve questions about which data to collect and how it should be reported. He is not alone in this regard. In fact, much of the impetus behind the creation of Missouri's Drug Court Commission was the desire to have greater control over "who gets funding and what they do," as Missouri Supreme Court Judge and Commission Chair William Price put it.

The lesson for drug courts is clear: to survive over time, they will have to collect reliable, standardized information about drug court impacts. Although implementing technology projects is notoriously difficult, one advantage of building a management information system is that it can help collect and analyze data more efficiently and produce useful recommendations to improve drug court outcomes.

Administrators may have to look beyond the 10 key components

The 10 key components have helped guide drug courts ever since 1996, when the federal government required all grant recipients to address the key components in their applications.

As drug courts have matured, however, it has become clear that there are several good reasons for practitioners to revisit the key components in light of more than a decade of drug court practice and scholarship. For one thing, new research can help tighten an understanding of what works and what doesn't in the drug court setting. Take the issue of "ongoing judicial interaction," which is Key Component 7: University of Pennsylvania scholar Doug Marlowe has written that regular contact with a judge, as opposed to a social worker, is more effective for high-risk offenders (e.g., low-functioning, long-term addicts with long rap sheets) than low-risk offenders.[29] For drug courts, the implication of Marlowe's research is that it may make sense to use the scarce resource of judicial attention where it can make the biggest difference.

There is another compelling reason for drug court practitioners to revisit the 10 key components: as a practical matter, they may need tweaking in the run-up to institutionalization. For example, many drug courts—particularly those in rural areas—are unable to adopt all of the key components, either because of funding shortfalls or a lack of access to treatment providers. Perhaps more critically, questions remain about whether certain components of drug courts, such as reduced adversarialism, are essential to the model. In Dade County, Drug Court Coordinator Robert Koch created a drug court sentencing option for each of the county's 19 judges. While the program reproduced many of the elements of drug court, court proceedings are still carried out in an adversarial setting. To Koch, retaining the adversarial system made it far easier to spread the model—at little apparent cost to program effectiveness. Other drug court practitioners, however, may disagree: after all, the "team" approach has typically been a defining feature of drug courts.

While many practitioners worry that drug courts will be "watered down" as they become institutionalized, the reality is that the movement has as much, if not more, to fear from excessive fidelity to the model. States going down the road towards institutionalization will have to decide which drug court components are essential to the model and which are not. In addition, they may need to explore whether new components should be added to the list. The challenge comes in balancing the desire for flexibility, and ease of implementation, with the need to protect the integrity of an innovative practice.

Conclusion

Drug courts have experienced an enviable evolution. Rarely has an idea caught on so quickly, especially an idea that touches on so many fields. Drug courts have required the good will and enthusiasm of all branches of governments and of professionals in the fields of medicine, social science, law and law enforcement. They have survived tough criticism, tight budgets and statewide referendums. By all accounts it looks as if drug courts are here to stay. States large and small have embraced them as an effective and appropriate way to deal with drug-abusing offenders.

But where drug courts will be in 10 years is hard to say. Will drug courts be recognizable by today's standards? Will they exist as separate courts or will they be available as an alternative approach to any judge who wishes to employ it? Will they be available across entire states to everyone who might be eligible? These are the questions that the process of institutionalization, now under way in a number of states, is attempting to answer.

CHAPTER THREE

Institutionalizing Innovation: The New York Drug Court Story

JOHN FEINBLATT, GREG BERMAN AND AUBREY FOX

It is difficult to overstate the impact that drugs have had on the American criminal justice system—and courts in particular—in recent years. The drug epidemic that began in the 1980s (and the war against drugs that continues to this day) has placed tremendous burdens on almost every part of the system.[1] The strain can be seen in the widespread overcrowding in correctional facilities.[2] It can be seen in the resources that police and prosecutors have had to dedicate to new enforcement programs.[3] And it can be seen in the courts that have struggled to keep pace with the resulting explosion in caseload volume.[4]

No state is exempt from these forces, of course, but New York offers a particularly vivid example of a court system grappling with the consequences of drugs and crime. According to New York State Chief Judge Judith S. Kaye:

> *While major crimes rates are heading toward record lows, filings in our criminal courts are soaring to all-time highs. And the substance of this caseload reflects some of the most daunting problems facing our society today. . . . Last year, nearly half of all felony filings in this state were drug-related. . . . Drug abuse was the fuel driving much of the criminal justice system's revolving door.*[5]

This essay was originally published as "Institutionalizing Innovation: The New York Drug Court Story" 28 Fordham Urb. L.J. 277 (2000).

Statistics confirm this bleak assessment: in 1980, there were 27,000 drug arrests in New York. By 1999, that number had skyrocketed to more than 145,000—a 430 percent increase.[6] Even when a defendant is arrested for a crime that is not explicitly drug-related, drug use often played a role. According to the National Institute of Justice, eight out of every ten defendants arrested in New York City in 1998 for all crimes tested positive for drugs at the time of their arrest.[7]

While the numbers are staggering, they only hint at the true scope of the problem. The challenge that this massive influx of cases poses for courts in New York and other states is not simply how to manage dockets more efficiently. It is how to do justice in cases that almost always involve litigants with complicated problems. As Kaye has written:

> *Not surprisingly, in many of today's cases, the traditional approach yields unsatisfying results. The addict arrested for drug dealing is adjudicated, does time, then goes right back to dealing on the street ... Every legal right of the litigants is protected, all procedures followed, yet we aren't making a dent in the underlying problem. Not good for the parties involved. Not good for the community. Not good for the courts.*[8]

Recognizing this reality, judges across New York have begun to rethink how courts respond to drug-related cases, testing new ways to halt the "revolving door" of drugs, crime and jail. The most obvious sign of this experimentation has been the creation of 20 "drug treatment courts" across the state. These are specialized courtrooms that take a problem-solving approach to addiction, linking nonviolent defendants to long-term, judicially supervised drug treatment instead of incarceration. Defendants are required to return to court frequently to report on their progress before the judge, who uses a variety of carrots and sticks to encourage participation in treatment. If defendants fail, they are subject to a range of graduated sanctions, including letters of apology, more intense treatment regimes and, if necessary, jail. Meanwhile, success in treatment often results in the original charges against defendants being dismissed.

Though a relatively recent phenomenon, drug courts in New York and other states have demonstrated that they are capable of achieving significant results. National research suggests that drug courts have succeeded in reducing drug use and recidivism among offenders.[9] Further, the research indicates that the retention rates for defendants in mandated treatment are about double the rates for those who pursue treatment voluntarily.[10]

These two realities—the crushing increase in drug-related cases in New York courts over the past generation and the demonstrated effectiveness of drug courts in promoting sobriety among offenders—underlie Chief Judge Kaye and Chief Administrative Judge Jonathan Lippman's recent announcement that they plan to restructure the New York State court system's response to drug-fueled crime. Among other things, their plan—the product of a six-month study by a blue-ribbon panel headed by Robert Fiske, Jr.—calls for adopting drug court principles in every jurisdiction in New York, offering judicially monitored drug treatment as an alternative to incarceration to nearly 10,000 addicted offenders annually.[11]

What makes this plan unique is that it is the most ambitious attempt to date to reassemble the DNA of a state court system with respect to drug-addicted offenders and litigants. In effect, Kaye has called for drug courts to move from their current status as isolated, boutique experiments into the mainstream of judicial operations in New York. While many states have gone out of their way to encourage the replication of drug courts, only New York has begun to ask whether it is possible for this experiment in judicial problem solving to lead to a full-scale reform of a state court system. For New York, the potential benefits of pursuing this course of action are enormous: safer communities, healthier families, substantial prison cost savings and improved public confidence in justice. But any large-scale reform effort also comes with challenges. Institutionalizing a small-scale innovation like drug courts will require new thinking, new resources and new ways of doing business.

This chapter looks at both the opportunities and the challenges of New York State's new statewide drug treatment initiative. It outlines the possible results that this reform might achieve, including both the obvious (e.g., reduced drug use and recidivism) and the not-so-obvious (e.g., expedited permanency decisions in cases involving substance-abusing parents and reductions in the length of time that children spend in foster care). In addition, it poses some of the tough questions that must be confronted as drug courts attempt to "go to scale": To what extent do drug courts require system players—judges, prosecutors, defenders—to alter their traditional roles? How willing are they to become active problem-solvers? Can any judge be a drug court judge? Are specialized courtrooms necessary, or can the tools developed in drug courts—judicial monitoring, early assessment of offenders, links to treatment—become part of the standard judicial approach? Is it desirable—and politically feasible—to extend the drug court approach to some offenders who have committed violent offenses in the past? How about property offenders? What about the up-front investment that any large reform effort requires? Do the resources exist to assess thousands of additional defendants, place them in treatment slots and pay for their care? Finally, how important to the success of drug courts has their small size been? Will going to scale have the ironic result of undermining drug courts' effectiveness? Will drug courts become a victim of their own success?

These are questions with profound implications not only for New York but for court reform efforts across the country. In 2000, New York State embarked on the most ambitious effort to date to institutionalize drug court innovation. Given the kinds of results that drug courts have achieved, it surely will not be the last. Any effort to follow New York's lead inevitably will have to address both the possibilities and the challenges of institutionalization. But before taking a deeper look at these issues, a brief overview of the problems posed by drugs in New York, and the results that drug courts have achieved to date, is in order.

The Problem

The rising tide of drug arrests in the last 20 years in New York has sent shock waves through the justice system. The costs of this increase can be seen in the courts, probation departments, prosecutors' offices, prisons and jails. In 1999 alone, the court system spent $115 million adjudicating drug cases.[12] The cost for the state's prison system is even steeper: close to $650 million annually to imprison drug felons.[13] In addition, local corrections departments, which house pre-trial detainees and offenders serving sentences of less than one year, received 21,000 drug sentences in 1999; the average cost of jail in New York City, where the majority of detainees are held, is $68,000 per year.[14]

Nor are the costs confined to the criminal justice system. Drug addiction has taken a toll on the state's family courts as well. Of the 465,000 children who are under the court-ordered supervision of New York City's Administration for Children's Services, an estimated 70 percent come from families with a substance abuse problem.[15] Lacking the capacity to assess and treat addiction and facing enormous caseloads, most Family Court cases drag on indefinitely, leaving parents in limbo and their children in foster care. Between 1985 and 1991, the number of children in foster care in New York City nearly tripled from about

17,000 to 50,000, while the average length of stay leapt from 1.81 years in 1985 to 4.5 years by 1997.[16]

Beyond the costs associated with incarcerating offenders or placing children in foster care, the impact of drugs can be felt in the quality of justice delivered by New York's courts. While drug arrests are up 430 percent over the last 20 years, there has been only a 15 percent increase in the number of state judgeships.[17] One result of this imbalance between supply and demand has been overwhelmed courtrooms where harried judges, prosecutors and defenders are forced to process cases as quickly as possible.

Not surprisingly, a large proportion of the drug offenders who pass through the court system without receiving meaningful treatment are rearrested quickly. Thirty-four percent of drug offenders released from state prison in 1998 were rearrested within a year; a similar cohort of prisoners released in 1996 had a 56 percent recidivism rate after three years. In New York City, the two-year recidivism rate for drug felony arrestees is 50 percent. Finally, close to one-third of parolees had their parole revoked for committing new felonies within three years.[18]

Drug Courts

New York's surge in caseload volume has created a window of opportunity for reformers throughout the court system. Many jurisdictions have taken advantage of this to create specialized drug treatment courts.

Drug courts are just one example of a growing trend in the world of court reform: the creation of "problem-solving courts" that seek to forge new responses to difficult problems like domestic violence, quality-of-life crime, child neglect and mental illness. Although they address very different problems, mental health, community, domestic violence and drug courts all share a common approach. They use the coercive authority of the courts to achieve more meaningful case outcomes.[19] They build new partnerships with treatment providers, community groups and others outside of the traditional criminal justice system.[20] Problem-solving courts broaden the focus of legal proceedings from fact finding and narrow legal issues to changing the future behavior of litigants (and the future well-being of communities).[21]

Drug courts focus exclusively on drug cases, linking substance-abusing offenders (who have voluntarily agreed to enter the program) to treatment. While there are many different drug court models (e.g., pre-plea, post-plea and diversion), in general, if a participant successfully completes treatment, the judge will reduce the charges or dismiss the case. In drug courts, unlike most criminal courts, the judge plays an ongoing, post-plea role, requiring participants to report back regularly to court for drug testing and to appear before the bench. The judge reviews participant progress through treatment programs, offering a set of graduated rewards and sanctions where appropriate. Eligibility for drug court participation is typically restricted to non-violent offenders with substance abuse problems. Individuals with prior violent convictions, or those believed to be involved in drug trafficking schemes, are usually ineligible.

The first drug court opened in Miami's Dade County in 1989 during the height of the crack cocaine epidemic. Since then, aided by the U.S. Department of Justice's Drug Courts Program Office (which distributed $50 million in grants in fiscal year 2000), drug courts have grown at a phenomenal rate. Today there are more than 500 courts nationwide, including one in operation or being planned in every state.[22] An additional 281 are in development.[23] In New York, drug courts were established first in Rochester and Brooklyn in the mid-1990s, and have now grown to include 20 operating courts, with an additional 20 in the planning stages. A statewide apparatus has developed around these courts in New York, including technology to track offenders, formal research benchmarks to evaluate the courts' impacts and an association that promulgates best practices as they emerge.

What accounts for this rapid expansion? One answer can be found in the research findings about drug courts. An emerging body of evidence credits them with keeping offenders in treatment, substantially reducing drug use and rates of re-arrest during the period of program participation and generating large savings in avoided jail and prison costs. Though less conclusive, there is also strong evidence to suggest that drug courts reduce long-term recidivism for participants.

The most authoritative review of drug courts comes from Columbia University's National Center on Addiction and Substance Abuse, which analyzed 30 independent evaluations of 24 drug court programs nationwide.[24] Some of the most striking findings from this meta-analysis include:

> Coercion works
>
> Drug court participants are far more likely to successfully complete mandated substance abuse treatment than comparable participants who seek help on a voluntary basis. One-year treatment retention rates are 60 percent for drug courts, compared to 10-30 percent among voluntary, residential treatment programs.[25]
>
> Drug use and recidivism are both substantially reduced during the period of drug court participation
>
> Drug court program lengths vary from court to court, although most require a minimum of one year's participation. For drug court participants, substance abuse is greatly reduced during the period of program participation. A survey of 13 drug courts found that, on average, 10 percent of urine tests were positive for drugs, compared to 31 percent for defendants in the same jurisdiction under probation supervi-

sion.[26] Rates of re-arrest for drug court enrollees are also quite low. In two evaluations where comparison groups were employed—in Jackson County, Missouri, and Ventura County, California—the re-arrest rates for program participants were four percent and 12 percent respectively, as opposed to 13 percent and 32 percent in the control groups, over a six- and eight-month period.[27]

Post-program benefits, while not conclusive, are positive

Drug court participants also have lower post-program re-arrest rates. Of nine drug court evaluations that used a comparison group, and included all drug court participants and not just graduates, eight found positive results.[28] One study conducted of the Maricopa County, Arizona, drug court showed a three-year recidivism rate of 33 percent for program graduates and 43.7 percent for a comparison group.[29] The average number of arrests for participants in the Multnomah County, Oregon, drug court after two years was 0.59, compared to 1.53 for a control group.[30] Less is known about post-program impacts on employment, education and drug use. Most drug court evaluations have tracked program participants for only a short period after their leaving the program. Other drug courts have not been in existence long enough to generate post-program results.[31]

Drug courts save money

Incarceration costs far more than either residential or outpatient treatment, and drug courts consistently save money even after factoring in administrative costs. The savings are particularly dramatic when other benefits, such as reduced recidivism, are factored in. A study of the Multnomah County, Oregon, drug court found that the court had achieved $2.5 million in criminal justice cost savings based on 440 participants over a two-year period.[32] Additional savings outside the criminal justice system—reductions in victimization, theft, public assistance and medical claims—were estimated to be an additional $10 million.[33] While no formal evaluation of drug court cost savings in New York has been performed to date, the potential for savings is enormous. In New York State, the average cost of incarceration is $29,000 annually (and jail in New York City costs $68,000 per inmate annually), as compared to $5,100 for outpatient and $18,400 for inpatient, or residential, treatment.[34] The state's Office of Court Administration estimates that Kaye's plan, if implemented fully, could result in annual government savings of $500 million.[35] This includes $130 million in savings in prison and jail costs and close to $400 million in saved public expenditures such as reduced recidivism, public assistance, foster care and health care costs.[36]

Opportunities and Challenges

With an eye toward these kinds of findings, Kaye and Lippman have recommended institutionalizing the drug court approach throughout the New York State court system. This will bring assessment, treatment and monitoring to thousands of defendants for an annual cost to the state court system of between $20 and $22 million.[37] It is fair to ask what kinds of dividends this substantial investment will pay. Drug courts have achieved remarkable results with non-violent offenders, helping them achieve sobriety and avoid further involvement in the criminal justice system. Bringing these kinds of results to as many addicted defendants as possible is a goal well worth pursuing. The potential ramifications of moving thousands of individuals from addiction and criminal behavior to sobriety and stable community life are enormous, both for communities and for families. For communities, it could mean safer streets and a measure of relief from drug-fueled crime and disorder. For many families, it could mean reunion with children lost to foster care. It could mean healthier families, too, with fewer "crack babies." At a recent graduation ceremony at the Rochester drug court, one program participant who had successfully completed treatment underlined the tangible, real-life benefits of the drug court model: "I had spent every day stealing for the money to buy drugs, and every free minute getting high. I got caught numerous times, but still I couldn't stop. I had no support system, and no incentive to stop. Drug court finally provided me with both."[38]

The potential benefits to the criminal justice system are also substantial. The most obvious are the cost savings that might be achieved by reducing both recidivism and reliance on prison. As mentioned above, the state's Office of Court Administration estimates that Kaye's plan could result in $500 million in government savings.[39] Reduced recidivism could also mean reduced caseloads, alleviating some of the pressure that judges, prosecutors and defenders feel to move through dockets as quickly as possible. And limiting caseloads could lead to more meaningful case outcomes and an end to "revolving-door justice." By achieving results like these, drug courts have the potential to affect not only how courts operate but how they are perceived. If drug courts do, in fact, become a permanent part of the judicial landscape in New York—and if they do continue to achieve demonstrable results—they might go a long way toward restoring the legitimacy of the court system, and helping to rebuild public confidence in judges, attorneys and police officers.

Large scale re-engineering of the courts is not without challenges, of course. What follows are a few of the issues that reformers must face as they attempt to institutionalize drug courts in New York.

Leadership

To date, New York's drug courts have been created in jurisdictions where entrepreneurial judges or prosecutors have been willing to exercise political and bureaucratic leadership. Their leadership has been critical, helping win over reluctant government partners, raise funds and build links with off-site treatment providers. How can court administrators reach beyond the cadre of initial drug court innovators to cultivate a new generation of local leaders? For New York's comprehensive drug treatment plan to be successful, it must reach out to new audiences in the 62 counties across the state, including judges, prosecutors, and defenders. Further, it must convince skeptics, agnostics and those who are unfamiliar with drug courts to embrace reform.

In building an outreach strategy, court administrators can draw upon five years of experience in drug court replication. In that time, New York has gone from a single drug court to more than 40 either in operation or in planning. The court system used several techniques to introduce new jurisdictions to the drug court approach. By making sure that results are well-documented and well-disseminated and by using existing courts as models, court administrators have been able to show system players across the state the benefits of the drug court approach. By not requiring local jurisdictions to conform to a one-size-fits-all model, they have been sensitive to local legal cultures. And by creating a statewide association of drug court professionals, they have helped legitimize drug courts, providing a vehicle for information-sharing among professionals and opportunities for the uninitiated to learn about drug courts.

Changing Roles

In drug courts, the traditional roles of "detached judge" and "zealous advocate" are altered in some important ways.[40] The judge's role is greatly expanded: from that of a neutral fact-finder to that of a problem-solver who uses the coercive power at his or her disposal to help address an offender's drug addiction. As judges step out of their conventional role, as they become active problem-solvers, it is crucial that they be provided with a clear set of guidelines. One way to do this is to articulate and broadly disseminate the outcomes that drug courts seek to achieve. Kaye's drug treatment initiative sends a loud message that the goal in adjudicating drug-related cases is not to move through court calendars as quickly as possible, but to achieve tangible results (e.g., increased sobriety, reductions in recidivism, etc.).

The role of advocates in drug courts shifts as well: from one that focuses on "winning" to one that creates case outcomes that serve the best interest of both addicted offenders and the community. For prosecutors, that might mean embracing new measures of success. As Portland, Oregon, District Attorney Mike Schrunk has said, "Dismissing 1,500 drug cases during the course of the year in a drug court is a better end product than 1,500 convictions in a regular court."[41]

For defenders, the issue is similar—attempting to achieve the least restrictive result may not be of long-term benefit for their clients if their drug addiction remains untreated. The culture of cooperation in a drug court may also be of concern for defense lawyers, because it departs from their traditional, adversarial role.[42] Drug court replication efforts must honor these concerns and take pains to include both defenders and prosecutors in the planning stages of any drug court. This need for joint strategic planning represents a challenge for any large, public bureaucracy unaccustomed to reaching beyond its doors to involve outside partners.[43]

Specialization

Eighty percent of those arrested in New York City test positive for drugs at the time of their arrest.[44] An estimated two-thirds of state prisoners are drug users.[45] Drugs are clearly a system-wide issue for the courts. This raises the question: are specialized courtrooms the answer for dealing with the problem of drug addiction, or should every courtroom be equipped with the technologies developed in drug courts? In making this decision, court administrators are faced with a basic trade-off: balancing the risk of watering down the effectiveness of drug courts by adopting them in every courtroom with the risk of limiting their reach by keeping them separate. This issue will become more important as drug courts move from experimentation to full implementation, and from urban centers to rural jurisdictions. If the answer is to give all judges in the state the tools they need to link defendants to treatment and monitor their progress, there will be a need for intensive training and new measures of success to ensure that the quality of the drug court approach is maintained.

A related question is whether drug courts require specialized judges. Some critics have wondered whether the majority of judges are capable of adopting a new approach to working with defendants and coordinating the work of partner agencies. Others argue that the qualities of a good drug court judge are not all that different from the qualities of a good judge. As Judge Truman Morrison III of the District of Columbia Superior Court has said, "It strikes me that [a drug court judge] ought to be . . . someone who is open to other people's ideas, who listens, who is informed, who is impartial. . . . If we put aside the real bad people who probably shouldn't be on the bench anyway, most judges could do this job, many more than do."[46]

Limits

In seeking to extend the drug court model to new populations, the state court system will have to confront a key question: What are the limits of the drug court approach? Are there some populations of addicted offenders for whom judicially monitored drug treatment is inappropriate? Three distinct populations of drug-addicted offenders have, for the most part, been excluded from drug courts. The first is substance abusers who have been arrested for violent offenses or who have prior violent felony convictions. There are several reasons for their exclusion, including concerns about the appropriateness of offering violent offenders an alternative to incarceration and the strict eligibility requirement imposed by federal funders explicitly limiting drug courts to non-violent drug offenders. A second group that traditionally has been excluded is low-level offenders whose crimes do not provide the criminal justice system with sufficient leverage to compel enrollment in a long-term treatment program. Finally, a third group is offenders who are not arrested for drug crimes but whose offense is driven by addiction. It is difficult to estimate how large these "missing groups" of potential drug court participants are. However, it seems clear that drug courts, as they are currently operating, are not reaching their maximum potential population.

Any attempt to add these various populations to the mix will face serious political and logistical obstacles. Including offenders with violent criminal histories is largely a question of local tolerance. Some jurisdictions will be uncomfortable with extending drug treatment to past violent offenders (e.g., someone with a ten-year-old robbery conviction or a five-year-old house burglary[47]); others may see the value in treating their addiction. In defining drug court eligibility, court administrators will have to balance the need to respect local preferences in each of New York's 62 counties with a desire to create uniformity throughout the state.

The question of what to do with misdemeanants is equally complicated. Kaye's plan suggests that there is a group of chronic misdemeanor offenders in New York City who, because of the length of their rap sheets, are potentially facing significant jail or prison terms. This is a group that might reasonably be placed in long-term treatment through a drug court. But what about the misdemeanants whose offenses do not rise to this level? This boils down to a question of what the legal marketplace will bear. It is unlikely that any defense attorney is going to allow a client arrested on a first-time shoplifting charge to accept one year of mandatory drug treatment, no matter how severe his or her addiction may be. One answer to this dilemma is suggested by the Brooklyn Treatment Court, which links first-time misdemeanants and others to a treatment readiness program that lasts for two days in an effort to encourage these offenders to seek out long-term treatment voluntarily.

Finally, reaching the third group—substance-abusing offenders who do not commit drug offenses but whose crimes are motivated by addiction—points to the need for comprehensive screening and early assessment for all offenders brought into the state courts. Building an infrastructure for achieving this will have to be part of any system-wide reform effort.

Capacity

Any proposal that calls for offering treatment to a large group of substance abusers must face the question of capacity: Will there be sufficient treatment resources to meet the demand? Will there be enough slots for everyone? Who will perform assessments of offenders to measure their addiction? In a changing welfare and managed care landscape, who will pay for treatment? These are, at base, questions of capacity. As suggested earlier in this essay, strong evidence exists to suggest that up-front expenditure on drug treatment saves considerable money in criminal justice and avoided costs of crime down the road. For drug court reformers, then, the challenge becomes convincing other branches of government—and the public—that such an investment is a sound choice. Drug court reformers must also be creative about tapping into unconventional funding streams. For example, foster care and welfare agencies share common cause with courts in helping individuals reach sobriety. Drug courts can make strong arguments for creating new funding arrangements to reflect these shared interests.

Size

One argument against institutionalizing drug courts is that they will lose their unique character as they increase in number. How can drug courts retain their intimacy? How crucial is it that judges be conversant with each offender's case history and progress through treatment? Is it possible to create truly individualized treatment plans for each and every eligible offender in the state? One tool that might help solve this problem is computer technology, which has the potential to help judges bring individualized attention to large caseloads. Many drug courts are already using computer applications to build and maintain a tremendous amount of information about drug court defendants, information that is made available to judges, advocates and other courtroom players as each case proceeds.[48]

Taking on the critics

Any new policy innovation is bound to attract critics, and drug courts are no exception. New York's drug treatment initiative will face criticism—from system players attached to old ways of doing business, skeptics who fear that courts may be overstepping their boundaries in attempting to address drug addiction,[49] civil libertarians concerned about any threat to the due process rights of defendants,[50] and, finally, observers who feel that offering treatment as an alternative to incarceration is "soft on crime." While serious, these are all concerns that might reasonably be addressed through strategic planning that brings all of the relevant players (judges, prosecutors, defenders, treatment providers, community groups and others) to the table to plot a course for local jurisdictions and through rigorous research that tracks—and disseminates—the results of this new judicial approach to drugs.[51]

It is also important to place the new initiative in proper context. There is no more convincing argument for change than the contrast between Kaye's proposal and the reality of the current system, one that continues to recycle drug-addicted offenders with little apparent value for the courts, the public or the offender. As Kaye has written, "Some may argue that such hands-on involvement [of the courts] clashes with our branch's traditional dignity and reserve. But what's the alternative? The flood of cases shows no sign of letting up. We can either bail faster or look for new ways to stem the tide."[52]

Conclusion

Institutionalization poses a unique set of challenges to public policy reformers in any field, whether in courts, health, education or welfare.[53] Creating successful demonstration projects is one thing. Implementing a new idea across a statewide system is quite another. Few public officials are willing to take on this challenge, particularly in states as large, as complex and as diverse as New York.

With their proposal to bring the ideas pioneered in drug courts to the rest of the New York State court system, Chief Judge Judith Kaye and Chief Administrative Judge Jonathan Lippman are attempting just this feat. The potential implications of their reform effort are far-reaching. By placing greater emphasis on achieving meaningful case outcomes, by encouraging judges and attorneys to play new roles and by working to solve problems rather than simply process cases, the New York drug treatment initiative seeks to change how courts work and what the public should expect of them.

Edited Transcripts

The chapters in this section look at critical issues faced by problem-solving courts from the perspective of leading policymakers, practitioners and scholars. In Chapter Four, Aubrey Fox and Greg Berman summarize a roundtable conversation about drug court efforts to enter into the mainstream of court operations. They identify a consensus among roundtable participants that the goal is to drill down to the "active ingredients" or "essence" of the drug court model and encourage the spread of drug court principles as opposed simply to expanding the number of drug courts.

In Chapter Five, Fox examines the role of research in drug courts. Although research may not have been integral to drug court development to date, this may soon change, as policymakers face pressure to show that states' investments in drug courts are paying off. Roundtable participants discuss how research can also help state policymakers make more informed decisions in such areas as identifying best practices, enforcing quality standards and determining whether drug courts should handle higher-level offenders.

In Chapter Six, Berman and Fox look beyond the court system to a variety of community justice programs—including community policing, prosecution, probation and corrections. Fox and Berman identify some important differences in the views of roundtable participants about these disparate initiatives—while some see them as an attempt to fundamentally redraw the relationship between criminal justice agencies and communities, others see them more narrowly, as a set of tools to deploy in specific situations, or as a vehicle for improving public confidence in justice.

CHAPTER FOUR

Going to Scale: A Conversation About the Growth of Drug Courts

AUBREY FOX AND GREG BERMAN

Perhaps no criminal justice innovation has spread as rapidly in recent years as drug courts, which offer judicially monitored treatment as an alternative to incarceration for non-violent addicts. The first drug court was launched in Dade County, Florida, in 1989. Today, there are more than 1,200 drug courts either in operation or in planning across the country. More than 226,000 defendants have participated in these programs.

Drug courts are the most prominent example of a wave of "problem-solving" innovation that has sought to change the way courts operate in this country. Alongside drug courts, domestic violence courts, community courts, family treatment courts, mental health courts and other specialized courts are using the authority of the judicial branch in new ways in an effort to improve outcomes for victims, communities and defendants. These problem-solving courts employ new tools and new methods—such as requiring defendants to appear regularly before judges to report on their compliance with court orders, or adding social scientists, drug treatment counselors and other service providers to the courtroom team.

This edited transcript originally appeared as "Going to Scale: A Conversation about the Future of Drug Courts," in *Court Review*, Fall 2002. Copyright © *Court Review*/American Judges Assocation. Reprinted with permission. The roundtable was supported by the Bureau of Justice Assistance, Office of Justice Programs, U.S. Department of Justice. Points of view and opinions do not necessarily represent the official position or policies of the U.S. Department of Justice.

The first generation of problem-solving courts has achieved some provocative results—none more so than drug courts. Independent research credits drug courts with reducing rates of drug use and rearrest among participants. Also, treatment retention rates—a key indicator of long-term sobriety—are twice as high for participants in drug courts as opposed to individuals who seek out treatment voluntarily.

To date, the drug court movement has largely been a grassroots phenomenon, driven by a highly motivated cadre of judges, prosecutors and court leaders. Based on the demonstrated success of drug courts—and the enthusiastic public attention these courts have generated—a number of states have begun to take the next step, seeking not just to replicate pilot drug courts, but rather to test system-wide the viability of new approaches to the problem of addiction. Their focus is on building systems at a state level, either through special judicial branch-led efforts (as in New York), legislation (Indiana) or collaborative efforts that bring together the heads of statewide agencies like corrections, courts and social services (Utah).

Clearly, drug courts are at the brink of moving into a new stage of development. Acknowledging this reality, in March 2002 the United States Department of Justice, working with the Center for Court Innovation, brought together a select group of judges, practitioners and thinkers from around the country to discuss the future of drug courts. The goal of the roundtable was two-fold: first, to unearth some of the strategic, conceptual, and practical challenges that practitioners face in attempting to bring drug courts into the mainstream of court operations, and second, to provide a road map to drug court advocates in addressing those challenges.

Perhaps not surprisingly, the topic proved to be a complicated one. During a day-long conversation, court administrators, judges, legal scholars and experts in other fields of social policy innovation grappled with a series of difficult questions. How do you "go to scale" with an idea like drug courts? Is the goal to promote continued replication of the drug court model? Or is the goal to advance drug court principles and strategies, making sure they take root in every courtroom? Most important, how do you institutionalize innovation? Will the drug court approach lose its effectiveness if it becomes business as usual?

Several key themes emerged from the discussion. Many, though not all, participants agreed that going to scale meant more than "hanging more signs on the door" (a phrase coined by University of Wisconsin law professor Michael Smith) or merely increasing the number of drug courts. Instead, participants seemed eager to distill the "active ingredients" or "essence" of the drug court model—and to encourage the spread of drug court principles as opposed to expanding the number of drug courts. Adele Harrell, a researcher at the Urban Institute who has written extensively about drug courts, put it best when she suggested that success for advocates might lie in drug courts fading "out of existence as their tenets become embedded in practice."

The desire to spread elements of the drug court approach—and not replicate drug courts per se—has some important implications. First and foremost, it means that advocates must identify which elements of the model that they wish to see incorporated into the broader court system. This is a more difficult task than it might at first appear. Participants at the roundtable articulated a number of core drug court elements. For Utah state court administrator Daniel Becker, the essence of drug courts is the creation of new partnerships between courts and state treatment agencies. For law professor Smith, it is "the idea that sentencing is a responsibility of the court over a long term." San Diego Judge James Milliken and Indianapolis prosecutor Scott Newman cited concrete goals: providing judges with more comprehensive assessments and more sophisticated management information tools to guide sentencing decisions and help track offender compliance with court orders. And for New York Deputy Chief Adminstrative Judge Joseph J. Traficanti Jr., who's leading an ambitious statewide effort to create drug courts in each of New York's 62 counties, the goal is to make it possible "for any defendant, in any jurisdiction, to go into treatment." The fact that participants in the roundtable (most of them drug court proponents) were unable to reach consensus on the core elements of the drug court approach suggests that more work has to be done before advocates attempt to mainstream them.

In addition to tackling conceptual problems, participants also addressed strategy questions. Participants returned again and again to the challenge of institutionalizing the drug court model without dampening the spirit of innovation that led to their creation in the first place. "[P]eople don't respond well to being told, 'You have to do this,'" said Lisbeth Schorr, an expert on social policy innovation based at Harvard University. She added: "You can't mandate belief in a program." Indianapolis prosecutor Scott Newman agreed, arguing that key leaders must have "[t]ransformative personal experiences" if they are to buy into the drug court idea.

Roundtable participants repeatedly articulated the tension between the need to ensure quality control as an idea goes to scale and the imperative to preserve local flexibility. One way this was expressed was the effort to distinguish "institutionalization" from "bureaucratization." "Bureaucracy creates a coercive style of leadership that forces other people to act in a certain way," Scott Newman said, while "institutionalization is a motivational style of leadership which gets people inspired." Many participants argued that the best way to promote institutionalization without bureaucratization was to create an intermediary entity that would provide the technical assistance and support necessary to ensure the quality of implementation at individual sites. This would help drug courts "move from a system based on charisma to one based on standards and principles," without sacrificing local control, according to Columbia University law professor Michael Dorf.

Participants also highlighted the need for drug courts to create new partnerships or strengthen existing ones as they mature. One example cited was the need to work with state drug and alcohol agencies, which not only manage large sums of money (from federal health and human service grants) but also have responsibility for guaranteeing the quality of treatment services. Going to scale will be "next to impossible" without involving the commissioners of state alcohol and drug agencies, said Valerie Raine of the Center for Court Innovation.

A second area for potential collaboration are state legislatures, which in many places are eager to create a statutory framework (and provide funding) for drug courts. Partnerships with state legislatures can either help or hinder drug courts, as the examples of Utah and Indiana suggest. While Utah provided a statutory framework that allowed federal treatment resources to be redirected to drug courts—clearly a positive development—in Indiana, pending legislation seeks to codify how drug courts are defined, a development that many feared would severely limit local flexibility. This suggests that drug court advocates will have to proceed cautiously in working with legislatures.

In addition to airing out conceptual and strategic challenges, participants shared their reservations about institutionalization—and in particular its potential unintended consequences. "Today's innovation is tomorrow's conventional wisdom," warned Michael Smith. "I think we need to find a way to go to scale that's open to constant change, revision and discovery. Otherwise, you just make it more difficult for the next innovator." In that vein, Adele Harrell cautioned against "overselling the promise" of drug courts, a shortcoming of past criminal justice innovations that have come and gone.

Despite these reservations, participants were cautiously optimistic about the prospects for institutionalization, pointing out that drug courts have already made significant strides forward. Perhaps the most heartening news of the day came from Lisbeth Schorr. Schorr, who has spent the greater part of her professional life thinking about government innovation, remarked that in discussing drug court institutionalization, participants had already reached an unusual level of sophistication. "[T]his is a far better, more rigorous discussion than I am used to hearing," she said.

What follows is a list of the participants and an edited transcript of the discussion, which took place over six hours in a conference room in Washington, D.C.

Participants*

Daniel Becker is the Utah state court administrator.

Greg Berman is director of the Center for Court Innovation, New York, New York.

Kevin Burke is a judge in Hennepin County District Court, Minneapolis, Minnesota.

Michael Dorf is a professor at Columbia University School of Law, New York, New York.

Chico Gallegos is staff counsel and chief financial officer of the Native American Alliance Foundation, Tulsa, Oklahoma.

Adele Harrell is a researcher with the Urban Institute, Washington, D.C.

Francis X. Hartmann (moderator) is executive director and senior research fellow of the Program in Criminal Justice Policy and Management at the John F. Kennedy School of Government, Harvard University, Cambridge, Massachusetts.

*Titles reflect participants' roles in March 2002.

Eric Lane is a professor at Hofstra University School of Law, New York, New York.

James Milliken is presiding judge of the San Diego Juvenile Court, San Diego, California.

Scott Newman is the elected prosecutor of Marion County (Indianapolis), Indiana.

Valerie Raine is director of Drug Treatment Programs at the Center for Court Innovation, New York, New York.

Marilyn McCoy Roberts is director of the Drug Court Programs Office, Office of Justice Programs, United States Department of Justice, Washington D.C.

Lisbeth Schorr is director of the Project on Effective Interventions at Harvard University, Washington, D.C.

Michael Scott is a police consultant, Savannah, Georgia.

Michael Smith is a professor at the University of Wisconsin School of Law, Madison, Wisconsin.

John Stuart is the Minnesota State public defender, Minneapolis, Minnesota.

Joseph J. Traficanti Jr. is deputy chief administrative judge of the State of New York.

William Vickrey is director of the California Administrative Office of the Courts, San Francisco, California.

Bernardine Watson is executive vice president, Public/Private Ventures, Philadelphia, Pennsylvania.

Setting the Stage

Francis X. Hartmann: Where are drug courts in the "going to scale" process?

Greg Berman: I want to read two quotes that I think speak directly to that question. The first is from John Goldkamp, a researcher at Temple University, speaking about drug courts: "What we have now is not a bunch of little hobbies that judges have in isolated jurisdictions, but rather a paradigm shift that larger court systems are trying to come to grips with. The question isn't, 'Are the courts supposed to be doing this?' It's, 'What are you going to do about it? How does it fit in?' It's no longer a question of whether this should be invented." The second is from Michael Smith, who's here with us today. He says, "It seems to me there are two different ways to go to scale. One is to use problem-solving courts as laboratories to improve the way they do business. The other is to build a new system devoted to proliferating problem-solving courts. That choice may turn out to be critical." These two statements underline the theme for today's conversation—an acknowledgment that drug courts are attempting to move from the margins of the court system to the mainstream. I think the challenge is: how do you go to scale in a way that is thoughtful and deliberate?

Marilyn McCoy Roberts: When the Department of Justice got into the business of supporting drug courts in 1994, there were about 30 or 40 drug courts around the country. Today we're nearly to the 800 mark and have quite a few more—400 or so—in the planning stages. What's remarkable is that drug courts, which initially didn't attract much interest from court administrators, have now been embraced by the leadership of court systems around the country.

James Milliken: One problem that going to scale will hopefully address is the exclusion of populations that need our services the most. For example, federal and state grants for juveniles exclude kids who have been violent or who have gang associations. Now that we know the medicine works, we need to expand the system so that we can provide the medicine to everybody who needs it.

Joseph J. Traficanti Jr.: I think institutionalization does mean, at least in part, the creation of more drug courts. I see it as a fundamental issue of fairness: two people arrested in different places for the same crime should have the same opportunity for treatment.

Michael Smith: For me, the question is: what are we taking to scale? The answer can't simply be to put more signs on the door. We have to know what the active ingredient of innovation is. Otherwise we won't be able to spread the idea.

Analogies

Hartmann: Drug courts are not the first criminal justice innovation to attempt to go to scale. What have we learned from other efforts in the field?

Smith: Let me offer two examples. The first is pretrial diversion programs developed in the 1960s. Public and professional opinion supported this idea, and it quickly became the norm. But nobody had really done the research to understand whether the program had the desired effects. Ten years later, when we finally did the research, we found that the diversions made no difference in outcomes.

The second example is point scales for the bail system. In the 1980s, I was visiting another state and came under attack for a point scale they'd instituted that wasn't working. I was told they'd come up with the scale based on an article I'd written about the Manhattan bail project in 1960. I said, "It's 1980. This is a different state. And we abandoned that scale in 1970 because we found it had no empirical basis. What are you doing?"

John Stuart: As a defender, I can tell you that my clients were being denied bail based on that point scale all through the 1980s in Minnesota. It's unfortunate that we didn't have this conversation 20 years earlier!

Smith: The lesson I'm trying to highlight here is the danger of replicating a specific model to another context. If you want to go to scale, you've got to know why, and you've got to be very careful to avoid harm creation.

Hartmann: Mike Scott, what can you tell us about your experience with problem-oriented policing?

Michael Scott: We've had some success in getting police officers to do beat-level problem-solving, using street savvy, common sense, and some rudimentary statistical analysis to target local concerns. We've had less success with higher-level problem solving, applying more rigorous research methods to study a class of problems experienced across a whole jurisdiction.

A police agency's enthusiasm for problem solving tends to wax and wane with the arrival and departure of individual champions within the department—when the champions leave, the innovation disappears as well. Many people still cling to fairly simple notions of what police departments can do, with no sense of what a broad range of responses could really be possible. Problem-oriented policing remains optional; it has not been institutionalized. One reason this is so is that there is no external constituency saying, "Give us more of that problem-solving stuff."

Hartmann: Is there a tension between trying to turn each police officer into a mini-problem-solving unit unto himself versus trying to arm departments with better analytical and research tools to problem solve on a higher level?

Scott: So far, the funding has been geared toward line officers who want to go forth, do good and interact with the community. Unfortunately, that's a heck of a lot more politically appealing than the idea of hiring a bunch of research analysts who work back at headquarters to study community problems. And I think it's fair to say that line-level cops have held up their end of the problem-oriented policing bargain a lot better than the police executives have. In fact, we have line officers to thank for much of the replication that we have seen. Policing is a profession that relies heavily on oral tradition; cops learn from talking to one another. We've come to the conclusion that stories are the best training tool—so at our annual conferences, cops spend the bulk of their time sharing examples of what they're doing. If you can get enough of the individual stories out, you can build a critical mass of support for a new idea like problem-oriented policing—or drug courts, for that matter.

Hartmann: Are there other criminal justice analogies out there?

Stuart: To me, the inescapable historical analogy is the juvenile court movement, which succeeded spectacularly in going to scale. The first juvenile court opened in 1899; every state had one within about 20 years. The most prominent problems with juvenile courts—as they became widespread and institutionalized—were lack of due process, poor fact finding, indefinite jurisdiction over people based on a small offense and idiosyncratic judging. It was a lawless court. As we develop drug courts, we need to keep this experience in mind.

Smith: It might also be useful to bear in mind that in its earlier days, the juvenile court was a mechanism thought to be useful in controlling immigrant populations. It was a strategy for dealing with groups that were marginalized, and making sure they stayed that way. If drug courts are falling into that part of the pattern, we may want to be very careful to leave this form of social control behind when we take them to scale. One way to avoid that problem is to bring drug courts to white university towns and suburbs, thereby legitimizing a system which is currently so pointed at African-American youth.

Scott Newman: I have a different take on the issue of race. What we've found is that young African-American males are opting out of drug court at a disproportionate rate; they are more likely to say, "I'll do my time instead." They simply aren't as fearful of the conventional system.

Hartmann: We've brought some outsiders to this discussion—experts who have been involved in taking innovative programs to scale in fields other than criminal justice. What have you heard so far? What lessons can you draw out for us?

Lisbeth Schorr: I see five key lessons regarding how to go to scale. The first is the need to distill the essence of an innovation. Unless you spell out what you're doing with some specificity, you can't spread the model. Another lesson is attention to those elements that don't travel easily from site to site. In many programs I've looked at, one of the essential components is the practitioners' belief in what they're doing. You can't mandate belief in a program when you replicate or systematize it, but you must take belief into account through training.

The third point is recognizing the importance of context. In my experience, the biggest mistake of replicators is thinking that because their program is wonderful, the surroundings won't destroy it when they plunk it down in a new place. But the surroundings do destroy the program unless you provide high-quality training. The context is the most likely saboteur of the spread of good innovations. Part of the context that can undermine innovation is the demand for evidence, and what that demand does to the innovation itself. The demand for proof by funders, elected officials and others has led practitioners to look for outcomes that are easy to measure rather than the outcomes they're really after.

The fourth point is that practitioners should arm themselves to look for patterns rather than proof. As you begin to notice patterns that reappear when you have success, and as those observations accumulate, you can start to offer some very persuasive evidence, if not "proof," of what works. Finally, almost all successful scale-up efforts I've seen have had an intermediary organization to provide legitimization and to articulate the essence of the program to be replicated. The importance of an intermediary cannot be underestimated.

Bernardine Watson: At Public/Private Ventures, we're very interested in alternative strategies for working with high-risk youth. We've developed three kinds of criteria for determining whether a program is ready for replication. The first is the program itself, and whether it actually addresses the recognized need or problem. Clearly this isn't an issue for drug courts. The second is whether it does so through methods that are considered credible by the field. Finally—and this is the thorny area that Lee Schorr talked about—we ask whether the program has proof of success and measurable results. The social service field has set a very high bar for how to prove that a program works: often the field requires a random assignment study to determine success.

But very few programs can muster this kind of data. We were able to do it in the case of Big Brothers, Big Sisters, an organization with a well-defined model, a name brand and funders willing to invest the money necessary for long-term and very expensive research.

Schorr: In the last 20 years, the rhetoric in the field has really improved. Everyone knows what they're supposed to say about their program. But that doesn't mean they're actually doing it.

Another function that an intermediary can play is to go beyond rhetoric in analyzing what makes a program work.

Assets

Hartmann: Are there reasons to be optimistic about the prospects of drug court institutionalization? Do courts bring any particular assets to the business of going to scale?

Eric Lane: The evolution of unified state court systems is one important asset, because it has allowed the judiciary to become a real branch of government in the sense that it can assign resources, delegate responsibilities and make things like drug courts happen that never would have been possible 25 years ago.

Hartmann: I would nominate a few more assets. One is that the judicial system is independent. Unlike police departments, the courts don't have mayors or the city council looking over their shoulders. They have much more freedom and power than almost any part of the executive branch. A second asset is that judges think in terms of precedent; they're willing to be guided. Finally, drug courts have received a lot of support and encouragement from the federal government.

Kevin Burke: Another asset, I think, is the willingness of drug courts to be evaluated. People are no longer prone to make policy by anecdote.

Stuart: I think drug courts appeal to people's desire to have hope. We have seen an awful lot of criminal justice programs in recent years that have not worked and have become more and more punitive. With drug courts, people see that we're not using leeches to cure disease: we're switching to antibiotics. The mainstream judicial system is still using leeches.

Newman: I would point to the favorable political climate as an asset. The public is much more receptive to this thing than it used to be.

Roberts: This is true. You can talk to almost any drug court professional in the country, and be told that there have been favorable newspaper articles and widespread community support for their drug courts.

Berman: We also know from public opinion surveys that while citizens may not be aware of what a drug court is per se, they do approve of the model's basic elements. In very high numbers, they like the idea of judges reaching out to clinicians and asking their advice on drug cases and they approve of court-mandated treatment as opposed to incarceration.

Spreading the Word

Hartmann: Last summer I visited the Red Hook Community Justice Center, where it's easy to see that all the people who work at the court are true believers in what they're doing. My question is what happens when the true believers leave? Can we talk about how to create and perpetuate local buy-in?

Berman: Whether it's a community court like Red Hook or a drug court or some other kind of innovation, I think it's possible to embed the new values we're talking about today in architecture, technology and research benchmarks—all kinds of things other than personnel. You've got to try to inoculate yourself against the inevitability of the first generation leaving.

Valerie Raine: Until recently, drug courts have been created from the grassroots up, thanks to entrepreneurial judges and attorneys. When drug courts are imposed from the top down, how will that change things? As you go to scale, do you take drug courts and make lots of them, thereby retaining some control over the process? Or is what we're seeking a new approach to judicial conduct? In which case, shouldn't our efforts be focused on inculcating this approach into judicial decision making in every courtroom? Of course, the risk is losing control and having what was once an innovative approach become just another case processing mill. These are difficult questions that don't have any easy answers.

Schorr: You're right to be aware that people don't respond well to being told, "You have to do this." I would be very leery of trying to impose the idea of drug courts on people who don't want to implement them. But it's a very different thing to say, "You have to do what is necessary to implement an idea you've already endorsed." You always have to invent some part of the innovation on site. You can't manufacture the desire to create something like a drug court from above. That's a recipe for disaster.

Newman: I wonder whether concepts like problem-solving courts can only be carried out if you're directly involved in building them yourself. Can you create a successful drug court—one that incorporates a process of mutual trust and buy-in among such diverse parties as judges, prosecutors and defense attorneys—without having everyone build it from the beginning?

Roberts: I think it all goes back to training. It can be done. The Department of Justice assembles training programs to help people plan drug courts, and we've seen the different stakeholders arrive and shake hands with each other because it's the first time they've met. Some are longtime enemies. We watch them go through a process of learning to appreciate each other's point of view, and developing the rudimentary skills of behaving like a team when they go back home.

Newman: I was part of one of those training teams several years ago. I was the hard-hearted prosecutor; our presiding judge was the hidebound traditionalist. I bonded with our drug court judge when I found out he snores very loudly on airplanes. Even workshop travel was part of the bonding process! I think transformative personal experiences among key figures are essential to institutionalization.

Watson: All the training in the world won't make a difference if the site you've chosen can't operate the program. In trying to spread drug courts, I think you have to be careful to pick places where the capacity exists to implement a new program.

Schorr: I'm not sure I agree with you on this point. I think you start by looking at places that really need the innovation and then try to create the infrastructure to support it. I would choose a place that's needy over a place that's ready to innovate.

Concerns and Obstacles

Hartmann: We've talked a lot about how you go to scale and how you spread the word about drug courts. Before we go any further, I want to make sure everybody's had a chance to air their concerns about the institutionalization of drug courts. What makes you nervous here?

Smith: I'd be concerned about an overreliance on arrests as a way of addressing drug abuse. There's an infinite supply of addicted persons out there. The more capacity you create, the more cases you're going to have. There may be no way to get ahead of demand. I worry that in creating drug courts, we may be holding ourselves back from coming up with other solutions to the problem.

Newman: I don't really share your concern. The idea that a judge in a drug court would recruit the police into gathering up fodder for his treatment program and get them to abandon opportunity deprivation or some other strategy doesn't strike me as real. In Indianapolis, we do both.

Adele Harrell: My big concern is that drug courts don't fall into the trap of overselling their promise, something I think we have to guard against very carefully.

Michael Dorf: I agree. What makes us think a court can solve a complicated social problem like drug abuse? The 1960s and '70s were the high water mark of optimism in the judiciary's ability to address problems like prison overcrowding, school segregation and a lack of mental health treatment services. What we've seen in the last 20 years or so is growing skepticism in judges' ability to address broad social issues.

Roberts: I think we have enough drug courts. What we need are more drug court clients. Most drug courts are fairly small experiments. Are they dealing with all the people they could be?

Newman: I have a public safety concern about allowing more serious criminals to be eligible for drug court. I get letters from inmates asking that I let them out early so they can continue their walk with Jesus. My feeling is that Jesus can walk in a reformatory just as well as outside, and so too can drug treatment.

Burke: I think there's a need to continue to explain to the 25,000 trial judges around the country that a drug court is an enjoyable assignment. Without that buy-in, you won't be able to build momentum to expand drug courts. Judges also need cover, because this is a profession that doesn't encourage risk taking and falling flat on your face.

Dorf: Another potential problem with going to scale is that drug courts today operate by penalty default—they use the threat of incarceration to get people to enter the program. If you go to scale, you take away that option. Entering drug court would no longer be voluntary.

Smith: I have a slightly different take on this question. Today's innovation is tomorrow's conventional wisdom—the standard operational procedure that's desperately in need of change. I think we need to find a way to go to scale that's open to constant change, revision and discovery. Otherwise, you just make it more difficult for the next innovator.

Lane: That's a very important point. I think drug courts are going to fail at some point. The question is how much good we do within that time frame and whether we're preparing an end game for the next innovation to come forward.

Treatment

Hartmann: Expanding the drug court approach will inevitably require new connections with the treatment community. What kind of challenges are presented by partnerships with treatment providers?

Burke: Accountability is one challenge. Drug courts hold the defendants accountable, but don't always do a good job of holding the treatment provider accountable.

Harrell: I agree. I think we have a real issue of quality control. When you start dealing with several thousand people instead of several hundred, you have to figure out how the courts can set up the right mechanisms to ensure treatment quality, and that treatment programs are holding offenders accountable. We're facing a serious problem with drug treatment capacity right now; some programs have a staff turnover rate of 50 percent each year.

Chico Gallegos: One major problem with ensuring effective drug treatment is that many assessment tools don't take into account the specific cultures and populations drug courts are dealing with. Cultural competence is important among both treatment providers and court personnel.

Roberts: Another issue is the question of where treatment begins and ends. Drug courts have expanded the concept of treatment beyond its traditional definition.

With drug courts the goal is not simply to get participants sober, as it might be in a straight-up treatment program, because then you just end up with a sober criminal. The idea is to work on the behavior that is problematic to the community. So for drug courts the goal is not just sobriety but also law-abiding behavior.

Harrell: Flexible thinking about treatment is key. Over the next few years, our ideas are going to change as knowledge in the field grows. The process of being able to react to and incorporate these changes in the definition of effective treatment should be part of how we think about taking drug courts to scale.

Leadership

Hartmann: Where is the leadership going to come from to expand drug court programs? Can the judiciary do it by itself?

Daniel Becker: In Utah, the leadership for drug courts originates from a judicial council that first put in place certain broad definitions—one being that our drug courts would be post-plea, and another being that treatment would remain an executive branch function. Those definitions helped transform the drug court judge from rogue status to legitimacy. More and more judges have since begun to express interest in drug courts. We are now reaching a critical mass. We have enough people engaged in the programs that we need much more intensive resources than what we've been working with up to this point. In our state, that need has meant bringing the legislature into play—and as the state becomes more involved in the administration of drug courts, a tension has developed between accountability and real innovation.

Hartmann: How valuable is something like the endorsement of problem-solving courts by all 50 state court chief judges and court administrators in convincing more people that the model is worth the investment?

Burke: The fact of the matter is that the Conference of Chief Justices is a pretty conservative group. This may be the first time they've passed an endorsement that is pro-active in nature, and it has been a great help in getting people's attention. As soon as it was passed, I went back to our judicial council in Minnesota and was able to argue that it was time to move our drug courts away from "pilot" status.

Stuart: Judicial support is obviously key, but it seems inevitable that state court systems will have to devise a strategy for approaching the state legislature. Federal grant money alone won't bring drug courts to scale over the next five years.

William Vickrey: In California, we have been fortunate to get the legislature to fund a separate committee to serve as the institutional voice on the planning, advocacy and guidance of drug courts. We also have legislation, initiated by the courts, that created a joint committee of the Department of Alcohol and Drugs and the judiciary to oversee drug court funding.

Becker: In Utah, we've passed a statute allocating 13 percent of every dollar of state funding dedicated to drug court to general court operations—to be spent by the judiciary, and 87 percent to testing, treatment and case management—to be spent by the Department of Human Services. I predict that states that successfully redirect federal money for substance abuse and treatment into the drug court arena will be the frontrunners in drug court institutionalization.

Raine: That's a critical issue. Health and Human Services block grants bring huge amounts of funding to state alcohol and drug agencies. Going to scale will be next to impossible without involving the commissioners of these agencies.

Hartmann: Scott, if you were the czar of drug courts in Indiana, what would you want from your state legislature?

Newman: I think it's important to be careful how you define what's being taken to scale. A bill in Indiana has proposed codifying the 10 components of drug courts into law. While I understand the urge, I don't think it's appropriate. I would instead structure the law to create an intermediary body that would help certify drug courts as well as provide incentives for their implementation. When Indiana created public defender commissions, for example, we allowed counties to tap into additional state funds if they had established a legitimate program. We preserved for each county the ability to qualify, within broad parameters, for matching funds, and work with an intermediary that was responsible for articulating standards. This approach avoids some of the problems of bureaucracy.

Dorf: On that note, I think one of the central challenges of going to scale is to have "bigness" and coordination without bureaucracy—and that's where the idea of an intermediary comes from. An intermediary can assess what's happening in the field; gather detailed, accurate information from local players; develop some sense of what the best practices are; and relay that information back to the players. This is the kind of institutional architecture I think you need if you want to move from a system based on charisma to one based on standards and principles.

Hartmann: Lee, let me put you on the spot. Institutionalization versus bureaucratization. What's the difference?

Schorr: If I knew, I would have written another book about it! That's a very hard question to answer. The term bureaucracy carries a negative connotation today that it didn't have in the Progressive Era. I think when we use a word like institutionalize, what we're suggesting is that we find the time and opportunity to allow for local variation and to move away from excessive rigidity.

Newman: To me, bureaucracy creates a coercive style of leadership that forces other people to act in a certain way. Institutionalization is a motivational style of leadership, which gets people inspired and allows them to build their own teams and create programs with some flexibility.

You have to move beyond that to a system less dependent on leadership, or you'll end up with a coercive situation in which other people feel they have to act a certain way. I think we all favor the kind of leadership that allows people some flexibility.

Looking Ahead

Hartmann: Where do you want drug courts to be in five years, and what single significant investment would you make to get them there?

Traficanti: In New York, my goal is to disappear by 2003, leaving in place the resources and infrastructure necessary for local sites to carry the drug court idea forward. In five years, I would like to see—in every state and across the country—the resources available for any defendant, in any jurisdiction, to go into treatment. This can be achieved by making it possible for judges to electronically access information from the bench, including available program slots and available beds.

Milliken: My goal is for every sentencing judge to have access to an assessment of the defendant that allows him to decide whether to make treatment a part of the sentence. In order for that to happen, we need state funding for treatment for the adult criminal population.

Smith: I would like to see the idea that sentencing is a responsibility of the court over a prolonged period of time gain wider currency.

Newman: The single most important investment that drug courts could make is in management information systems. Building more uniform operating systems for drug treatment courts would really advance the ball on institutionalization.

Becker: I'd like to see less emphasis placed on drug courts per se, and more emphasis on making treatment a mainstream enterprise by developing partnerships between courts and state agencies that oversee treatment.

Lane: I'd like to find a way to define success, figure out how to measure it and then invest in the tools to measure it. We would then have an opportunity to really find out what it means for a drug court to "work."

Scott: I would love criminal justice practitioners to understand their roles more broadly than they currently do. Prosecutors should see themselves as more than just the chief law enforcement officers, but also as the chief lawyers who help us think about community standards and public safety. Judges should see themselves not just as decision-makers but as concerned leaders of the community.

Gallegos: I'd like to see evidence that drug courts have made inroads in the broader, loftier goal of rebuilding communities.

Stuart: I would like to see every court in my state thinking of itself as a substance abuse court, and operating with the kind of consciousness about these issues that we've been talking about today. The investment to be made is in the time needed to talk about what the justice system is really doing and whether it's working.

Harrell: I share the vision of making this a way of doing business across the justice system, and maybe even fading drug courts out of existence as their tenets become embedded in practice.

Schorr: I feel very envious of all of you because this is a far better, more rigorous discussion that I am used to hearing. And as I walk away from this table, I think what's most exciting is the idea that drug courts open doors for the court system in general to become more problem-solving, in terms of thinking more broadly about problems and solutions.

CHAPTER FIVE

Bridging the Gap: Researchers, Practitioners and the Drug Court Model

AUBREY FOX

In an effort to bridge the worlds of research and practice at a critical moment in the life of drug courts, the Center for Court Innovation, working with the U.S. Department of Justice, brought together in November 2003 a select group of state administrators and drug court scholars to discuss a series of important questions: What can researchers tell state officials about drug court operations and impacts? What can't they tell them that they need to know? Going forward, are there a handful of strategic investments in research that would reap significant dividends for the field as a whole? And how will state leaders know if their efforts to promote statewide drug court reform are successful?

One thing became quickly apparent during the conversation: as in many areas of social policy, researchers and practitioners rarely talk to one another. Indeed, the scholars at the table lamented that research had not played a particularly influential role in shaping drug court policy to date.

Why is that so? There were several reasons cited at the roundtable, but they all spoke generally to a single theme: the cultural

---

This edited transcript was originally published in May 2004 by the Center for Court Innovation as "Bridging the Gap: Researchers, Practitioners and the Future of Drug Courts." Its publication was supported by the Bureau of Justice Assistance, Office of Justice Programs, U.S. Department of Justice. Points of view and opinions do not necessarily represent the official position or policies of the U.S. Department of Justice.

divide between research and practice. This divide has several dimensions. One is philosophical: Urban Institute researcher Shelli Rossman summarized this neatly when she observed that "researchers start with the assumption that an intervention does not work and try to disprove it. . . . Practitioners, however, want to start from the position that they're doing something that they already know works."

Another dimension is practical: researchers tend to talk to one another, rather than to practitioners whose work they are studying, observed University of Pennsylvania scholar Douglas Marlowe. For Hennepin County, Minnesota, Chief Judge Kevin Burke, the issue is the differing reward systems for both professions. While researchers worry about getting papers published, judges worry about getting re-elected and re-appointed.

Although research may not have been integral to drug court development to date, this may soon change. While the first phase of the drug court movement was dominated by individual judicial leaders at the grassroots level and the second phase by drug courts' success at attracting the attention of decisionmakers at the federal level, the action seems to be shifting more and more to the state level. All across the country, states are increasingly assuming fiscal and programmatic authority over drug courts. Along with this new authority comes the pressure to document results—and to identify best practices, enforce quality standards and determine eligibility criteria (including whether drug courts should handle higher-level offenders). Research can help administrators make better, more informed decisions in all of these areas.

Albeit frustrated by their lack of a voice in drug court policy-making decisions to date, scholars at the roundtable did report widespread consensus in the research community that, when properly implemented, drug courts offer a powerful means for changing the behavior of addicted offenders. As Doug Marlowe said, "There's no room for debate: the application of certain, swift and appropriately modulated sanctions and rewards improves behavior over time."

Participants around the table identified the following elements as crucial to successful drug court implementation:

- enrolling addicted offenders into treatment quickly;
- imposing sanctions and rewards swiftly and appropriately;
- bringing high-risk offenders back before the judge regularly;
- creating effective screening mechanisms to identify eligible cases;
- graduating a significant percentage of participants; and
- ensuring that drug court participants feel they are being treated respectfully by the judge and are being listened to in the courtroom.

At the same time, researchers also acknowledged that there was much still to be learned about what makes drug courts work. "What we know [about drug courts] is very small and what we think we know is much bigger," said Urban Institute researcher John Roman.

For researchers, the critical question is whether drug court implementation will heed the wisdom of drug court research, or if resource constraints will force administrators to cut corners and thus decrease the effectiveness of the drug court model. For example, roundtable participants raised questions about whether drug courts with heavy caseloads could afford to schedule weekly or bi-weekly judicial status hearings with the high-risk offenders who appear to benefit most from interacting regularly with a judge. In addition to resources, other participants raised concerns about a potential "novelty effect": the idea that drug courts, like many demonstration projects, will show less positive results over time as the novelty wears off.

Both scholars and practitioners agreed that certain aspects of the drug court model needed improvement. Treatment emerged as a critical area of concern, with several roundtable participants noting that treatment programs in the field were slow to catch up with emerging best practice standards. While University of Maryland researcher Faye Taxman suggested that one obstacle to change was that these new treatment models appear to "threaten practitioner discretion," other roundtable participants said that drug court judges could help move the process along, arguing (in Doug Marlowe's words) that "if anyone is going to hold the treatment system accountable, it's the court system."

The issue of race also came up a number of times in the discussion, mostly by practitioners looking for guidance with regard to how to work effectively with minority populations. Hennepin County, Minnesota's chief judge, Kevin Burke, said the key to working with this population was to "build a sense of hope. . . . If there's anything a judge can do, it's to convey to a young person that they can be something." Taxman concurred, pointing out that research showed that young African-American males need "positive reinforce[ment]" from authority figures to succeed. However, Burke also raised concerns about fairness, contending that drug courts needed to be careful not to put excessive pressure on African-American defendants to forego an opportunity to challenge the constitutionality of an arrest in exchange for being offered drug treatment.

The "Bridging the Gap" roundtable was part of a series organized by the Center for Court Innovation and the Department of Justice. Previous roundtable events have addressed such topics as the reintegration of drug court graduates into their home communities, mental illness, community justice and due process in problem-solving courts.

What follows is an edited transcript of the discussion, which took place over six hours in a Washington, D.C. conference room.

Participants*

John Baron is executive director of the Coalition for Evidence-Based Policy, Washington D.C.

Steven Belenko joined the Treatment Research Institute at the University of Pennsylvania, Philadelphia, in November 2002 as a senior scientist.

Donna L. Boone is president-elect of the Congress of State Drug Courts and executive director of the National Program for Therapeutic Courts, William & Mary Law School, Williamsburg, Virginia.

Kevin Burke is a district judge in Hennepin County, Minnesota, and currently the Hennepin County chief judge, Minneapolis, Minnesota.

Karen Freeman-Wilson is chief executive officer of the National Association of Drug Court Professionals and executive director of the National Drug Court Institute, Arlington, Virginia.

Francis X. Hartmann (moderator) is executive director and senior research fellow of the Program in Criminal Justice Policy and Management at the John F. Kennedy School of Government, Harvard University, Cambridge, Massachusetts.

Cary Heck is director of the Louisiana State Supreme Court Drug Court Program Office, New Orleans.

Lars Levy is administrative director for treatment services for the 16th Judicial District Drug Courts in the parishes of St. Mary and Iberia, Louisiana.

Douglas B. Marlowe is director of Law & Ethics Research at the Treatment Research Institute at the University of Pennsylvania, Philadelphia.

Janice T. Munsterman is a senior social science analyst at the National Institute of Justice's Office of Research and Evaluation, Washington D.C.

---

* Titles reflect participants' roles in November 2003.

William Ray Price Jr. was appointed to the Missouri Supreme Court in 1992 and served a two-year term as chief justice. Judge Price also serves as the chairman of the Missouri Drug Court Commission, Jefferson City, Missouri.

Valerie Raine is director of drug treatment programs at the Center for Court Innovation, New York, New York.

Michael Rempel is director of research at the Center for Court Innovation, New York, New York.

John Roman is a research associate in the Justice Policy Center at the Urban Institute, Washington D.C.

Shelli Rossman is a senior research associate in the Urban Institute's Justice Policy Center, Washington D.C.

Richard Schwermer has been a court administrator since 1990 and has served as Utah's Assistant State Court Administrator since 1995.

Michael Stringer has served for the last 14 years as division chief for the Ohio Department of Alcohol and Drug Addiction Services, Columbus.

Faye S. Taxman is director of the Bureau of Governmental Research and an associate professor in the Department of Criminology and Criminal Justice at the University of Maryland, College Park.

Douglas Young is a senior faculty research associate with the Bureau of Governmental Research at the University of Maryland, College Park.

Setting the Stage

The conversation began with a discussion of the strategies that states are using to promote drug courts within the judiciary. Increasingly, state leaders in the judicial, legislative and executive branches are assuming fiscal and programmatic authority over drug courts. While research identifying the benefits of drug courts has played a role in fueling drug court growth, so too has frustration with "business as usual."

Francis X. Hartmann: There are a number of state drug court administrators here at the table. Give us a sense of what's going on with drug courts in your state.

Richard Schwermer: We now have 21 drug courts in Utah. We've been fortunate in terms of funding, with tobacco settlement money getting diverted to us. Early on, we agreed that for every dollar that came in for drug courts, 87 cents would go to treatment, testing and case management and 13 cents for additional judge and clerk time. The state court administrator, the head of the department of corrections and the head of the department of human services decide where the money goes. The only ground rules are that all programs have to be post-plea, and they have to follow, in some vague way, the 10 key components. I tend to think that we will continue with this approach, though it may be time to add more requirements.

Cary Heck: Last year, the Louisiana legislature provided $13 million in drug court funding, which is a lot of money for a state with only four million people. At the Supreme Court, where I serve as statewide drug court coordinator, we've developed a fiscal monitoring and oversight plan to make sure the money is being spent appropriately. We're developing a number of initiatives, including starting a certification program for drug court professionals, releasing a statewide case management system and requiring that drug courts follow a set of best practices that we've developed.

William Ray Price Jr.: I'm the chairman of the board in Missouri that oversees all the drug courts in the state. In Missouri, drug courts grew from the bottom up: people did things differently from drug court to drug court. Now my job is to figure out what works, how to quantify it and what to require.

Valerie Raine: In New York, drug court momentum was initially driven by a small group of charismatic judges. Today, that is no longer the case. In 2001, the state's chief judge, Judith S.

Kaye, pledged to expand drug courts throughout New York. Judge Joseph J. Traficanti Jr. was given the job of developing a set of tools to advance institutionalization, including training, management information systems and research. Our challenge in New York is ensuring quality control and making sure that all eligible offenders receive the drug court option. We also have some questions about how to achieve the goal that Judge Kaye articulated, which is not necessarily to continue to create more drug courts, but to take the components that work in drug court and build them into the DNA of courts across the state.

Michael Stringer: Leadership for drug courts in Ohio comes from a slightly different direction—the state's treatment agency, where we've taken a broad look at how you connect treatment with the justice system. More than 40 percent of our clients have a court relationship. Recognizing this, over the last decade we've established 60 drug courts, 15 in-prison therapeutic communities and 20 diversion programs that are linked to the courts. Our goal is to improve our treatment system, and match up the right offenders with the right treatment.

Hartmann: What role, if any, has research played in helping you advance the case for drug courts?

Raine: In New York, drug court expansion has been built on a set of operating assumptions that seem to be backed by research. One is that treatment works. Another is coercion: the notion that judicial coercion works with addicted offenders and that they are more likely to succeed when ordered into treatment as opposed to when they seek it out voluntarily. Another idea is that early intervention works.

Schwermer: In Utah, we really haven't had to use research to sell drug courts. We've said, "They work and they probably save money." The important thing with elected officials is getting them in the door. The best two hours ever spent on Utah drug courts was the two hours the governor sat in the Salt Lake City drug court and asked questions about the program. He saw one of the defendants come up to the judge and say, "Thank you for saving my son's life," and he was hooked from then on.

Kevin Burke: To me, the question of what the evidence shows or doesn't show about drug courts is almost beside the point. In Hennepin County, where I serve as chief judge, our drug court is already to scale—we take everyone who is charged with a drug offense, one-third of all our felonies. My attitude in creating a drug court of that size was that there was compelling evidence that the system was completely broken. There is something liberating when the patient is critically ill. The doctor has some liberty to take risks because, absent something dramatic, they're going to die anyway. Courts need to be honest in evaluating how broken (or critically ill) their present systems are.

Donna L. Boone: Coming from a southern state, I should say that many people don't think that what they're doing is broken. Putting more people in prison, executing more people, doesn't really bother folks in the South. Still, they are concerned about the increasing costs of incarceration, and we should emphasize that drug courts are a cost-effective crime reduction strategy.

What the Research Says

The researchers around the table identified a number of components as essential to drug court success, such as early intervention, active judicial supervision and immediacy. By making investments in these areas (for example, working to guarantee that participants are enrolled in treatment on the same day as their first drug court appearance), state leaders can help improve drug court effectiveness. At the same time, researchers raised concerns about obstacles that might prevent courts from making these kinds of investments, citing, for example, the pressure on drug courts to schedule less frequent judicial status hearings to save on court costs or the failure of many drug courts to offer rewards for program compliance with sufficient regularity.

Hartmann: I'd like researchers to pretend that your brother or sister has been given the job of carrying forward the drug court movement in a given state. And your sibling calls you and says, "Help me understand what we know about drug courts." What would you tell him?

John Roman: I would tell my brother that what we know is very small and what we think we know is much bigger. We know that drug courts reduce recidivism and drug use among participants when they are in drug court, though we don't know how long the effect lasts. We know that people tend to respond to sanctions when they understand them, when they're proportionate and delivered with a high degree of certainty. However, there's also a lot about drug courts that we don't know, such as differences between pre- and post-plea drug courts and the effect of requiring participants to pay fees.

Douglas B. Marlowe: I would tell my brother not to take the job.

Hartmann: Pretend he already took it.

Marlowe: I'm sort of being facetious, because in my opinion, drug courts are the only criminal justice intervention that's been implemented that can, in theory, apply appropriate principles of behavior modification. There's no room for debate: the application of certain, swift and appropriately modulated sanctions and rewards improves behavior over time. We also know that the judge is a critical component of drug courts, and that outcomes for the most severe offender populations are improved if they see the judge on a regular basis. The problem is what happens in practice: the drug courts I've seen give one reward for every 60 or 70 appropriate behaviors, and while the ratio is better with sanctions, most infractions still go undetected. As for judicial monitoring, the reality is that judges don't see clients often enough; in large jurisdictions handling thousands of cases, status hearings are being held every six to eight weeks. My worry is that drug courts are very intensive, very expensive interventions, and as money gets tight, people are going to start picking at them. There's isn't a lot of good research out there that tells us what elements of drug courts you can't dispense with.

Schwermer: Doug, are you suggesting that drug courts used to work better than they do now, or that the first studies of drug courts weren't any good?

Marlowe: What I'm saying is that a universal law of behavioral research applies here: all demonstration projects show extraordinary effects and all replication studies either don't show them or show a greatly reduced effect size. Partly that's due to a novelty effect—any time you do something new, you improve outcomes. But there are other issues as well. The first drug court judges were believers, and believers always do a better job than those who get assigned to drug court. Another issue is publication bias: you only hear about positive results because they're the only ones that get published or talked about.

Faye S. Taxman: I would tell my brother that he should set up a screening system to get high-risk, high-stakes offenders involved in drug court, because that's where you're going to see your results. Most systems screen on legal criteria—the challenge is including behavioral issues like co-occurring mental health and substance abuse disorders, anti-social personalities and substance abuse dependency that are equally as important as arrest history in determining whether a participant will succeed in drug court.

Burke: If I understand you correctly, you're saying that the high-risk offender is most likely to respond effectively to drug court. However, most of the early drug courts took lower-level offenders. The design was flawed to begin with, and bringing it to scale is going to be incredibly difficult because inevitably it means working with a different group of people.

Steven Belenko: The treatment field is ripe with examples of interventions that target low-risk offenders because it's politically expedient. It's a very difficult political issue—while there are examples of drug courts that target high-risk offenders, they are few and far between. It's a dilemma both politically and analytically to establish programs that will target the appropriate population.

Jennifer Columbel: I don't agree with the idea that drug courts are only focused on low-end offenders. Early drug courts were focused on diversionary populations, but in the last eight years we've seen a great increase of offenders with decades of substance abuse problems and long rap sheets.

Michael Rempel: I would highlight three points for my imaginary brother. First, immediacy: across the board, participants do better when they are linked to treatment very soon after they enter the drug court. Having formalized screening and assessment systems that are able to rapidly process cases and get participants into treatment is critical.

Hartmann: One quick observation about immediacy: I sat in the Red Hook Community Justice Center in Brooklyn, New York, some time ago, and I saw a young man get sentenced to treatment. A staff member got on the subway and took him to the treatment center, instead of calling and setting an appointment eight weeks later. That's a powerful example of what we mean about immediacy.

Rempel: That's right. It speaks to resource allocation—the time to spend money is early on in the process. If you have to save resources somewhere, it should be when a participant has been in a program for over a year and they can report to court less often. The second thing I would tell my brother is to read Doug Marlowe's study on judicial status hearings, which shows that they have a great impact on high-risk populations. Importantly, it's not just the hearing itself, but the quality of interaction that matters—judges with the longest and most direct connection with participants had the best results. My final point would be about graduation. In our study of six drug courts in New York, we found that while drug courts were effective, the entire impact came from graduates. In other words, there was no benefit to receiving large amounts of treatment and then failing. One implication is that it's important for drug courts to increase graduation rates, and in some instances that may mean toning down graduation requirements.

Taxman: Picking up on Mike's research on graduation, if you look at drug courts nationally, a large percentage of participants don't graduate. We haven't thought through the criminal justice consequences of failure.

Boone: I think I would tell my brother that we know something about public opinion. In Virginia, we've asked the public about the role they think judges should be playing. Do they just adjudicate or do they have some responsibility for the effectiveness of dispositions? And the public is saying yes, we hold these judges accountable for dispositions. So I think that if you can argue that what courts have done in the past does not work, it gives you more latitude to take some risks. Putting drug courts in this context might help sell them to the public.

Hartmann: What do administrators at the state level need to know about drug courts? Where are the holes in our knowledge?

Price: The number one thing I need to know is, do I have a successful program? How can I quantify it or show that success to others? And how can I improve the program? I also need to know what data I should be collecting and how to analyze that data.

Rempel: Here is the bare bones data I think drug courts should be collecting. Get the arrest charges, criminal history, the date a participant entered drug court, what their status is—open, out on a warrant, graduated or failed—and when graduation or failure took place. To everyone in this group, that type of data collection might seem obvious. But it doesn't consistently occur. So my priority number one is to collect that information for everyone.

Burke: I think we need to know how to do a quick assessment of mental health issues. We had psychiatrists associated with the Veterans Administration conduct full-blown psychiatric exams of defendants, and they found that 41 percent had a major mental illness. Obviously, we can't afford to do this all the time.

Taxman: Another thing you should be collecting on drug court participants is their level of drug usage. It's important to distinguish between people who are drug users versus those who are drug dependent, because the first group is probably not suitable for drug court. There are standard assessment tools in the public domain, such as the one developed by Texas Christian University, that are well validated and deal with both criminal factors and substance abuse dependency.

Burke: You need accountability for the people who are doing the screening. In my experience, the level of sophistication of the screeners is all over the map.

Taxman: That's true, but the good news with using tools in the public domain is that they've been tested in the field and they can help reduce the number of errors or biases that counselors bring to an assessment.

Marlowe: Our discussion so far has focused on adult drug courts, but juvenile drug courts have spread quite rapidly in the last few years in the absence of any decent research or an effective treatment model for adolescents. The adolescent treatment field is in its infancy, and drug court programs are bringing kids who are not addicted into a very high level of social control. We don't know anything about their impacts.

Hartmann: Let's talk about cost-benefit analysis for a minute. John Roman, can you distill your 15 years of knowledge into four minutes?

Roman: Taking an economic lens can help policymakers decide what population drug courts should focus on. For example, it may be worth investing more in a younger population that is more likely to commit crimes that pose high costs to communities. But you have to be careful about the kinds of questions you ask: some populations that are most responsive to drug courts, like long-term heroin users, aren't likely to show great economic benefits. They're probably not committing a lot of costly crimes in their community. They're going to continue to need public resources, even after they leave the drug court. From a cost-benefit perspective, they might be a net loser to your program. Finally, let me mention my opinion of the movement to encourage individual courts to do cost-benefit analysis as part of their evaluation. I think it's a mistake, because drug courts with small sample sizes are very sensitive to outliers.

John Baron: Just a quick observation. There is a lot of evidence from different social policy fields that small differences in the way a social intervention is administered and the population it's administered to can make an enormous amount of difference in its effect. For example, it matters a great deal that nurses, not paraprofessionals, make visits to poor families. In drug courts, it could be small differences in implementation that make all the difference in whether the intervention is going to work.

The Relationship between Research and Practice

The relationship between research and practice was a heated issue during the roundtable. Many of the scholars and policymakers at the table lamented that research had not played a particularly influential role to date in shaping drug court policy. Some policymakers felt that researchers did not understand the political, professional, fiscal and institutional pressures they faced. The key, participants agreed, was to balance the desire to "create an environment where people can take risks" with the need to collect objective, realistic information about drug courts.

Hartmann: How important has research been to drug courts? What role should it play going forward?

Rempel: What I've heard today is that research has not been terribly influential in terms of the major statewide institutionalization movements that have occurred. I think the only type of research that's been mentioned as important in selling drug courts to the legislature is cost-benefit analysis.

Marlowe: Unfortunately, research has zero penetration into practice in the drug treatment field. We don't know how to explain what we're doing to practitioners. What goes on in the laboratories and what goes on clinical practice are two completely different worlds.

Burke: What I'm hearing is frustration—researchers asking, "Why don't judges listen to me and why don't they read what I write?" And for the most part we haven't. I don't want to disabuse you of that. However, there's been no discussion of the complex nature of judging and I get the feeling that researchers don't really understand us. We went to law school because we didn't want to work for somebody and we went on the bench to get rid of our partners. We're a very independent group. And many of us are elected. For me, the risk of failure is "I've got to go back to private practice." That's not something that I want to do. Our goal should be to create an environment where people can take risks.

Hartmann: Picking up on Kevin's point, I've been involved in the community policing conversation for the last 20 years, and key changes in policing didn't come until individual police chiefs said that the old system didn't work any more. They realized that you could double their resources and it wouldn't make any difference because what they were doing wasn't working. Researchers operate with a different need for evidence than people who are making decisions in the policy arena. Is it possible to bridge the two worlds? Is it possible to make research operate on the time frames and the standards of evidence that policymakers employ? When do we know enough that it is okay to say, let's take this new practice to scale?

Roman: I don't think you can answer the questions practitioners want answered without the threat of finding answers that they won't like. The drug court industry has done itself a disservice by trying to tailor its evaluations to come to the conclusions that they want to come to. We've all read evaluations that are so positive that they are almost impossible to believe. That puts the courts in the situation of having to demonstrate a level of efficacy that's just not possible.

Marlowe: Picking up on John's point, the drug court field started out with these tremendous enthusiasms and expectations, and I think that has affected how we think about the type of outcome studies that need to be done. There is a sense that drug courts will change people's behavior forever. How long do you observe people after they complete drug court? Is a short-term effect an adequate basis for expanding drug courts? If you don't get an effect after three years, does that mean drug courts are not effective?

Rossman: There's a disconnect between research and practice. Researchers start with the assumption that an intervention does not work and try to disprove it so we can feel confident that it does. Practitioners, however, want to start from the position that they're doing something that they already know works. Researchers and administrators have different missions and different constituencies. The challenge is how to use research to manage expectations and be accountable, but with enough flexibility to permit you to acknowledge that this is virgin territory.

Heck: Most judges I know see evaluation as sort of like a medical exam—you only get bad news. In Louisiana, we have worked to change that mentality with our judges through continual training and our annual conference.

Hartmann: Let's assume that the federal government funded one of the researchers around the table to help you take the next steps with drug court. What would you want from that person?

Heck: I would want outside objectivity. I would want someone to come in, validate our measures and say, "This is good data and this is good research." We don't have the option of having a randomized study. It's not politically feasible. Being an academic, I know that all research falls on a continuum. While we try to get as close to pure experimental design as possible, we would want someone to come in and say, "This is about as good as you are going to get, given political circumstances."

Burke: I've been intrigued by why the first generation of drug courts worked when they were all so different. There's a researcher at New York University named Tom Tyler who's found that people are more likely to obey the law when they have a sense that they are being listened to. I think what made drug courts work is that defendants felt that judges were listening to them, and that when defendants left they felt like they knew what they were supposed to do. This is not normally the case in state courts. I would encourage researchers to go beyond looking at program details such as how often drug treatment occurs or which type of treatment people receive to these broader questions of whether defendants feel listened to.

Treatment

Most roundtable participants agreed that treatment is an issue that requires more attention from drug court advocates. The problem is one of implementation—participants agreed that many successful treatment modalities were not being adopted by treatment professionals. This pointed to a role that drug court judges and court administrators could play: as "potent customers" of treatment services, they could potentially help shape the behavior of the field.

Hartmann: What do administrators need to know about what works and what doesn't in the treatment arena?

Rempel: In the research field generally, and our own research into drug courts in New York in particular, methadone maintenance for heroin users is shown to be an effective treatment.

Raine: A quick question on the issue of methadone. When I was a public defender and saw people on methadone come through, I remember thinking that this was not a population for whom methadone was working very well. I mean, they were only seeing me because they were doing other drugs and getting involved in crime. When we say that "methadone works," have we done field tests to confirm that it does?

Taxman: Val, your personal observations are correct: the way we distributed methadone was in many cases counterproductive. The good news is that there are new regulations in place to change that.

Marlowe: In addition to methadone, there are probably 12 to 14 types of drug abuse treatment interventions that have absolute, indisputable proof of efficacy. The problem is that these interventions aren't being delivered in treatment programs.

Heck: Doug, if they're not being implemented, how do you know they're effective?

Marlowe: It's because they've been proven effective in a number of controlled, clinical trials—the same criteria the FDA would use to say a medication is effective.

Hartmann: So why aren't they getting out to treatment professionals in the field?

Marlowe: There are a number of reasons. First, if you want to get tenure at the University of Pennsylvania, you publish in refereed journals that practitioners don't read and you talk to other researchers about your work at conferences that treatment professionals don't attend. Second, the treatment field is in many respects impenetrable to new knowledge. It talks a different language and has a different set of values. Finally, the kinds of interventions that we're talking about are hard to do well. They are hard to implement and take a lot of training.

Lars Levy: As a drug treatment professional myself, I can say it's frustrating as hell to try to make people change.

Taxman: Part of the reason for this intransigence is that treatment models that work are structured interventions, which is a big change from established models that involve counseling and therapy. Structured models are threatening to practitioner discretion. More research needs to be done in terms of thinking about how we help professionals understand that there's a lot of room for professional judgment, even within structured interventions.

Hartmann: The point that's coming to the fore is that courts don't get to invent the treatment options that are available.

Marlowe: Yes, but judges make pretty potent customers. If anyone is going to hold the treatment system accountable, it's the court system.

Roman: I agree. The judge is the best-positioned person to hold treatment accountable, but I find that judges often don't feel like they are educated customers. Treatment in general is a black box that judges and courts are reluctant to open.

Boone: I agree with John. When I worked at the Supreme Court in Virginia, I suggested that we try to measure treatment impacts in drug court. The response I got was, "Well, treatment is like electricity. Nobody asks why electricity works if you turn on the light and it works." Thank goodness one person had pity on me and said, "Yeah, but if the light only turned on two times out of 10 somebody would start asking how it works."

Taxman: There are some resources out there for courts that want to better understand the treatment field. Several years ago, the Center for Substance Abuse and Treatment created regional centers, called Addiction Treatment Technology Centers, to help improve treatment services. They've been underutilized so far, particularly in the criminal justice field, as a way of helping to transform treatment.

Stringer: I'm feeling a little bit out of melody over here. I'm the only person at the table who works in a state division of treatment services. While I understand what people are saying about needing accountability from treatment, this goes both ways. We do about 15,000 assessments for drug courts every year. What our system can do is give the judge that takes risks with clients some assurance and some predictability that there is a net beneath them. Negotiating these relationships respectfully is hard—it's easy to offend people on both sides.

Karen Freeman-Wilson: One thing that strikes me about our conversation is that we can't underestimate the political implications of the issues we're talking about. We've mentioned some small "p" political issues, such as "How do you get into a treatment field that is closed to outsiders?" and "should drug courts use methadone?" And we've talked about some large "p" political questions, like "How do I sell my governor, my state representative, on taking higher-level offenders?" Even as we think about the research that needs to get done, we need to look at how to address political issues as well.

Race

The issue of drug courts and race also emerged as a significant issue at the roundtable. For some, it is an issue of effectiveness: many drug courts struggle to address the unique issues posed by African-American participants, particularly young men. At the same time, several participants felt that drug courts have the potential to help build a sense of hope among minority populations, and in the process build confidence in the fairness of the criminal justice system.

Hartmann: What is the impact of race on drug courts?

Price: In Missouri, our most difficult people to treat are young African-American males. We need to know more about how to work with this population—I can't go to the legislature asking for more money unless we can say we know what to do with our biggest problem. I want to go home with some hope that we know how to treat young urban males who get in trouble with drugs.

Freeman-Wilson: As a former judge in Gary, Indiana, I can tell you that there are at least two populations here. When I was a judge, I would refer to the first population as "piss-poor wannabe drug dealers," much to my staff's dismay. These are young men who have been raised well, come from intact homes, but who are hangers-on and emulators. They would be the last person to use any type of substance other than marijuana. This group does not need drug court. There's another demographic, however, of people who have been using since they were kids. They are totally different from the first group, and may in fact benefit from treatment interventions. The key is to distinguish and understand that the group is not monolithic.

Taxman: For the 16- to 22-year-old African-American male, what the literature says is to focus on positive reinforcers. This tends to be a population that didn't do well in school and has a lot of other failures. Unfortunately, in the criminal justice arena, it's hard for people to congratulate offenders for small stuff that we think they should be doing anyway.

Burke: To pick up on Faye's research, my experience in dealing with this population is that they don't have a sense of hope. If there is anything a judge can do, it's to convey to a young person that they can be something. This population doesn't need any more sticks—they need to build a sense of hope.

Belenko: There are a number of strength-based interventions or family-focused interventions that have been studied extensively in clinical trials. Multi-systemic therapy is one example.

Another is mentoring. The good news is that there is a lot of literature about successful interventions with this population.

Stringer: This is not just a drug court issue, it's a correctional issue. Part of the dialogue has to be with the correctional system. In Ohio, we've started the process: our director of corrections is working with us to identify candidates for judicial release who can be treated in their communities.

Burke: I want to raise some other issues regarding race. There's a lot of complicated stuff going on out there on the streets. Young people are forced to make the choice: do I go to treatment or become a snitch, or can I do both? There's also the issue of constitutional rights: should defendants be forced to choose between treatment and their right to challenge racial profiling? Though we need to be careful about how we approach this issue, I think there is potential to positively impact communities of color and their distrust of the justice system. This is a population that has no confidence in the justice system's fairness. The potential here is to show that courts are a place where people are treated with respect and in a positive manner.

Raine: I'm in agreement with Judge Burke. If people feel they are treated fairly in the system, because of the drug court experience, then we've done really well.

Measuring Success

The roundtable concluded with a discussion of how to measure success with drug courts. Some participants offered concrete measures, such as a decline in the use of incarceration or positive impacts on individual drug court participants. Others suggested more sweeping targets, such as changing the culture of the courthouse to support problem solving or building public support for the treatment of addicted offenders.

Hartmann: Each of us is in some manner involved in this enterprise of drug courts. How will we measure success five or six years down the road?

Schwermer: I would use a few standards. The first is, are there sufficient resources to meet demand? The second thing I would look at is the extent to which drug courts have been mainstreamed. Are drug courts part of a standard judicial curriculum? Has a body of case law developed around due process and equal protection concerns? Finally, some impact questions. Have we changed the composition of our prisons? Have we diverted addicts, allowing us to use the resource of prison more effectively?

Burke: Picking up on Rick's point, I was told once that in 1963, New York State had 85,000 inpatient psychiatric beds and 15,000 prison beds. By the early 1990s it had completely reversed itself. When I went back to Minnesota I discovered that it was true there as well.

Roman: Let me offer a concrete example of how we can change correctional practice. Birmingham, Alabama, ran a program called "Breaking the Cycle" that used some drug court principles less intensively over a broader population. The results of the program were such that they actually had a new jail planned in Birmingham that they didn't need to build.

Rempel: One area I'm interested in is attitudinal changes among judges and attorneys. Have drug court practices like judges speaking directly to defendants and collaborative relationships between attorneys and treatment providers filtered throughout the state court systems more widely? Has it led to institutional change?

Belenko: Like Mike, I want to offer a broad view of success. I think we need to look at the political and public opinion context of drug courts. Can we measure the changes in public opinion and media coverage around treatment interventions for offenders? Can we build better systems for educating the media, the public and elected officials about addiction and crime? Elected officials often make assumptions about what the public thinks about criminal justice, and they're often not consistent with what people really think.

Rempel: I think it would be valuable to know if there is an impact in areas of income, employment and life outcomes for participants.

Taxman: I would look at system-level integration efforts. Have you changed how justice system and treatment actors work together, not just on drug court cases but on the larger number of people who are under criminal justice supervision?

Stringer: I would like to see state sentencing laws reflect the success of drug courts by mandating court-supervised treatment for first-time offenders and parole violators. I'd also like to see active alumni associations, where recovered addicts participate over the long haul.

Raine: Five years down the line, I'd like to see other kinds of traditional courtrooms incorporate some of the active ingredients of drug courts. One indicator of success might be the number of people who have the option of being linked to treatment. My second goal would be to institutionalize problem-solving ingredients into the various educational systems that impact criminal justice, whether it's law schools or training for new assistant district attorneys, defenders, probation and court officers.

Freeman-Wilson: We're only hitting four to eight percent of the eligible population now. We won't really be a successful institution until a large number of folks are able to access drug court. I don't know if it's 60 percent, but I do know it's more than 10 percent.

Taxman: I take a slightly different position: we should only use drug courts for the people who need it most. We don't have a good picture of whether that is five percent or 20 percent or 50 percent. My guess is that it probably under 10 percent, because if you target high-risk cases, there is a small percentage of people who need the structure and oversight of drug courts. There is probably a larger population of people who need other types of treatment intervention than drug court.

Roman: What would a person who's not involved in drug courts call a success? They might say it's a success if drug courts were to pop up everywhere, in almost every large community. They might also look to see if the drug court model was being applied to other populations. The reality is that all this has already happened.

Conclusion

By the end of the day, roundtable participants agreed that research can play a number of important roles in guiding drug court growth. First, by providing state policymakers with good, reliable information about drug court outcomes, research can help build a case for the model.

Equally important, by identifying characteristics of drug courts that promote program success—such as immediacy, frequent court appearances for high-risk offenders and an environment in which drug court participants feel they are being treated respectfully—research can be used to improve day-to-day operations. The challenge for the field going forward involves opening up lines of communication between researchers and practitioners—a shared responsibility for both groups.

CHAPTER SIX

From the Margins to the Mainstream: Community Justice at the Crossroads

GREG BERMAN AND AUBREY FOX

Across the United States, a variety of new ways to solve public safety problems in neighborhoods plagued by crime and disorder are being tested:

- Beat cops working with tenants to fix broken windows and doors in a public-housing development;
- Judges sentencing low-level offenders to pay back the community by cleaning local parks;
- Prosecutors using civil ordinances to close down crack houses and pursue gang members;
- Probation officers reaching out to the relatives of probationers in an effort to offer better supervision; and
- Ministers working with the police and probation officers to identify and assist young people at risk of criminal offending

These are just a few of the kinds of creative, problem-solving efforts that are happening across the country. Many have described these initiatives as examples of "community justice." What does this mean? In what ways—if any—is community justice different from the traditional justice system? Is there a coherent philosophy or set of principles that unites all those who

---

This edited transcript was originally published as "From the Margins to the Mainstream: Community Justice at the Crossroads" in *The Justice System Journal*, Volume 22, Number 2 (2001).

espouse or practice community justice? Is community justice a good or bad thing? These are the kinds of questions that motivated the U.S. Department of Justice's Bureau of Justice Assistance, in collaboration with the Center for Effective Public Policy and the Center for Court Innovation, to bring together a small group of leading practitioners and thinkers from around the country to participate in a day-long exploration of community justice. The group's charge was deceptively simple: to begin to build an intellectual framework for community justice, defining its borders, articulating its values and describing its best practices.

This task was complicated by the diversity of the projects falling under the community justice banner. Beginning with the rise of the community policing in the 1980s, prosecutors, courts, probation officers and even defender services have engaged—both at their own instigation and at the urging of community advocates—in community-focused and community-based work. Community justice programs have been created to solve local problems ranging from drug trafficking to underage drinking, from gang violence to shoplifting. They have taken place in context big and small, from large urban areas to isolated rural jurisdictions. And they have relied on community members to play a wide range of roles in "doing justice"—from participating in local advisory boards to determining sanctions for offenders.

A number of community justice projects have achieved remarkable results and attracted considerable public acclaim. This includes Boston's Operation Cease Fire, in which a coalition of local and federal criminal justice agencies, researches, social workers and clergy nearly halted an epidemic of youth violence in two inner-city neighborhoods; the Midtown Community Court, which helped reduce low-level crime like prostitution and illegal vending in the Times Square neighborhood of New York; and Boise County, Idaho, where courts have taken the lead in developing mediation programs in schools and home visitation programs for pregnant women. Other community justice projects have been less ambitious. In many places, what passes for community justice is simply community relations—a police officer or assistant district attorney attending neighborhood meetings. In short, the umbrella of community justice has included both ambitious efforts to rethink how the criminal justice system goes about its work and more modest initiatives that seek simply to improve communication between justice agencies and the citizens they seek to serve.

Defining Community Justice

Given this kind of variety—of quality, of geography, of purpose—participants in the Department of Justice's roundtable struggled to arrive at a common definition of community justice. This comes as little surprise—it is hard to imagine two words that carry more baggage than "community" and "justice," both independently and together. As the judges, prosecutors, law professors, defense attorneys and community representatives at the table groped for common themes, several distinct lines of thinking about community justice emerged. While participants did not fall neatly into clearly marked camps, it was possible to identify important differences in their views of community justice.

A first group of roundtable participants saw community justice as a moral critique of the current criminal justice system. For these participants, community justice is an effort to repair the "harm" done by this system, to "rebuild society" and to rethink "how we live together as human beings." This means fundamentally altering the balance of power—and the division of labor—between criminal justice agencies and communities. According to Vermont Commissioner of Corrections John Gorczyk, "For me, the goal of community justice is to provide nonexperts in communities with the infrastructure and capacity to do conflict and dispute resolution and become the primary providers of public safety. For the last 60 years, we've been moving the responsibility and the authority for resolving disputes out of the community and into some sort of governmental function. And it's made communities dysfunctional."

A second set of participants saw community justice more narrowly, as a set of new tools to be deployed strategically to address specific problems in specific situations. For these participants, community justice is "a problem-solving model" that "breaks down jurisdictional barriers" in an effort to achieve tangible benefits, such as "safer cities." Scott Newman, the district attorney in Indianapolis, articulated this point of view neatly: "I think community justice is something that is problem oriented, something that is geographically tailored in some way, in which power is not jealously guarded but is shared with the community." John Feinblatt, director of the Center for Court Innovation, amplified this point, identifying a group of community justice proponents who "think we should adopt these characteristics because it's the right strategy—if we do it, there will be a number of benefits, such as safer cities and more people using parks and fewer living under the highway."

A third group focused less on the strategic value or transformative power of community justice, emphasizing instead community justice's potential to engage citizens and restore public confidence in the justice system. For this group, community justice is not about "gutting the traditional criminal justice system and replacing it with something different." Nor is it about solving "specific problems . . . that have proven resistant to traditional approaches." Rather, community justice is an opportunity to enhance citizen engagement in the process. According to Robin Kimbrough-Melton of Clemson University, "If we want to have an effective justice system, we have to enable people to participate." Cheryl Steele of the Washington State Department of

Corrections added, "I think [community justice] is a perfect opportunity for government to reacquaint itself with society in smaller groups. . . . It's about reviving participation in democracy."

A final group was dubious about community justice, asking whether it is simply a "rallying cry" that drains resources from other worthy efforts and widens the net of governmental control over poor and minority populations. "I find myself skeptical of community justice and wondering if there is anything really new here," said Eric Lane of Hofstra University Law School.

At the end of a day's worth of discussion, no clear consensus emerged about the definition of community justice, its underlying values or where the roles of communities and criminal justice agencies should begin and end. As Scott Newman concluded, "The problem right now for community justice is definitional. We have to be careful to not let it get too broad a concept or to sweep too much within it, because at some point it will be such an umbrella that it won't mean anything."

Despite this concern, participants at the roundtable acknowledged that community justice had emerged in response to a real crisis—the declining sense of public faith in the criminal justice system and those who work within it. "[Community justice] is what our customers are asking us to do," said Marti Kovener, a victim advocate in Denver, Colorado. "We're getting pretty clear messages from people who are involved in the justice system that what we're doing isn't working, it's not meeting their needs." Participants returned again and again to this theme, saying that "community justice is an effort on the system's part to regain legitimacy." Moreover, many participants felt that community justice initiatives around the country had begun to make strides in addressing this crisis, building new bridges between government and citizens and tackling neighborhood problems that would otherwise go unaddressed.

What follows is an edited version of the broad-ranging discussion about community justice, which took place over the course of six hours in a Washington, D.C., conference room in September 2000.

Participants*

Alex Calabrese is presiding judge of the Red Hook Community Justice Center, Brooklyn, New York.

Walter Dickey is the Evjue-Bascom professor of law at the University of Wisconsin-Madison Law School.

John Feinblatt is director of the Center for Court Innovation, New York, New York.

John Gorczyk is commissioner of corrections for Vermont.

Francis X. Hartmann (moderator) is executive director of the Program in Criminal Justice Policy at the John F. Kennedy School of Government, Harvard University, Cambridge, Massachusetts.

Leo Hayden is president and CEO of the National Center for Violence Interruption in Chicago, Illinois.

Robin Kimbrough-Melton is professor at the Institute on Family and Neighborhood Life at Clemson University in Clemson, South Carolina.

Marti Kovener is program director of Victim Services 2000, Denver, Colorado.

Brad Lander is executive director of the Fifth Avenue Committee, Brooklyn, New York.

Eric Lane is the Eric J. Schmertz distinguished professor of public law and public service at Hofstra University School of Law, Hempstead, New York.

Peggy McGarry is senior associate at the Center for Effective Public Policy, Washington D.C.

---

* Titles reflect participants' roles in September 2000.

Timothy J. Murray is director of the Program Development Division at the Bureau of Justice Assistance, U.S. Department of Justice, Washington D.C.

Scott Newman is the elected prosecutor in Marion County (Indianapolis), Indiana.

Leonard E. Noisette is director of Neighborhood Defender Services, New York, New York.

Tom Potter is the former chief of police of Portland, Oregon.

Kay Pranis is a restorative justice planner for the Minnesota Department of Corrections.

Bill Ritter Jr. is the elected district attorney in Denver, Colorado.

Cheryl Steele is the community mobilization manager for the Department of Corrections in the State of Washington.

John M. Stewart is the Minnesota State Public Defender based in Minneapolis, Minnesota.

Patricia Young is a judge in the Fourth Judicial District of Idaho.

What is Community Justice?

Francis X. Hartmann: We're going to begin by asking the big question: What is community justice? How might you recognize it if you saw it?

Eric Lane: Community justice is an opportunity for citizens, working with government, to identify problems and look for ways to resolve them. So I see it as problem solving. It's about asking how the criminal justice system can use strategies to resolve specific problems such as drug-fueled crime and quality-of-life crime that have proven resistant to traditional approaches.

Alex Calabrese: In addition to problem solving, I think of community justice as prevention. As a judge working in a traditional courtroom, I was like a plumber with one tool or an artist with two colors: jail or out. That wasn't effective. Now that I sit at the Red Hook Community Justice Center, I can bring many more tools. I can bring counseling sessions. I can bring community restitution projects. And I can bring anger management classes. I know these kinds of alternative interventions are not appropriate for every case. But for many of the cases that I see—disorderly conduct, low-level drug offenses, shoplifting—I've got a real chance at getting at the root cause of the offender's problems so the person doesn't come back before me again and again.

Peggy McGarry: I think Eric and Judge Calabrese are right to highlight problem solving and prevention as central features of community justice. One of the forces driving community justice is that the criminal justice system is, in fact, uniquely positioned to see social problems like child neglect in a way that cries out for doing something about it. Why should the criminal justice system care about prevention? I think it comes from the sense that there are two sides of justice—that if we're going to hold people accountable for bad behavior, we should also hold ourselves accountable for guaranteeing that people start out with a chance at having a successful life.

John Feinblatt: I think that under the rubric of community justice, we're seeing institutions like courts and prosecutors become much more outcome oriented. They're thinking about reintegrating offenders into the community. They're thinking about restoring victims. And they're thinking about community health and getting addicts off drugs.

Cheryl Steele: I'd like to nominate another definition for community justice. I think it's a perfect opportunity for government to reacquaint itself with society in smaller groups and help build community. In many respects, it's about reviving participation in democracy.

Robin Kimbrough-Melton: I agree that community justice is about participation. In a lot of the communities I work with in South Carolina, it's the norm for families to feel that the justice system has not served them particularly well. On the other hand, when I sat down recently with some women who had been through a family drug court and talked to them about why the program had been successful, I heard them talk about how the court had taken them seriously and let them participate in the decision-making process. They felt it helped them make progress with the issues they were facing like neglect and substance abuse. So I'm encouraged by the community justice movement because if we want to have an effective justice system, we have to think about how we enable people to participate.

Marti Kovener: For me, this is sort of a déjà vu moment, because a lot of what's being said about participation I've heard for years and years out of the victim advocacy community. When I was a court advocate, the victims I worked with were always saying, "Do I get to say something now? Is this when I get to say how I feel and how this has impacted me?" And we kept saying, "No, not yet, not yet." I think that desire to be an actor rather than acted upon is what community justice is really about.

Scott Newman: What's clear to me so far is that community justice is something different from conventional case processing. The question is, in what ways? No one element fully captures community justice, which makes it hard to explain to the public. Is community justice about getting out of the courthouse and into the neighborhood? Let's take prosecutors in police stations, for example. If all they're doing is screening felony cases, they're nothing more than a convenience for the detectives so they don't have to come downtown. But if they start to notice particular crime trends and then make suggestions to police and other agencies, then that starts to look more like community justice, I think. Is community justice a willingness to deal with root causes and prevention? That, too, is an element, but only when those efforts are integrated with the justice process. Is it a willingness to break down jurisdictional barriers? Take the example of neighborhood sweeps where police and probation officers go out together to ensure compliance with probation conditions. If you link those sweeps up with a gang problem, as they did in Boston, that starts to look like community justice. So I guess I think community justice is something that is problem oriented, something that is geographically tailored in some way, in which power is not jealously guarded but is shared with the community, and the community is allowed to have a sense of ownership. It's more willing to look at what's happening, not just at what happened in a particular incident.

Hartmann: I hear us struggling to define the boundaries of community justice. I've heard problem solving. I've heard prevention and expanded sanctioning options. I've heard participation in democracy. I've heard power sharing and a geographic focus. My concern is that we don't want to end this meeting by saying "doing good and avoiding evil is community justice." So let me try a different approach. I wonder if it would help us if I asked, what do you think community justice is a solution to?

John Gorczyk: The first thing community justice is a solution for is a criminal justice system that is totally unsustainable fiscally. In the state of Vermont, where I'm commissioner of corrections, one out of seven men from the ages of 18 to 21 is under correctional supervision. We need to add 265 new taxpayers to the state rolls a month just to pick up the bill for the growth in our incarcerated population. That's unacceptable.

Kay Pranis: I think community justice is a solution to the harm the current system is causing to individuals and to communities, which I think is substantial. It's a solution to the disempowerment of those communities most impacted by crime, and a real shift in the relationship between the criminal justice system and communities. It's about letting the community take a leadership role, while criminal justice professionals learn to listen and ask themselves, "How do we support the community and its goals towards building a healthier community?" I also think that community justice is about rebuilding a society in which people actually care about one another and take responsibility for the well-being of one another. In many respects, what we're talking about here today is what we think the term "justice" ought to mean.

Tom Potter: Community justice is a solution to the problem of the lack of responsibility of parents for their children, of citizens for other citizens. It has the potential to begin to engender more personal responsibility. There's a belief out there that "the government will fix it. We don't have to do it." One of the models that I envy is the environmental movement. Right now every citizen knows that there's something they can do as an individual to help with the environment. It's called recycling. So everybody has their little yellow recycling bins. They can put things in it, and they can do something every single day to make the environment a little bit better. In the issue of personal and public safety, we haven't given the same kind of choices to people that the environmentalists have.

Lane: I think there's a legitimacy problem in the criminal justice system today, and community justice is an effort on the system's part to regain legitimacy. It's one solution to the lack of public confidence in the justice process.

Feinblatt: I hear a lot of agreement that community justice be problem oriented, locally focused, that there should be power sharing. Where I don't think there is a lot of agreement so far is why those characteristics are necessary. I think I detect three strains of thought here. There's a group of people who think community justice is necessary because those are the right values. It's moral—it's what we should be doing and how our society should be organized. And I think there's a second strand of people who think we should adapt these characteristics because it's the right strategy—if we do it, there will be a number of benefits, such as safer cities and more people using parks and fewer living under the highway. And finally there's a third strain, which says we need to do these things because the criminal justice system has done such a lousy job that we have no choice but to share power until we right the boat. And then when we right the boat, the necessity to share power might recede. It's important to think through these different philosophies now, before we consider expanding and institutionalizing community justice.

Why Now?

Hartmann: My next question is, why now? What are the forces driving the rise of community justice?

Patricia Young: I think a lot of it has to do with people within the criminal justice system wanting to do a better job. I'm starting my twentieth year on the bench, and like Judge Calabrese, I kept feeling that I was not being very effective because by the time I would get a case, the damage had already been done, whether it was a child who had been abused or a drunk driver who had hit somebody. And I kept thinking, there's got to be a way that we can get on the front end of some of this. For me, this has translated into a real need to explore prevention programs so that we don't just have a reactive response to problems.

Leonard E. Noisette: My sense is that, with prison expansion and the criminalization of more and more conduct, there's a recognition that the justice system is headed in the wrong direction.

Gorczyk: Fundamentally, we have a colonial system of justice. When you see overrepresentation of minority populations in correctional systems, that's not a reflection of a system being broken. That's a reflection of it doing what it's designed to do.

John M. Stuart: I want to return to the point that community justice is being driven by the frustration of system players with "business as usual." I work with the public defender's office in Minnesota, where we routinely have prosecutors and defenders who handle a thousand cases a year. We have set up a very expensive prison system and a bottleneck in the middle. The court system handles cases on a kind of McDonalds basis. Now we're talking about a system of community justice in which each disposition is going to be cooked to order. The problem that we have to work out is that we don't have enough cooks to do that.

Bill Ritter Jr.: Part of the reason for this feeling of frustration, I think, is that in the last 20 years the justice system has had foisted upon it more in the way of social problems than ever before. Drugs may be the best example, as well as domestic violence. We don't have all the means we need to address these problems because they're social problems, and we're a legal system.

Walter Dickey: I think we can also relate the rise of community justice to a larger political context. Political debate today often consists of false choices: tough on crime or soft on crime is one example. One way of looking at community justice is that it's an attempt to break down false choices and create other options. It's a way of trying to bring nuance to the political debate about public safety and crime in this country.

Kovener: I think there's another reason for the rise of community justice, and it's because it's what our customers are asking us to do. We're getting pretty clear messages from people who are involved in the justice system that what we're doing isn't working, it's not meeting their needs.

Timothy J. Murray: Another answer to the question of "Why now?" is the increasing alienation that citizens feel from the criminal justice system. To most lay people, the criminal justice system doesn't make sense. When they go to a courthouse, they go to a place that is architecturally designed, staffed, equipped and populated with people trained for something that hardly every happens in that place, and that is a trial. All of us in this room know that trials hardly ever happen in state criminal courts. We're just moving cases, plowing through the day's calendar with plea bargains. And so when my mom and dad go to watch court, they say, "What was that? What were all those guys doing there?" I think if we can expose ourselves to some of the common sense that people bring into the process, the process will get better.

The Role of Communities

Hartmann: What is the role of the community in all this? How does community justice change the relationship between the community and the justice system?

Stuart: Traditionally, crime is seen as a breakdown of community life that has to be handled outside of the community in a special courthouse downtown, with marble columns and so on. What we're talking about here is bringing the criminal justice process back into the neighborhood to address community needs.

Potter: I've spent 35 years watching police around America operate, treating communities as people we did things to, not with. With community justice, I think we have the opportunity to see communities as part of the solution and a real partner.

Pranis: I think that we, in the criminal justice system, have a responsibility to use our authority to help build stronger communities. It's a huge challenge, but I think the criminal justice system can play a role as a convener. If you call a meeting to build a stronger community, not many people show up. But if you call a neighborhood meeting around crime, people will come. The issue of crime becomes an opportunity to gather people to build stronger communities.

McGarry: I think the criminal justice system has to understand the need not just to partner with communities, but to let them lead. There's a really high level of distrust of government and the criminal justice system in large parts of the country. Unless we get partnership and leadership from the community—and from a broad cross-section, not just the usual suspects like the chamber of commerce—that level of distrust is not going to change.

Dickey: One of the threads that's been running through this conversation has been the loss of legitimacy in the criminal justice system, and that the way to restore it is through community participation. But what makes us think that what the community would do would be different?

Calabrese: Walter, what I've found—and I was surprised at this—is that when you ask the community what they want, they want defendants to be given an opportunity to use services, even people with longtime records. I thought that would be a little bit of a problem to convince people in Red Hook before the court opened, but right away they were saying, "No, let's give them a chance."

Steele: I don't think the community wants to change the criminal justice system. In my experience working with the community, they don't say, "Well, let's not have judges or prosecutors." The fundamental system they believe in, but they're concerned about all the ways in which the system isn't functioning.

Murray: As I listen to what's been said so far, I think it's important to note that we're not talking about using the criminal justice system to fix society and we're not talking about gutting the traditional criminal justice system and replacing it with something different.

Hartmann: So what's different about community justice?

Dickey: What interests me about community justice is that it can evoke or invoke naturally occurring forces that drive human behavior in ways that have the potential to advance public safety. For example, it seems to me that our desire for the respect of others is a powerful force in our lives. Why would we think that's not true of offenders? They desire love, respect, all that sort of stuff just as people in this room do. Most of us don't respond very well to threats, and yet we continue to threaten people with the idea that that's going to motivate them or change them. I think the question is, how can the criminal justice system tap into informal, community-based means of enforcing appropriate standards of behavior and promoting public safety?

Gorczyk: I'd like to expand on that point. Punishment does not work to change behavior in any kind of positive direction. It's a fact. For me, the goal of community justice is to provide non-experts in communities with the infrastructure and capacity to do conflict and dispute resolution and become the primary providers of public safety. For the last 60 years, we've been moving the responsibility and the authority for resolving disputes out of the community and into some sort of governmental function. And it's made communities dysfunctional.

Newman: I disagree that punishment doesn't work. In drug courts, using the coercive power of the court to coerce treatment and keep people in intensive outpatient treatment is working. And I also believe punishment works to incapacitate the most dangerous people and make sure they don't hurt anybody.

Pranis: I agree with John Gorczyk. All of our institutions have to rethink what it is for us to be human beings and live together. We are trying to develop processes that invoke the deepest desires of human beings to be in positive connection with others.

Lane: I think we ought to be cautious about romanticizing human nature. Even as we talk about tapping into the positive desires and forces that drive our behavior, I think we need to acknowledge that fear and violence are part of the deep nature of human beings as well. I worry about the idea of just leaving things to communities to decide for themselves. I was thinking about the example of the Voting Rights Act, where the only way we could solve the problem was by sending federal marshals into communities to ensure that people got to vote. And I use that as an example only to show that some problems are resolvable on a community basis, and some problems are not resolvable that way.

Pranis: I recognize that there's a concern about what communities would do if given decision-making power. I know of an experience that defies everything everybody at this table would assume about communities. There was a neighborhood in Oregon where the city was placing a sex offender transition house. Even though the project did not require community approval, the city knew how difficult it would be to go forward without consulting neighborhood residents. A woman I know offered to do a circle in the community, and the city agreed to abide by what the circle wanted. After some negotiations, the community agreed to support the transition house and even helped fix it up. Three months later, the city decided that there had been a mistake in zoning and said the house couldn't be there. And the neighborhood was angry at the city and got up in arms to defend the house because somehow the occupants had gone from a "they" to a "we." And I share that story because there are times when communities and neighborhoods do things that are very exclusive, and there are times that the dark side of humanity comes out, but it seems to me that we've been overemphasizing that. We've built all of our policy on the Willie Horton story and none of our policy on the stories like the one that I just shared.

Feinblatt: I can imagine the process that you're describing producing that kind of result, but I can also imagine three blocks away that same process producing a very different decision. And I wonder whether that's tolerable, that two communities could follow the same process and have a different outcome. One of the hallmarks of our current justice system is a sense of predictability and certainty. When I think about the balance between community and the judicial branch of government, what I keep thinking about is that the judiciary is the branch that's not supposed to be influenced by the political process or public opinion or the concerns of one community versus another. They're supposed to be the ones who are responsible for a more detached form of justice. And so one of the issues I have to come back to is the balance between community involvement and the role of government. Where does one start and the other begin?

Leo Hayden: I submit to you that evenhandedness looks very uneven as it relates to my community. Look at the disproportionate number of people of color in the prison system. What happens when they go to prison is that their families break up and children don't get financial support. We end up creating a cycle of deprivation. What looks evenhanded may in reality have very uneven or unintended consequences for a particular community.

Dickey: We've been talking about the role of communities in the criminal justice system. But what if we turned the question on its head and asked, what role should the criminal justice system play in communities? My friend Herman Goldstein, who is widely thought of as the father of problem-oriented policing, tells a story of visiting a town in Italy. And there are two murals on the wall. One is obviously meant to depict a healthy, vibrant community, and the other an unhealthy one. And in the healthy, vibrant community, there's all kinds of commerce going on. People are in the park, playing, interacting with one another. There are individuals alone who are having their privacy respected. The criminal justice system is a very, very small part of this mural. The point obviously is that a healthy, vibrant community doesn't have a very big criminal justice system. Then, in the unhealthy mural, there's a big criminal justice system. There are soldiers all over the place, there are police officers and the amount of commerce is very small. And that, of course, is meant to indicate an unhealthy condition that people basically don't want to be in. The question becomes, "What is it about community justice that will move us from the unhealthy to the healthy place?" One thought that occurs to me is "first do no harm." That's been a consistent theme in our discussion today—that a lot of harm has been done by the conventional justice system. And my second thought is that we're really talking about a realignment and a different role for government. The challenge for community justice is to figure out what the criminal justice system can do, knowing that it's not the primary producer of public safety and community well-being.

Values

Hartmann: What values underlie community justice? Is it possible to identify them?

Gorczyk: That's an important question. Earlier Scott Newman listed a number of points about community justice, which I agreed with. But it struck me that they were a little bit more oriented to the process side and less focused on the values and principles that I think we need to have if we're going to ensure that community justice is consistent with who we are as a culture and what kinds of outcomes we want to produce.

Newman: I think the point's well taken. I think the tricky thing is figuring out whether we can, at a national level, delineate a set of values or whether that needs to be left to individual communities.

Pranis: I've resisted the term "community justice" because I've always had at the back of my mind the recognition that lynching was a form of community justice. And so I'm insistent in my own work that we never talk about any terminology without saying what values bound whoever it is that's making decisions. The work I do is about a fundamental rethinking about what we mean by justice. It's much, much bigger than the criminal justice system. This is about how we live together as human beings.

Stuart: I have an anecdote that gets to the issue of what values animate community justice. I was at a sentencing circle on the Mille Lacs Reservation, and the people in the circle were dealing with a guy who had 14 drunk-driving convictions. It had gotten to the point where every time he'd show up in court, the local judge would give him a year in jail, pretty much automatically. And he'd had a year in jail five or six times through this process, and it had done absolutely no good. But since he'd been participating in the sentencing circle, he had been sober for two years. And I heard some of the elder women from the Ojibwa band critiquing this guy at the circle, and they said, basically, "Look, we saw you going over to your cousin's house last week, and we know those guys drink a lot of beer over there. We want you to watch it." And he replied, "Yeah, you're right. I've got to be careful about that." And through that kind of weekly dialogue with this guy, he'd been sober for two years and had not been in jail and had not been driving drunk. To me, that was an illustration of a lot of the principles we're talking about—how communities, if given the opportunity, can be far more effective in changing behavior than the traditional justice system.

Dickey: Your story is a great example of how basic human impulses can be tapped to change behavior in community justice. What happened was that this man realized he was part of a group whose respect he desired, who cared about him and who were watching. They weren't going to give him a free pass, but, on the other hand, they were very decent in their approach to him. And all of a sudden it had engendered an alteration in his behavior that hadn't been achieved in five years of sitting in prison.

Lane: I don't feel as comfortable as Walter Dickey seems to about communities trying to change someone's behavior. I've lived for a long time in a very small town, and there are wonderful advantages to it. But there are also a lot of horrible things about small towns. For example, they tend to be exclusive. So I'm not sure I always trust the values of people acting in the name of "community."

Newman: I'm wondering if there is in fact a coherent set of values behind community justice. In the description of the Ojibwa sentencing circle where the guy went to his cousin's house, and they drink a lot of beer, and somebody said, "Well, you shouldn't be going to your cousin's house." I mean, what values are at play here? Is it self-determination? Or is the value sobriety and community control? I think you've got a conflict here. What does community justice stand for? Is it the dignity of the individual? Is it the interconnectedness of community? If so, what about all those people who want to be left alone, who would rather have a back deck than a front porch, who would rather be on the Internet than in the park with their kids? So each of these values sounds good, but when you start to peel away the layers of the onion, you still have other questions underneath.

Gorczyk: I think we can learn a lesson from the private sector, which is to ask customers what they want. In Vermont, we used focus groups and telephone surveys to find out what the public wanted from their criminal justice system, from corrections and from offenders. What did we find? We found that they wanted to be safe from violent offenders and wanted offenders to be held accountable and make reparations to victims and the community. At the same time, they wanted offenders to receive treatment to reduce the risk of reoffending. Finally, they wanted to be directly involved in the justice process themselves, and had the most confidence in the system when they were involved. We used this input to construct reparative boards staffed by community volunteers across the state. My sense is that if you talk to the customers and find out what they value, then design your system within those parameters, it will flourish, particularly if you give people a role to play in the system.

Ritter: The difficult thing here is that we don't have a sufficient consensus on what the right values are. We can all probably agree on the value of citizen participation. But I think it's a lot deeper than that. And it has to do with what "quality of life" means in a given community. And we don't, quite frankly, have a consensus that allows us to say, "Quality of life should look like this in any given community."

Skepticism

Hartmann: What are some of your concerns about community justice? Do we have any skeptics in the room?

Lane: I find myself skeptical of community justice and wondering if there is anything really new here. American history is filled with examples of groups attempting to participate in governance, whether it's with the criminal justice system or other parts of government. Community groups rise and fall, fight to identify problems and try to resolve them. And I worry about adopting a phrase like community justice that seems like a solution or sounds like an easier answer when it's really more of an ongoing struggle. The term community becomes a rallying cry, and I'm concerned about using it because it carries with it such baggage.

Newman: I want to add a second historical note of caution. It may be kind of unfashionable and maybe a bit mundane, but part of the reason that we're in the situation we're in today is because concerns about corruption caused us to centralize and "professionalize" police departments. I don't know if those concerns have evaporated completely. It's still something we need to be aware of.

Kimbrough-Melton: My concerns are a little bit different from the others I've heard. I'm cautious about community justice because I see a trend of people looking to the justice system for answers. I see schools pushing kids out into the justice system when they don't want to deal with them. I see families sometimes pushing family members. I think there are a number of institutions in our communities that are giving up and are absolving their responsibility to the justice system. So how we take that on and how we deal with people who are coming into our system and how we provide leadership back to our communities, I think that's a very critical point.

Newman: I'm wondering whether the justice system is even capable of providing any answers to the kinds of problems we're talking about here today. We've talked about the idea that one reason we do community justice is because other segments of society have abdicated or are not occupying the field appropriately. And my question is, who are we talking about? And if they failed, why did they fail? And what can we learn from their failures? More to the point, what is it about courts, or appendages of courts, that's different, that means that we will not fail when other so-called social programs have failed? Is it in part because courts are the new kids on the block? Is it because of the awe that many people hold our courts in and the relative remoteness of the way they exercise authority? The question will arise in community justice, do you lose some of the coercive power of the court that is created by a certain amount of remoteness? Are we throwing out the baby with the bathwater?

Noisette: My reservations come from my perspective as a defender and seeing and experiencing community justice, at least as I understand it, mostly in the formal justice system, primarily in the reconfiguration of courts and specialty courts. I worry that community justice may have a tendency to expand the court's role in solving problems. I have a couple of concerns about it. One is the allocation of resources. There are limited resources. And if more and more of those resources are thrown into the justice system, then those resources have to come from somewhere. I also have concerns about widening the net. I wouldn't want to find people under the control of the criminal justice system who would otherwise not be there and who could resolve their problems without big brother watching over them. Then I have broader cautions about community participation. I think this is a nice aspirational goal, but I think we have to be very, very careful about promising something that we can't deliver on. Communities where crime is a big concern have been made promises many, many times. You had better deliver in these communities when you talk about community participation and involvement.

Brad Lander: I'm skeptical about whether community justice is really getting at the root causes of crime. In my neighborhood, the obstacles to community health can't be resolved after a crime's been committed. The problems run so much deeper. It's great to be able to offer people who have committed an offense a second chance at some things they didn't get the first time around: drug treatment or education and job development and housing. But there are a host of issues that cannot be addressed through the justice system at all. What people in communities care about is access to real opportunities to earn a decent wage and access to housing. Yes, they also care about living in a safe place. I don't want to underestimate it, but I don't feel like it's primary. I don't think people don't have good jobs, housing and decent schools because their neighborhoods aren't safe.

Hayden: I'd like to follow up. For communities of color, community justice is either a blessing or a curse. Every solution that the justice system has come up with to solve the issue of crime and dispense justice in a fairer way always seems to have unintended consequences. We wind up with more people of color being arrested, more in the court system. So there are real issues of trust and respect that need to be dealt with.

Ritter: As a prosecutor, my biggest concern is that with community justice, you could end up with parallel justice systems, that there could be a separate community justice track where some practitioners work with communities but other prosecutors, defenders, probation officers just keep doing what they're doing in the traditional sense. The danger there is that you end up with people being treated differently depending on which track their justice system was operating on.

Newman: The problem for community justice right now is definitional. We have to be careful to not let it get too broad a concept or to sweep too much within it, because at some point it will be such an umbrella that it won't mean anything.

Going to Scale

Hartmann: We've covered quite a bit of ground today. We've attempted to define community justice, looked at some of the forces driving its adoption and examined the relationship between communities and the criminal justice system. We've also talked about some reasons to be skeptical about community justice. Now I want to ask a different question. What would have to be true in order for community justice to move from the margins to the mainstream of the justice system?

Murray: I think we first have to talk about the institutional objections to community justice. The institutions within which each of us work aren't famous for seeking out and nurturing innovation. Community justice kind of looks like and smells a little bit like an innovation. And judges dress funny, talk funny and work in funny places. Most of them like it that way. Scott Newman has talked about holding court in a trailer. And I've actually been to community courts that look a lot like trailers. And those communities and those judges have done that on purpose. But it has caused a lot of weeping and gnashing of teeth among the judicial brethren in that community. What do we do about courts that have spent a hundred years centralizing? We're now talking about decentralizing them. We're talking about collaborating with defenders and prosecutors to address problems rather than simply move the maximum number of cases.

Dickey: I think Tim's hit the nail on the head. He's asking, "Does the system have the capacity to do the things we're talking about?" For example, take drug courts. The things that drug courts do—monitoring an offender's progress through drug treatment—are exactly what probation and parole agents were supposed to do. Why do we think courts are going to be able to succeed where probation and parole failed?

Noisette: Following up on Tim Murray's point, I think what we haven't explicitly said is that community justice requires those of us in the criminal justice system to be prepared to change our role substantially. For community justice to be successful, it's going to require system players to step back and be prepared to do things differently.

Stuart: I agree that community justice requires system players to change their roles, but changing roles raises some difficult resource issues. Let me give you an example. In Minnesota, we had a client named Angel Hernandez who was a minor leader of the Latin Kings and was supposed to go to prison for a number of minor crimes he had committed. Our social worker found a Latino fraternity at a local college. And they said, "We'll take Angel Hernandez, and he can stay at the fraternity and go to college and we'll supervise him." Now, that's the kind of resource that the people who work in the criminal justice system either don't know about or don't have time to find out about because they're doing 800 or 1,000 cases. So one of the things that would have to be true in order to make community justice work is that the people who handle criminal cases would have to have the skills and the time to get to know community resources on the same level the social worker did when she found the fraternity for Angel Hernandez.

Newman: I think the one thing that I would say is most necessary for this effort is that we all need to be our best selves in order to make community justice work. It's not going to work without the good faith to be empathetic to each other's roles and to presume good faith on the part of other people. If someone was proposing that Angel Hernandez be placed in a fraternity instead of sent to prison, I would want someone to acknowledge what my problems as a prosecutor might be; that is, he may kill someone or open floodgates for similar cases. How is Angel's case different? Why is it fair to treat Angel in this way? Someone has to acknowledge my role and be empathetic in their style of collaboration.

Kovener: One of the things we have to do is challenge the cultural assumptions that are implicit in our current system of justice. For example, in working with traditionally underserved communities in Denver for the treatment of domestic violence offenders, representatives of both Latino and African-American organizations told me, "Your standards aren't going to work if you assume treatment for victims and offenders can't happen in the same place. In our community, you can't do treatment unless it's in the context of family and couples." There is no such thing as one community, and we have to honor the identities of different communities and ask questions without already having our minds made up.

Kimbrough-Melton: I'd like to switch our focus a little and encourage us not to forget rural areas in community justice. Rural areas are dealing with unique issues that are difficult to overcome and become much more magnified in a small context. For example, I work in a number of communities with deeply entrenched racial attitudes and power structures that have been in place for a long, long time. These communities are very difficult to change. I think there are also resource issues—rural areas often have traveling judges who affect the consistency of how we can implement community justice initiatives. These are issues that affect urban communities very differently.

Stuart: I'd like to raise two points. The first is from the perspective of a public defender. I'd like to speak up for including public defenders on the ground level of trying to work with community justice, because we have some issues that I think if they can be addressed successfully will make the programs work better. Second, in terms of the most important step to move it forward, in the specific context of Minnesota, where we have a great deal of stuff going on at the grassroots level, the most crucial issue for us now is sustainability. People have started this up on enormous energy, a lot of it volunteer energy. The projects that do have funding have soft funding that will go away after a couple of years. We need to be able to shift resources to have system people stop doing some of the things that they're currently doing that are ineffective and to get those resources to community-based groups that are doing these other kinds of things.

Kovener: John Stuart mentioned the need to include public defenders in community justice. I also think the victim advocacy community has a ways to go to really embrace this concept. There are victim advocates who don't realize that victims want to have a voice in a different way, who don't realize that victim and offender issues in many communities are not separated. When I talk to victims and communities in Denver, they say it's not about splitting victim and offender, right and wrong, good and bad, help and punishment—it's about my family, my community, which have been traditionally underserved by the justice system.

Ritter: Nobody has talked much today about community justice being a resource drain and how difficult it is to sell to local city councils or other funding authorities when other kinds of traditional prosecution are so expensive and so demanding.

Lander: I'd like to see some experimentation that isn't led only by criminal justice organizations. There are somewhere between two and three thousand community development corporations in the neighborhoods that we're talking about, and almost none of them are involved in this.

Feinblatt: I think that where we've made significant progress today is in defining why we are here, what drove this, why are we even having this conversation. I think that where we're still a bit stuck is where's the fit. Community justice is here, we can describe it somewhat, but is it a universal fix? Is it a fix for some things and not for others? What do we expect to get out of community justice? What are the results we are looking for? Are we looking for reduced recidivism? Are we looking at better allocation of resources? Are we looking at lowering costs? Are we looking at healthier communities? Or would it be enough to say that we're looking to establish legitimacy, and that part of establishing legitimacy is having a government that's responsive to its citizens and can actually interact with its citizens in a meaningful and honest way? Perhaps establishing legitimacy for justice institutions, which have long suffered without it, is a goal in and of itself.

Newman: When I started as a prosecutor 15 years ago, as far as I was concerned, when I convicted a criminal, a trapdoor opened underneath him, they fell through, and they were never seen again. And I took a lot of joy in that, I'll admit. Over time, my view has changed to the point where I take great joy—I still take joy in convicting criminals—in going to a drug treatment court graduation and being able to address people who were cases and say, "Can I call you Tanya? Can I call you Bill?" I have on the wall of my office a letter from Chi Chi's restaurant commending one of the drug treatment court graduates as Employee of the Month. There's a lot to be said for harnessing the desire for positive connections with others as a core concept of community justice—both the community connecting to the justice system on a more egalitarian basis, and the offender having a more positive relationship with the community.

Dickey: I happen to think that if community justice has a future, it's really going to be because of its problem-solving quality. I don't know that it will stay a problem-solving endeavor only, but that seems to me to be the most likely place for it to take root.

Now, what would have to be true for community justice to thrive, if it is basically a problem-solving model? First of all, you have to listen. I'll bet everybody in the room has had the experience of going out into communities and discovering that what's on their mind is not necessarily what we expected. We did this exercise in Milwaukee where we went into the area of the city with the highest homicide rate. And we found out that what was on people's minds were kids stealing screen doors. I also think leadership is required. One of the interesting questions for community justice is the tension between community and government. Sometimes problems are of such concern to a community that they start to yell "screen doors," but an awful lot of this stuff is below the level of visibility. A final element is imagination and a certain amount of flexibility because sometimes the obvious answers don't work. I happen to believe there's enormous energy in communities and the agencies we're talking about. What's needed is a system that's organized to release that energy and not keep it bottled up.

Research

In Chapter Seven, Greg Berman and Anne Gulick review the state of knowledge about drug courts, community courts and domestic violence courts and outline a research agenda for the field.

In Chapter Eight, Michael Rempel and co-authors summarize their evaluation of six drug courts in New York and offer lessons for state policy makers attempting to improve the quality of drug courts.

In Chapter Nine, Don F. Farole Jr. and co-authors discuss results of focus groups, held with judges in New York and California, about how to apply problem-solving principles in conventional courtrooms. While participants cited barriers to transferability, such as limited resources and the pressure to resolve cases quickly, they also identified practices they believed could be broadly adopted. Among the practices mentioned were ongoing judicial monitoring of treatment and social service mandates, direct interaction with defendants and the creation of links between courts and social service agencies.

In Chapter Ten, Aubrey Fox summarizes the results from a 2001 phone survey of over 500 state court judges. The survey found that while overwhelmingly satisfied with their jobs (and mostly unfamiliar with problem-solving courts), judges are nonetheless very interested in, and supportive of, problem-solving approaches in cases involving addiction, domestic violence and mental illness.

CHAPTER SEVEN

Just the Facts: What We Know and Don't Know About Problem-Solving Courts

GREG BERMAN AND ANNE GULICK

> *Policymakers often think, incorrectly, that an evaluation is like an "audit" or trial in which the results are usually clear cut and definitive. Either the funds were spent or they weren't; either the program served its intended beneficiaries at a reasonable cost per client or it didn't. Such "audit" questions are much easier to answer than the "evaluation" questions of cause and effect, often stretching out over a lifetime of the targets of crime prevention efforts.*[1]

> *The expected value of any net impact assessment of any large scale social program is zero.*[2]

Robert Martinson's seminal 1974 *Public Interest* article, "What Works? Questions and Answers About Prison Reform," offered a bleak assessment of rehabilitative initiatives aimed at criminal offenders.[3] This literary review of prison-based treatment programs—from vocational training to psychotherapy—concluded that, "with few and isolated exceptions, the rehabilitative efforts that have been reported so far have had no appreciable effect on recidivism."[4] Martinson determined the failure of treatment pro-

---

This research review was orginally published in *Fordham Urban Law Journal* as "Just the (Unwieldy, Hard to Gather, But Nonetheless Essential) Facts, Ma'am: What We Know and Don't Know About Problem-Solving Courts," 30 Fordham Urb. L.J. 1027 (2003).

grams by demonstrating a failure of research because the more than 200 studies he reviewed gave little evidence that the programs studied were linked to a reduction in crime.[5] Yet, what seems to have most frustrated the author were the studies themselves, many of which left unclear whether the programs had not worked, or whether the system under which they were administered prevented successful implementation.[6]

Martinson's hugely influential article cast a pall over rehabilitative criminal justice programs for years. To this day, reformers in the field find themselves grappling with the suspicion—held by many academics, policymakers and citizens—that "nothing works." The 1996 report, "Preventing Crime: What Works, What Doesn't, What's Promising," confronted this mindset head on:

> *Merely because a program has not been evaluated properly does not mean that it is failing to achieve its goals. Previous reviews of crime prevention programs, especially in prison rehabilitation, have made that error, with devastating consequences for further funding for those efforts. In addressing the unevaluated programs, we must blame the lack of documented effectiveness squarely on the evaluation process, and not on the programs themselves.*[7]

Sherman attempted to infuse hope into the field by throwing out the "nothing works" conclusion.[8] But the more accurate conclusion he offered in its place—that very little is known about what works[9]—comes with its own set of frustrations.

Problem-solving court research,[10] most of it conducted post-Sherman, faces a political climate that prefers definitive answers over cautious preliminary findings, and is still likely to mistake uncertainty for proof of failure. Yet, at present, cautious preliminary findings are the best tools. The research to date on these new judicial experiments does not offer many definitive conclusions. Projects that fall under the "problem-solving" umbrella have been around for a relatively short time—anywhere from a decade to a few months. It takes time and money to track recidivism over the long term, to meaningfully weigh program costs and benefits and to compare new practices to one another, as well as to business as usual.

The best research designs use a random assignment model, splitting a single pool of defendants between an experimental track and normal case processing, but in most cases this "gold standard" is not feasible for studies of problem-solving courts. Quasi-experimental comparison groups range from the good (defendants in traditional court with carefully matched characteristics to drug court participants), to the not so good (less rigorously selected groups of defendants undergoing normal prosecution), to the bad (defendants who refused to participate in the problem-solving court).

In truth, many programs are not subject to even a bad quasi-experimental evaluation. While the demand for criminal justice research is high, both among policymakers and practitioners, the financial support lags.[11] Outside of the National Institute of Justice, there are few sources of funding for criminal justice research.[12]

Nevertheless, problem-solving courts have begun to leave a paper trail. Many problem-solving courts have produced, are producing or plan to produce process evaluations with detailed information about how the programs have been implemented. Sherman noted that newer programs have the advantage of more rigorous standards for evaluation,[13] and in the long history of criminal justice innovation, it is indeed difficult to locate many new ideas that have been better documented or more well-researched than problem-solving courts.

What is known about problem-solving courts? After more than a decade of practice, what conclusions, if any, can be drawn about these judicial experiments? Where are the gaps in the current knowledge and which areas are ripe for further study? This chapter attempts to answer these questions. It is not a piece of original research, but rather an effort to map the territory of this new field, offering for the first time both a review of current problem-solving research and a sketch of a future agenda.

I. Drug Courts

Any review of problem-solving court research must begin with drug treatment courts, the first projects to fall under the problem-solving court umbrella, and the most extensively studied. Since 1989, when the first drug court opened, the model has been replicated widely.[14] There are now hundreds of drug courts in operation or in planning.[15] Moreover, these courts have generated a sizeable body of research on their operations and outcomes. Drug courts now have enough of a track record to promote an informed discussion of how they work, how well they work and why they work.

What We Know

Steven Belenko's reviews of drug court evaluations are the most authoritative source of information on the what, where and how of drug court research to date.[16] His *Research on Drug Courts: A Critical Review 2001 Update* reviewed 37 evaluations from 36 different drug courts and only included studies conducted by outside evaluators.[17] Most of the studies included were process evaluations, but some included limited outcome measures and cost analyses as well.[18] Based on Belenko's review and other drug court studies, the following can be stated about drug court programs:

- Drug courts are popular and serve a needy population. According to Belenko, "drug courts have achieved considerable local support and have provided intensive, long-term treatment services to offenders with long histories of drug use and criminal justice contacts, previous treatment failures and high rates of health and social problems."[19]

Court-mandated treatment programs result in higher retention rates. The estimated national average one-year retention rate for mandatory treatment is 60 percent.[20] By way of contrast, reported retention rates for voluntary treatment programs range from 30 to 60 percent over a three-month period (one-year rates not available).[21]

- The longer participants stay in treatment, the better the outcomes. A 1978 study of an Oregon program demonstrated that people who dropped out of treatment were less likely to be rearrested if they had stayed in treatment for at least 90 days.[22] This finding pointed to the importance of looking beyond what happens to graduates of drug courts. Outcomes for other participants (even those who "fail" in treatment) can be substantial and are worth studying.

- Drug court participants have lower rates of recidivism and drug use while still in the program, than did comparison groups undergoing normal prosecution.[23] Lower in-program recidivism rates demonstrated that offenders in drug court pose a reduced risk to public safety, at least during the multi-year period when they are under drug court supervision.[24]

- Even absent treatment, graduated sanctions can have a statistically significant impact on offenders' behavior. An Urban Institute study of the District of Columbia Superior Court suggested that ongoing monitoring and graduated sanctions and rewards could help drug offenders avoid rearrest in the year after sentencing, even if offenders were not linked to treatment.[25] The results point to the value of intensive judicial monitoring.[26]

- The certainty and severity of drug court sanctions are crucial to the model's effectiveness. Criminal justice researchers looked at the effects of punishment in terms of certainty (whether the sanction will be enforced), severity (how harsh the sanction will be) and celerity (how quickly the sanction will be imposed).[27] One recent study surveyed college students about the likelihood that they would drive home from a party drunk, given the possibility of being caught and punished for the crime.[28] Respondents showed less concern for how quickly the punishment would come, and more concern with its certainty and severity in deciding whether to commit the crime.[29] Extralegal consequences were also important factors, but the study's most prominent conclusion was the weakness of a punishment's celerity as a deterrent.[30] Another study by Adele Harrell of the Urban Institute compared the graduated sanctions programs in three drug treatment court settings, and found that the severity of the sanctions had the greatest effect across the board.[31]

- Well-designed post-program studies about the recidivism of drug court clients are relatively sparse. Of the more than three dozen evaluations included in Belenko's latest review, only six looked at post-program recidivism rates.[32] Of these, two showed a statistically significant reduction in recidivism.[33] Clearly, there is a need for more information in this area.

- Cost analyses reveal savings for drug courts compared to traditional adjudication. Nearly all studies showed significant savings to the criminal justice system when drug courts were implemented. For example, a Multnomah County, Oregon, study reported that for every dollar spent on drug court treatment and program administration, the system saved $2.50 in avoiding the costs of conventional adjudication.[34] This figure excluded costs related to victimization, theft reduction, public assistance and medical claims.[35] When those costs were added in, the savings were 10 dollars for every one dollar spent.[36]

- Cost savings for jail and prison beds are less clear. A 2000 Vera Institute of Justice report cited the need to look at multiple factors in evaluating a drug court's impacts on jail and prison costs.[37] While faster case processing and reduced recidivism among program graduates may lower these costs, other factors may offset these savings.[38] For example, costs accrue when judges use jail time as a sanction for participants who slip up. The authors also questioned whether some drug court participants would have been incarcerated had they undergone traditional adjudication.[39] The report concluded that "we simply do not know enough about the interaction of these elements to accurately predict overall bed savings."[40]

Unanswered Questions

Even with the relatively extensive body of drug court research, there are a lot of unanswered questions. Variations in research quality and program design make it difficult to draw general conclusions about the drug court model. Recidivism rates among program participants as compared with those undergoing normal prosecution, arguably the most important measure of a drug treatment court's success, are still mostly unknown. Post-program studies are few and far between, and relatively little funding is in place for this kind of research. Many of the studies that do exist fail to distinguish between recidivism during and after program participation.

Post-program effects, other than recidivism, have received even less attention. Belenko cited the need for information on participants' future drug use, employment, family stability and use of social services, pointing to the benefits of tracking the work of drug courts and the progress of their participants over a substantial period of time.[41] One-shot evaluations, Belenko noted, were far less useful than multi-year analyses, since impacts may fluctuate, particularly in a program's first years of operation.[42]

Studies also frequently fail to track the progress and failure of defendants who do not graduate from drug court programs, but instead drop out early. Drug court graduates will almost always have lower recidivism than drug court failures and comparison group defendants.[43] The proper comparison, however, is of all drug court participants with comparison group defendants. Tracking drug court failures is important not simply for the sake of a thorough comparison but because we know that treatment can benefit even those participants who do not complete their entire regimen. In addition, the fate of less successful defendants might shed light on the effectiveness of some of the program's components.

New Types of Drug Courts

More research is also needed to assess the efficacy of adaptations of the drug court model. The two most prominent adaptations are family treatment courts and mental health courts, which apply drug court principles to cases involving addicted parents charged with child neglect, and cases involving defendants with chronic persistent mental illness.

A 1999 Urban Institute evaluation of the implementation of three family treatment courts cited many of the challenges particular to this emerging model (client confidentiality, juggling the rights of the parent and the welfare of the child, the use of sanctions, and extensive service needs).[44] A future research agenda for family treatment courts emerges out of the lessons learned from implementation. These authors felt that the focus should be on detailed process evaluations that document parents' and children's service needs, outcomes, both immediate and long-term, for parents and children,[45] system impacts for courts and other agencies,[46] and the direct expenditures and the value of contributions required to operate these model projects.[47] Any effort to seriously evaluate family treatment courts will run up against a number of obstacles, including the need to track multiple parties (parents and children) and serious confidentiality restrictions.[48]

Mental health courts pose a somewhat different set of challenges. They require an individualized approach to defining success for participants, each of whom must receive a treatment regimen, and graduation requirements based on her unique affliction.[49] For this reason, outcome measures are difficult to standardize even within a single court. As John S. Goldkamp and Cheryl Irons-Guynn of the Crime and Justice Research Institute wrote in their 2000 review, "courts cannot say, 'be cured within 12 months.'"[50] Research must take this reality into account.

It is too soon to examine recidivism rates for mental health courts, but self-reported data on retention and jail savings has begun to surface. For example, the Seattle Municipal Court's Mental Health Court reported that more than two-thirds of all participants continued to be successfully engaged in treatment at the end of their first year.[51] The Santa Clara County Mental Health Court Progress Report assessed the total cost savings to the county in unserved jail days of moving 56 clients from jail custody to community treatment at 65 dollars and 80 cents per client, per day.[52] Moreover, advocates marshaled significant anecdotal evidence to support the notion that mental health courts offered more resources and a more sensitive approach to the needs of mentally ill defendants than did conventional case processing.[53]

While these findings are interesting, this question remains—how do you define success in a mental health court? As the programs develop, there will be significant pressure to demonstrate reduced recidivism, a goal that may not be realistic for many participants. What other measures are there? Improved functionality and quality of life? Cost savings? A reduction in the frequency of arrests? Given the difficult population the courts work with, mental health courts may want to make a deeper investment in qualitative research by conducting interviews with participants and their family members to assess both their functionality and their satisfaction with the process.

II. Community Courts

Each community court is more or less a model unto itself, designed to address quality-of-life problems within a specific neighborhood or group of neighborhoods.[54] Among the nearly two dozen community courts currently in operation there is wide variety in the types of cases each court tackles—prostitution, landlord-tenant disputes, truancy, public urination, and unlicensed street vending, to name a few.[55] Community courts seek to have an effect on both individual litigants and on the community as a whole.[56] A community's quality of life, however, is a much more complicated outcome to measure than, for instance, drug treatment retention rates. Benefits to neighborhood residents range from the concrete (less graffiti), to the intangible (how safe people feel, and how people relate to each other and their physical space).[57] Therefore, factors to take into account when evaluating the effectiveness of a community court project might include the neighborhood's perception of the court, its staff and its mission, the impact on local hot spots and eyesores, and the way government and citizens relate to one another.[58] Community courts thus call for a research agenda that goes beyond counting cases and tracking dispositions. Surveys, ethnographies, interviews and other narrative records are essential to a critical examination of whether these programs work.

Midtown Community Court

The most thorough community court study to date is the National Center for State Courts' evaluation of the Midtown Community Court in Manhattan, which was conducted in two stages. The first, completed in 1997, included a process analysis and preliminary impact measures.[59] The second, in 2001, evaluated the long-term impacts of the court over three years and included a cost-benefit analysis.[60]

The first stage of research documented the following:

Case Outcomes

One of the threshold questions for the Midtown Community Court was whether the court could change outcomes in cases involving misdemeanor and quality-of-life crimes (prostitution, shoplifting, illegal street vending, low-level drugs). During the period studied, quality-of-life offenders who went through conventional case processing in Manhattan tended to receive either jail or no sanctions at all from the criminal justice system.[61] Offenders received a larger amount of intermediate sanctions, like community service or a social service referral, in Midtown than in the downtown court.[62]

Community Service Compliance Rates

Midtown achieved a 75 percent compliance rate in contrast with 50 percent in the downtown sample.[63] Midtown also tracked defendant characteristics in tandem with compliance rates and found that the faster offenders were assigned their service, the more likely they were to comply.[64]

Reduced Crime

The first evaluation of Midtown included an ethnography designed to provide insight into the daily lives of street offenders, to elicit their opinion about the court and to examine how the street scene had changed in the neighborhood since the court's opening.[65] Prostitution arrests dropped 56 percent in Midtown during the court's first 18 months of operation.[66] Unlicensed vending arrests dropped 24 percent.[67] Ethnographic data suggested that the court was responsible for increased pressure, and a subsequent drop in local activity.[68] In both industries, sex workers and vendors complained about the inconvenience of frequent court appearances and community service sanctions, and some reported exploring other ways to make a living as a result.[69]

Community Attitudes

Focus group research revealed that in the months following the court's opening, the police department moved from skepticism to support for Midtown.[70] Community members expressed positive, but less dramatic, feedback in the first phase of the evaluation.[71]

The second stage of the National Center for State Courts' evaluation of Midtown unearthed some of the complexities of measuring long-term success of a community court. The court opened during a period of dramatic neighborhood turnaround for midtown Manhattan. Many factors contributed to the positive changes, including the improved local economy and the Giuliani administration's concerted effort to clean up the Times Square area. The Midtown Community Court undoubtedly played a role in the transformation, but it is not possible to accurately apportion the credit.[72]

The second stage of the evaluation also demonstrated that fewer Midtown offenders were initially sentenced to jail.[73] Unlike conventional criminal courts, Midtown has rigorously monitored the compliance of offenders with community and social service sentences.[74] Offenders who did not comply were often sentenced to jail when they reappeared in court.[75] In other words, Midtown used jail less frequently than other Manhattan courts hearing comparable cases, but when offenders were sentenced to jail, it was for longer periods because they had already been given a chance to fulfill intermediate sanctions.[76] This use of jail as a "secondary" sanction in response to non-compliance led to a reduction in the net jail savings generated by Midtown.[77] The evaluators concluded: "after accounting for the greater use of secondary jail at the Midtown Court, the net jail saving of the project over three years was reduced to roughly 12,600 jail days—or approximately 35 jail years."[78]

Finally, as part of a cost-benefit analysis, researchers made use of a neighborhood survey, which revealed that two-thirds of residents would be willing to pay more taxes to keep the court in operation.[79] "Overall, the survey demonstrated that local respondents saw the benefits of the Midtown Court as equal to or greater than its costs and supported public funding for comparable projects."[80]

Future Research

Needless to say, it is impossible to draw any firm conclusions about community courts based on the results of a single study, no matter how encouraging. In the days ahead, society's understanding of community courts will undoubtedly become much richer. Each community court in operation is documenting its own impacts. Two research projects are particularly worth watching. Taken together, they demonstrate the multifaceted approaches that research in this field must take in order to capture a full picture of a community court's outcomes. The first is the Columbia University Center for Violence Research and Prevention's study of the Red Hook Community Justice Center in Brooklyn. Red Hook departs significantly from the Midtown model. The court is multi-jurisdictional and serves a diverse set of neighborhoods.[81] Offenders tend to live within the community, as opposed to Midtown, where most serious offenders do not.[82] The primary neighborhood demonstrates less social organization, and its demographics are entirely different (public housing tenants, as opposed to a mixture of middle-class residents and businesses).[83] The current evaluation will focus on qualitative measurements of community improvements and perceptions of procedural justice, and look for results in the form of enhanced community involvement and support.[84] Key research questions include the following: To what extent does the Justice Center bring a new approach to case processing, the roles of court personnel and the disposition of cases? How does local knowledge and information sharing affect the business of the court? How are community members involved in the Justice Center, and how does the Justice Center get involved with the community?

A second study of note is underway in Hartford, Connecticut. Since opening in 1998, the Hartford Community Court differs from Midtown most sharply in terms of its target population. The court serves all of Hartford's 17 downtown neighborhoods (though the total number of residents is still smaller than the number in Midtown's jurisdiction).[85] Hartford has developed a process evaluation to document nine key elements of the court: target problems; target locations; target populations; court processing focus and adaptations; identifying, screening, and enrolling participants; dispositional options and the structure and content of services; community involvement; productivity (services delivered and impact per resource); and extent of systemwide support and participation.[86] The evaluation strategy, similar to Midtown's, is a two-tiered initial study of implementation and immediate outcomes.[87]

III. Domestic Violence Courts

The primary stated objective of most domestic violence courts is the enhancement of victim safety.[88] Other outcome measures include reduced recidivism, improved monitoring and accountability for defendants, improved case processing speed and systemization and better coordination among all the players in domestic violence cases.

As domestic violence courts have only begun to yield published evaluations, most of what we know about the model's outcomes derives from studies of its core components, particularly batterer intervention programs, judicial monitoring and orders of protection, within the context of regular criminal court.

Batterer Intervention Programs

Intervention programs, usually "re-education" programs that give an overview of the history and context of domestic violence, are widely used in conventional criminal courts as a sanction for batterers. Recent research estimates that nearly 80 percent of individuals in batterer programs were sent by probation officers or the courts.[89] In some cases, as in Florida, state law requires program participation of all domestic violence defendants. Batterer intervention is popular, but how well does it work? An August 2001 literature review conducted by Larry W. Bennett and Oliver J. Williams cited three measures for a program's success: "(1) Are batterers held accountable for their crime (or, has justice been served?) (2) Are victims safe? And, (3) Has the batterer changed his attitudes and behavior?"[90] The authors reached two conclusions: "(1) Batterers [sic] programs as currently configured have modest but positive effects on violence prevention, and (2) there is little evidence at present supporting the effectiveness of one BIP approach over another."[91]

To date, few studies address the relative effectiveness of different types of batterer programs (the Deluth "re-education" model has dominated the field in the past, but now faces competition from other emerging models). Thankfully, there is significant interest within the research community in this area. As a result, the next few years may yield much more information on how different program models compare with one another. Bennett and Williams cited a number of questions for comparative study, including the following: What roles do program structure and length play in effectiveness? How do programs that adopt an integrated approach to other issues—such as drug abuse and mental health—fare in comparison to more narrowly defined programs? And what about cultural specificity?[92] Three studies suggested that African-American men who participated in batterer intervention programs experienced higher rearrest and reoffending rates, lower rates of program completion and lower levels of "trust, comfort, willingness to discuss critical subjects, and participation in treatment."[93]

Judicial Monitoring

Evidence suggests that rigorous court monitoring may have more of an effect on recidivism than do batterer reeducation programs. Most telling in this regard is a recent random assignment experiment in Brooklyn, which compared offenders assigned to community service to those linked to batterer intervention.[94] There were three experimental groups: one community service track, one 26 week batterer intervention program track, and one eight-week program track (while the length of the programs was considerably different, the total number of hours was the same).[95] Perhaps predictably, more participants successfully completed the eight-week program than the 26-week program.[96] Only participants in the 26-week program exhibited lower violence rates than those of the community service group.[97] Neither program track group provided evidence that participants had learned anything as a result of their treatment, but the ones least likely to reabuse were those who were under court supervision for the longest period of time.[98] In other words, judicial monitoring, not batterer intervention, seems to have made the difference in victim safety.

Two other studies are worthy of note here. In 2000, San Diego court administrators conducted an internal study that underlined the importance of judicial monitoring by showing that highest rates of recidivism in domestic violence cases took place between the time of arrest and the time of a case's disposition.[99] In the first year, with only a batterer program in place, recidivism was at 21 percent.[100] The next year, when the court added a judicial monitoring component, recidivism dropped to 14 percent.[101]

A 1997 study of two projects in Milwaukee examined the effects of two changes in the court system with respect to domestic violence cases—the establishment of a specialized court, and a change in the district attorney's screening policy that increased the pool of cases to include uncooperative victims.[102] The creation of the specialized court resulted in a 50 percent reduction in case processing time, a 25 percent increase in convictions, and a decline in pre-trial crime.[103] The change in prosecutorial policy detracted from some of these positive effects, causing a case backlog, a decline in convictions, an increase in pre-trial crime, and lower levels of victim satisfaction.[104] Researchers found that shortening court processing time in domestic violence cases was a good idea, introducing domestic violence cases with reluctant victims into the criminal justice system should be carefully considered and undertaken only with sufficient resources for prosecution and adjudication, and in deciding whether or not to prosecute, the victim's voice should be taken into account.[105]

Orders of Protection

Do orders of protection keep victims safer? Research suggests that the answer is no. A 1996 study by Adele Harrell and Barbara E. Smith pointed to some of the limitations of restraining orders.[106] Findings were based on interviews of female complainants and the men named in their orders, as well as court and police records.[107] The researchers found that women who sought orders of protection reported serious incidents of abuse (severe violence, including punching, choking, forced sex and threats on their lives).[108] Harrell and Smith concluded that the orders were generally not sought "as a form of early intervention, but rather as a signal of desperation following extensive problems."[109]

Unfortunately, permanent orders of protection made no difference in the likelihood that victims would experience physical abuse in the future, nor did they reduce the probability of contact between the victim and the abuser.[110] Permanent orders of protection were effective in significantly reducing psychological abuse, and victims generally agreed that it was worthwhile to file the order—even if they still had concerns about their safety.[111] Harrell and Smith concluded their report by recommending that courts tailor orders of protection to the needs of individual victims, coordinate with other criminal justice agencies to improve enforcement, help victims develop a safety plan and encourage women to return to court to report future violations.[112]

Harrell and Smith's findings were echoed by a 1997 study by Susan Keilitz, Paula Hannaford and Hillery S. Efkeman that reviewed the effectiveness of civil protection orders.[113] This report also highlighted the need for courts to link victims to additional services, specifically citing the need for victim counseling and safety planning, the need for the court to address petitioners' specific concerns and the need for more detailed knowledge of alleged abusers' histories of crime and substance abuse.[114]

The Role of Victims

A recent study of a specialized domestic violence court in Toronto revealed that a case was seven times more likely to be prosecuted if the victim was perceived as cooperative, even in a court specifically designed to minimize reliance on victim cooperation.[115] How do the roles that victims play in their own cases influence the ways in which domestic violence courts work to ensure victim security? What effects do victim advocacy, prosecutorial policies and other court procedures have on outcomes for victims?

The role of victims in case processing is a topic that has generated significant interest among domestic violence researchers. For example, a 1993 Indianapolis Domestic Violence Prosecution Experiment examined a number of different prosecutorial policies designed to reduce repeat incidents abuse among misdemeanor domestic violence defendants.[116] In the six months following case settlement, regardless of prosecutorial policy, researchers found significant rates of battery.[117] The victims in the greatest jeopardy of renewed violence were those who dropped charges after the batterer was summoned to court.[118] The researchers concluded that "prosecutors can help victims minimize the chance of violence by affirming the legitimacy of their criminal complaints and by respecting their decisions about what is best under their unique circumstances, even if contrary to the prosecutor's administrative concerns."[119]

Other research qualified the above findings by indicating that mandatory arrest policies result in a net reduction in domestic violence offenses, regardless of how the victim participates in the process.[120] Victim cooperation is not the only variable in domestic violence case outcomes, but its importance should not be overlooked.

Taking the needs of victims into account and studying impacts on victim safety present some distinct challenges for domestic violence court researchers. Police and court records may not indicate how much abuse has actually occurred, and victims—if they are involved in the court process at all—are often reluctant to participate in formal studies.

Most research to date on specialized domestic violence courts takes the form of process evaluations, not experimental designs. Preliminary findings from an Urban Institute study of the Brooklyn Felony Domestic Violence Court, for example, point to some significant outcomes.[121] The study reveals improved coordination among stakeholders both inside and outside the court system. Lawyers, judges and representatives from victims' services and batterer programs started meeting together for the first time under the new specialized court structure.[122] Victim advocates were assigned to 100 percent of victims who came through the court, up from 55 percent under the old system.[123] Among defendants released on bail, 44 percent were sent to batterer programs (up from zero) and five percent were sent to substance abuse treatment (up from two percent).[124] An additional four percent were mandated to both batterer programs and substance abuse treatment.[125] Before the specialized court opened, 73 percent of domestic violence felony defendants entered a guilty plea.[126] After, 88 percent entered guilty pleas.[127]

A pending experiment in the Bronx, conducted by the Center for Court Innovation with funding from the National Institute of Justice, seeks to explore the relative effectiveness of court monitoring and batterer intervention as responses to domestic violence.[128] Convicted batterers in the Bronx will be divided at random into four 200-person test groups.[129] One group will participate in a batterer intervention program and receive monthly monitoring, a second group will participate in a batterer program and receive court monitoring on a graduated schedule, a third group will not participate in a batterer program and receive monthly monitoring, and a fourth group will not participate in a batterer program and receive graduated monitoring.[130] This study, scheduled to conclude in 2004, presents an opportunity to simultaneously test two components of the specialized court model, both batterer programs and court monitoring, under experimental conditions and within the context of the specialized court itself.

IV. Perceptions of Problem-Solving Courts

While problem-solving courts are designed to improve case processing and court outcomes, they also seek to make an impact in the world of public opinion. How are these courts perceived by relevant stakeholders? Do they have the potential to improve public confidence in justice? How about the job satisfaction levels of judges and attorneys?

Recent surveys conducted by the National Center for State Courts have attempted to document public attitudes toward problem-solving courts.[131] These surveys have demonstrated that the public shares problem-solving court innovators' concerns about court efficiency, fairness and responsiveness to communities.[132] The research also indicated high levels of public support for problem-solving methods aimed at improvements in these areas.[133] A 2001 survey found strong support, particularly among African-American and Latino respondents, for common problem-solving strategies, including the hiring of treatment staff and social workers, bringing offenders back to court to report on their progress in treatment, coordinating the work of local treatment agencies to help offenders and bringing in relevant outside experts to help courts make more informed decisions.[134]

What do judges think of problem-solving courts? A recent study of state court judges commissioned by the Center for Court Innovation and conducted by the University of Maryland's Survey Research Center suggested that the judiciary shares the public's endorsement of basic problem-solving tools.[135] More than 500 criminal court judges were surveyed.[136] Participants supported treatment as an alternative to incarceration for addicted, nonviolent offenders (over 70 percent agreed that treatment was more effective than jail).[137] They overwhelmingly agreed that the bench should be involved in reducing drug abuse among defendants (91 percent).[138] They also cited the need for more information about past violence when deciding bail and sentences in domestic violence cases (90 percent agreed).[139] Sixty-three percent of criminal court judges and 71 percent of problem-solving court judges said they should be more involved with community groups in addressing neighborhood safety and quality-of-life concerns.[140] This runs counter to the popular assumption that judges, concerned with neutrality and independence, are unwilling to engage with the community.

How do defendants perceive problem-solving courts? While no national survey has been undertaken, as part of the National Center for State Courts' evaluation of the Midtown Community Court, researchers conducted individual interviews with defendants, who commented on the court's better facilities and faster case processing time.[141] Interestingly, they found the sentences meted out by the court tougher than those issued in conventional courts.[142] When asked which court they preferred, however, they chose Midtown because personnel treated them better.[143]

V. Developing a Future Research Agenda

While problem-solving courts and related innovations have generated a solid and growing body of research to date, there remain more unanswered questions than firm conclusions about these judicial experiments. Further, new models are quickly moving to the forefront and producing their own preliminary research findings and future directions. An Urban Institute study, published in April 2002, evaluates the performance of 14 courts (where low-level juvenile offenders are adjudicated by their peers), and sets parameters for further research in this area. Teen courts and other new models must be integrated into a problem-solving court research agenda, drawing upon the same questions and approaches that have been used so far while also helping to shape what the research of the future will look like.

Going forward, the operative questions for problem-solving court researchers may be both the open-ended "Do they work?" query and some more specific questions: How do these programs work? For what populations and under what circumstances? With that in mind, what follows is an attempt to define an agenda for the future of problem-solving court research. It is intended to spark conversation rather than foreclose it. Inevitably, the most provocative questions will emerge at the local level—the product of a dynamic conversation between researchers and practitioners.

Studies of the Components

Recognizing that complex problems call for complex solutions, problem-solving courts employ a vast array of ideas and strategies. Nonetheless, as the current Bronx Domestic Violence Court experiment suggests, it is worth isolating some of their core components, such as treatment, graduated sanctions or judicial monitoring, to more precisely understand how the pieces within the problem-solving court model affect outcomes. What is the "active ingredient" in these experiments? To answer this question, it may make sense to look across projects, for example, studying the role of the judge in drug courts, community courts and domestic violence courts.

Long-Term and Post-Program Outcomes

Researchers face tremendous challenges when they try to gather data about problem-solving court participants, particularly those who have left the programs, either due to graduation or failure. If program drop-outs or failures end up in jail, "post-program" only begins once they get out, which could be years from the original arrest that diverted them to a problem-solving court in the first place. Many studies do not currently track what happens to participants who do not graduate from a problem-solving court but instead return to traditional adjudication. Nevertheless, post-program outcomes are vital to understanding the long-term effects of problem-solving courts and how they compare to the effects of conventional practice.

Other Outcomes for Program Participants

While recidivism may be the holy grail for problem-solving court outcomes, there are a number of other potential effects that bear investigation, particularly as these courts broaden their scope to include difficult populations with histories of mental illness and violence. Graduation exit interviews can shed light on how participants' lives have changed since their first contact with the court. Offenders who were homeless upon arrest may now have a place to live, women who were pregnant and addicted may have given birth to drug-free babies and people without high school diplomas may have GEDs. Alternatively, participants in long-term treatment may have lost their jobs or their marriages while getting help for their addiction. There are potentially endless consequences, some intended, others not, that might occur from participating in a problem-solving court. Studies can track these types of changes with relative ease while defendants are under the court's control, but again, post-program effects are harder to assess. If all goes well, a problem-solving court graduate will never again have formal contact with the criminal justice system after program completion. Unfortunately, this best of all outcomes makes it difficult for researchers to track other events in the lives of graduates over a longer period of time. For example, it is nearly impossible to determine whether drug court graduates remain sober over time if they are not rearrested.

Speed

With increases in caseloads every year, state court systems are looking for ways to reduce backlog and repeat appearances. In some cases, problem-solving courts may alleviate some of the burden on the traditional system by diverting certain types of offenders, but they also require more face time between defendant and judge, better tracking and record-keeping and more administrative resources while the case is in the system. It is uncertain whether problem-solving courts speed up or slow down the administration of justice.

Coercion and the Protection of Rights

Problem-solving courts exert—or threaten to exert—legal force as part of their efforts to change the behavior of offenders. Some critics have argued that no one should be coerced into treatment.[144] Others have wondered if problem-solving courts diminish the ability of defenders to engage in zealous advocacy on behalf of their clients.[145] Advocates have argued that problem-solving courts have done little to alter the practice of lawyering or the nature of due process but have simply given attorneys and judges more tools to work with.[146] Future research could investigate whether problem-solving courts do indeed represent a change in the way defendants' rights are protected. This might include both qualitative work (how defendants and their attorneys perceive coercion and representation in a problem-solving court) and quantitative work (for example, comparing the number of objections and plea bargains with those of a conventional court).

Net Widening

Critics with concerns about defendants' Fourth Amendment rights and the decline of adversarialism in the problem-solving court model are uneasy about the effect of these courts on the actions of other players in the criminal justice system.[147] Does the existence of a drug court, for example, lead police to make arrests they otherwise would not have made? Does an increase in information sharing lead to more scrutiny of specific groups of offenders? Or, more glibly, is there a "build it and they will come" phenomenon at work here? Having created problem-solving courts, will criminal justice agencies feel compelled to ensure their caseloads by any means necessary? Research can help answer these questions by studying arrest patterns and prosecutorial and judicial decision making.

Community Impacts

In recent years, a number of new theories (social capital, bowling alone, community efficacy) have been advanced to explain why some neighborhoods are safe, healthy and economically viable for problem-solving courts and others are not. One of the key ideas running through these theories is that strong communities promote information sharing and coordination among civic institutions, whether they are churches, schools, civic associations or government agencies. Because of their emphasis on inter-agency collaboration and public engagement, problem-solving courts hold out the possibility that they might contribute to the healthy functioning of the neighborhoods in which they reside. This idea is ripe for further exploration. Does the coordination of services within the court lead to new levels of cooperation among community stakeholders beyond the courthouse? Can courts serve as a bridge between government and citizens? How might researchers document and assess this? These are questions that as yet have attracted little attention in the field.

Conclusion

It goes without saying that this essay only touches the surface of the possibilities for problem-solving court research. The rapid proliferation of these experiments has been driven by more than rhetoric or funding. It has been driven by the ability of problem-solving courts to generate demonstrable results, however provisional or inadequately studied. Framing a research agenda for problem-solving courts is much more than an academic exercise—it is of vital importance to the future of the problem-solving movement. If problem-solving courts hope to continue to thrive, and to move from experiments to institutionalization, they must answer the concerns of critics and continue to win over the agnostics. The only way to do this is through rigorous, independent research that focuses on the questions that matter most to practitioners and policymakers.

CHAPTER EIGHT

Evaluating Drug Courts in New York: Policies, Participants and Impacts

MICHAEL REMPEL, DANA FOX-KRALSTEIN, AMANDA CISSNER, ROBYN COHEN, MELISSA LABRIOLA, DONALD J. FAROLE JR., ANN K. BADER AND MICHAEL MAGNANI

By combining drug treatment with ongoing judicial supervision, drug courts seek to break the cycle of addiction, crime and repeat incarceration. While practice varies widely from state to state (and county to county), the outlines of the drug court model are clear: addicted offenders are linked to treatment; their progress is monitored by a drug court team composed of the judge, attorneys, and program staff; participants engage in direct interaction with the judge, who responds to progress and setbacks with a range of rewards and sanctions; and successful participants generally have the charges against them dismissed or reduced, while those who fail receive jail or prison sentences.

This report evaluates adult drug courts in New York State, one of a handful of states that is engaged in a coordinated effort to institutionalize drug courts statewide. With funding from the Bureau of Justice Assistance of the U.S. Department of Justice, the Center for Court Innovation, in collaboration with the New York State Unified Court System, has spent the past three years documenting the policies, participant characteristics and performance of participants in 11 of the state's oldest and largest drug courts. Among other analyses, this chapter evaluates the impact of six drug courts on recidivism and identifies the partic-

---

This research report was originally the executive summary of "The New York State Adult Drug Court Evaluation: Policies, Participants and Impacts," co-published in October 2003 by the New York State Unified Court System and the Center for Court Innovation.

ipant characteristics and programmatic features that increase the likelihood of successful drug court outcomes.

Methodology

This report includes an analysis of drug court policies and participant characteristics in 11 drug courts.[1] Four are from large urban counties of New York City (Bronx, Brooklyn, Manhattan, and Queens); one is suburban (Suffolk); three are from medium-sized cities (Syracuse, Rochester and Buffalo); and three are from small city/semi-rural areas (Tonawanda, Lackawanna and Ithaca).

This study is also among the first to demonstrate consistent and meaningful recidivism impacts across a large number of sites and over a relatively long-term tracking period. At each of six sites, the recidivism analyses compare the reconviction rates of drug court participants with similar defendants not entering the drug court. These comparisons include among the longest measurement periods in the research literature—at least three years following the initial arrest (four years in Brooklyn and Rochester); and, in separate analyses, at least one year after program completion or final case disposition (two years in Brooklyn and Rochester).[2]

In developing comparison group criteria, a uniform set of research design principles was implemented. Comparison defendants had to have no contact with the drug court on the instant case, meet the same paper eligibility criteria as drug court participants and be convicted on the instant case. In four sites (Bronx, Queens, Suffolk and Syracuse), the comparison group consisted of defendants arrested just prior to the opening of the drug court. In two sites (Brooklyn and Rochester), the comparison group consisted of defendants arrested during a contemporaneous period but not referred to the drug court for reasons unrelated to program eligibility or defendant interest in participating.[3]

For each site, comparison samples were further refined using a propensity score matching methodology (e.g., see Rubin 1973; and Rosenbaum and Rubin 1983). Propensity score matching is among the strongest methodological alternatives to random assignment, since the approach ensures that each drug court's final comparison sample closely matches the drug court participant sample across a range of important background characteristics, such as sex, age, race/ethnicity, specific charges and criminal history.

Impact on Recidivism

All six drug courts (Bronx, Brooklyn, Queens, Suffolk, Syracuse and Rochester) produced recidivism reductions compared with conventional case processing. The six courts represent a mix of geographic areas and policies (e.g., regarding eligibility criteria, screening and assessment protocols, graduation requirements, approach to sanctions, and supplemental services). Since the measurement periods tracked defendants at least three years after the initial arrest and at least one year after program completion, the results indicate that positive drug court impacts are durable over time.

The six drug courts generated an average 29 percent recidivism reduction over the three-year post-arrest period and an average 32 percent reduction over the one-year post-program period. Major findings are as follows:

Reduced Post-Arrest Recidivism

Drug court participation led to a lower probability of recidivism three years after the initial arrest (significant in five courts and $p < .10$ in the sixth). Depending on the drug court, recidivism reductions ranged from 13 percent to 47 percent (average reduction = 29 percent) relative to the comparison group level.

Reduced Post-Program Recidivism

Drug court impacts extended beyond the period of program participation. Drug court participation led to a lower probability of recidivism at one year post-program (significant in three courts, $p < .10$ in one court, and suggested by the numbers but not significant in two). Post-program recidivism reductions ranged from 19 percent to 52 percent (average reduction = 32 percent).

Survival Over Time

When comparing in-program to post-program recidivism rates for drug court participants, recidivism did not rise in the post-program period, but rather declined in three of the six courts. Further, when comparing participant and comparison group recidivism rates after each additional year following the initial arrest (a "survival analysis"), in only one of the six courts was there clear evidence of attenuation of the drug court impact over time. This was contrary to the expectation that the magnitude of the drug court impact would peak immediately following the arrest (when judicial monitoring is most intensive); instead, results in most sites revealed positive long-term impacts persisting beyond the period of active judicial supervision.

Impact of Drug Court Graduation

Drug court graduates were far less likely than comparison defendants to recidivate in all six courts; however, drug court failures were as likely, if not more so, as comparison defendants to recidivate in four of the six courts. Translation: the benefits of drug court participation largely accrue to those who successfully graduate.

Impact of Arrest Charge

In Rochester, participants arrested on drug charges performed better relative to the comparison group than participants arrested on a select number of non-drug charges. Although the analysis is relatively limited in scope and requires future replication, the findings suggest that drug courts may be more successful in curtailing drug-based criminal behavior (indicated by drug charges) than in curtailing criminal behavior driven by other criminal propensities.

Other Predictors of Recidivism

Among drug court participants and comparison defendants alike, those with prior misdemeanor convictions and of younger age were generally more likely than others to recidivate across all courts and analyses.

Impact on Case Processing and Case Outcomes

For the same six sites, the impacts of drug courts on criminal case processing and case outcomes were analyzed. Key findings include:

Initial Case Processing Speed

Drug court cases reach initial disposition more quickly than conventional court cases. Participants in all six drug courts spent significantly less time from arrest to initial disposition/program entry than comparison defendants.

Total Time Pending

When in-program participation time was included in the calculation, processing time for participants was far longer than for comparison defendants (due to the length of the drug court program). Hence to achieve positive impacts such as lower recidivism, drug courts require a significant up-front investment of court resources.

Sentencing

Average sentence length stemming from the initial criminal case is sometimes shorter than in conventional prosecution—and sometimes not. Whereas graduates are never sent to jail or prison, drug court failures receive longer incarceration sentences than comparison defendants in five of the six courts. This highlights the importance of drug court graduation in reducing the use of incarceration. When considering initial case outcomes for all participants at once (combining graduates and failures), drug court participants averaged significantly shorter jail or prison sentences in three of six courts; but in one court, drug court participants were sentenced for significantly longer on average and in the remaining two courts, there was no significant difference.

Program Retention Rates

Retention is a key measure of program success. A one-year retention rate indicates the percentage of participants who, exactly one year after entering drug court, had either graduated or remained active in the drug court program. Earlier research finds that retention not only indicates success in treatment but also predicts future success in the form of lower post-program recidivism and drug use. Drug courts generally produce higher retention rates than community-based treatment programs accepting a combination of voluntary and court-mandated treatment participants.[4] Key findings about program retention and graduation rates across the 11 drug courts studied here include:

Retention Rates

The one-year retention rate exceeds the national standard of

60 percent for drug courts in eight of 11 courts studied (five New York State courts exceeded 70 percent).

Long-term Retention/Graduation Rates

When the retention period is extended to two and three years, more than half of participants in eight of 11 New York State courts are retained —and the rate exceeds 60 percent in three courts. The three-year retention rate gives a close approximation of each drug court's final graduation rate.

Predictors of Success

Across five drug courts (Bronx, Brooklyn, Queens, Suffolk and Syracuse), several characteristics consistently predicted both drug court graduation and lower recidivism:

Participant Characteristics

Consistent with earlier studies, age predicted success; older defendants were more likely to graduate and less likely to recidivate. A primary drug of heroin made graduation less likely (in two of three courts examined for this effect) and prior criminal convictions were near universally predictive of future recidivism. Also, participants entering on property charges were somewhat more likely to return to criminal activity than those entering on drug charges.

Immediacy

Immediate engagement in treatment (e.g., avoidance of early warranting) universally and strongly predicted drug court graduation.

Importance of Graduation

Graduation is itself a powerful predictor of avoiding post-program recidivism; those who failed drug court were far more likely to recidivate in the post-program period.[5] Further, contrary to previous research with non-drug court populations, no benefit was found to spending more total time in treatment only to fail in the end. Among those who failed, more time in the drug court program (measured in four courts) or more days specifically attending treatment (measured in one court) had no impact on post-program recidivism. These results strongly point to drug court graduation as the pivotal indicator of long-term outcomes.

Drug Court Policies and Participant Characteristics

In considering the drug court policies and participant characteristics in 11 courts, the analysis produced four general findings:

Diversity of Approaches

There is no single drug court model. All 11 courts mandate community-based treatment, regular drug testing, case management visits, updates before a dedicated judge and rewards and sanctions in response to progress or noncompliance. However, policies vary considerably across several domains—legal eligibility criteria, whether a guilty plea is required prior to entry (the pre-plea or post-plea models), approach to treatment and case management, specific sanctioning practices, graduation requirements, legal consequences of graduation (e.g., case dismissal or charge reduction), and legal consequences of failure (e.g., length of resulting jail or prison sentence).

Drug Use Patterns

The 11 courts also treat participants with different presenting problems. The median duration of drug use ranges from eight years (Manhattan and Queens) to 18 (Brooklyn); and while the five most common primary drugs are similar statewide (heroin, crack, cocaine, marijuana and alcohol), they are used in different proportions in each jurisdiction.

Socioeconomic Disadvantage

In all 11 courts, nearly half of the participants (and a much higher percentage in several) were neither employed nor in school at intake. More than a quarter of participants in seven courts were currently or formerly homeless.

Female Participants

The challenges faced by female drug court participants were particularly acute (including more severe drug use, treatment histories and socioeconomic disadvantage than males), highlighting the need for supplemental services for this population.

Treatment and Recovery

Major findings about the treatment and recovery process include:

Treatment Capacity

Despite early questions about whether there is sufficient treatment capacity in New York State to serve the increased demand for treatment generated by drug courts, so far participants have been able to enter treatment rapidly. The median time from drug court intake to treatment placement is less than one month in eight of nine courts examined and less than 10 days in three courts.[6]

Treatment Modality

Over half of participants begin in an outpatient modality, in all but two courts. When clinically feasible, most courts prefer to begin participants in outpatient treatment and then upgrade to inpatient in response to relapses or other compliance problems. Characteristics generally indicating a higher probability of inpatient care are primary drug of choice (heroin), living situation (homeless), employment status (unemployed) and age (younger defendants).

Relapse

Relapse and noncompliance are common, even among those who ultimately succeed. In seven of eight courts examined, at least half of all graduates had at least one positive drug test, and many had several positives—usually in the earlier stages of participation. This highlights the value of drug courts according multiple chances to participants experiencing early problems.

Graduated Sanctions

In responding to noncompliance, drug courts apply sanctions, such as writing an essay, observing drug court for several days from the jury box, more frequent court appearances or case management visits, community service, or short jail stays. However, drug courts vary widely in the type and severity of sanctions most frequently used. Across three courts examined in depth (Brooklyn, Queens and Suffolk), none routinely follow a "graduated sanctions" model, where successive infractions are met with increasingly severe sanctions. Instead, some infractions are always met with a similar sanction response. For example, a warrant or new arrest in Brooklyn nearly always incurs a jail sanction. Also, drug court teams frequently make individualized decisions based on what they believe will be most effective with a particular participant rather than adhering to a rigid schedule of graduated sanctions.

Achievements Beyond Substance Abuse Recovery

Beyond substance abuse recovery, drug courts seek to promote further achievements and lifestyle changes in the areas of employment, education, vocational training, housing and family reunification. Consistent with these goals, across all nine courts examined, graduates were significantly more likely to be employed at graduation than intake. Also, graduates in five of the nine courts were significantly more likely to be in school at graduation than intake.

Conclusion

This study provides strong evidence that drug courts produce lasting changes in their participants, persisting even after the period of active judicial supervision. In general, the study reveals impacts consistent with those detected in other evaluations that covered shorter timeframes and fewer courts. This study also finds that final program status is a critical predictor of subsequent outcomes. Drug court graduates had far lower recidivism rates than comparable defendants not entering the drug court, while drug court failures had similar or, in some courts, higher recidivism rates than the comparison group. Accordingly, future research should seek to pinpoint which policies and practices can help drug courts produce both more graduates and lower recidivism rates. With drug courts demonstrating considerable diversity in their geography, policies, and practices, the next generation of studies should seek to answer *why* drug courts work and *how* they can produce positive outcomes for more of their participants.

CHAPTER NINE

Applying Problem-Solving Principles in Mainstream Courts: Lessons for State Courts

DONALD J. FAROLE JR., NORA PUFFETT, MICHAEL REMPEL AND FRANCINE BYRNE

In recent years, an array of innovative courts has emerged throughout the country in an effort to address the underlying problems of defendants, victims and communities. Drug courts, which seek to break the cycle of addiction, crime and repeat incarceration by mandating addicted defendants to treatment, represented the first such innovation. However, since the original Miami Drug Court opened in 1989, other analogous models have also arisen—domestic violence courts, juvenile drug courts, family treatment courts, mental health courts, community courts, peer/youth courts and homeless courts. Generally known as "problem-solving" or "collaborative justice" courts, these innovations are distinguished by a number of unique elements: a problem-solving focus, team approach to decision-making, integration of social services, judicial supervision of the treatment process, direct interaction between defendants and the judge, community outreach and a proactive role for the judge inside and outside of the courtroom.[1]

At the same time that the number of problem-solving courts has grown, several states—including California, New York, Missouri, Louisiana and Ohio—have begun to go further, developing efforts to coordinate at least some of their problem-solving

The California Administrative Office of the Courts supported the research and writing of this article. Points of view and opinions are not necessarily those of the California Administrative Office of the Courts.

initiatives on a statewide level. For example, California, which now features approximately 250 such courts, coordinates its efforts through a special Collaborative Justice Courts Advisory Committee to the state's Judicial Council. These institutional efforts reflect, in part, the demonstrated effectiveness of drug courts[2] as well as the public attention and support all of these innovations have garnered.

While specialized problem-solving courts have proliferated, and we have learned a great deal about the practice of problem solving within them, interest has recently begun to surface around the new question of what potential exists to apply problem-solving court practices outside the specialized court setting. In other words, will problem solving be restricted to stand-alone specialized courts dedicated to discrete interventions (e.g., for substance addiction, domestic violence or mental illness) or can its core principles and practices be productively applied throughout court systems, provoking more sweeping changes in the administration of justice? Understanding the answer to this question can directly inform the growing efforts in many states to institutionalize, or "go to scale," with a problem-solving approach. Contingent upon what is feasible and appropriate, institutionalization can involve the system-wide expansion and coordination of specialized problem-solving courts and/or the incorporation of problem-solving practice throughout conventional court operations. Interest in this issue among justice system representatives was enhanced by an August 2000 resolution of the Conference of Chief Justices and Conference of State Court Administrators, which advocated:

> *Encourag[ing], where appropriate, the broad integration over the next decade of the principles and methods of problem-solving courts into the administration of justice to improve court processes and outcomes while preserving the rule of law, and*

meeting the needs and expectations of litigants, victims, and the community.[3]

This article presents results of an exploratory study, conducted by the California Administrative Office of the Courts in collaboration with the Center for Court Innovation, concerning the opportunities and barriers to applying problem-solving principles and practices outside of the specialized problem-solving court context—in conventional courts and on general (as well as other specialized) calendars. Focus groups and interviews were conducted among a diverse group of judges in California and New York with experience in drug, domestic violence, mental health and other problem-solving courts. The research addressed three principal questions:

1. Which problem-solving principles and practices are more easily applied in conventional courts (and which are less easily applied)?
2. What barriers might judges face when attempting to apply these principles and practices in conventional courts (and how might those barriers be overcome)?
3. How might problem solving be disseminated among judges and judicial leaders throughout the court system?

We begin with a brief review of the study background and methodology. We then present key emergent themes and findings from the focus groups and conclude by discussing the implications of these findings for court managers as well as future research.

Background

Many of the issues associated with the application of problem-solving principles in conventional courts are so new that justice system representatives and researchers are only beginning to consider them. Thus the available literature consists largely of descriptive accounts chronicling individual judges' perspectives or personal attempts to apply problem solving in conventional courts.[4] A related literature considers how judges and attorneys might apply "therapeutic jurisprudence"[5] in various contexts.[6] In addition, others have considered opportunities and challenges of institutionalizing or "going to scale" with specialized problem-solving courts.[7] While these literatures are varied, three consistent themes emerge throughout:

1. The broader use of problem solving requires changing traditional attitudes and role orientations of judges, attorneys and other justice system actors;
2. Resource constraints (lack of time, money, and staff) can pose serious barriers to attempts to apply specific problem-solving practices more widely; and
3. Judicial leadership is critical in any efforts to expand problem solving, either through the expansion of specialized courts or the integration of problem-solving practice in conventional courts.

Different perspectives also exist regarding the extent to which the practice of problem solving—and therapeutic justice—requires specialized courts (and judges) or, alternatively, can be productively applied in conventional courts.[8] Most writings that address these issues, however, do not examine discrete, specific problem-solving principles and practices (e.g., direct interaction between litigants and the judge) that may be more or less easily applied on general court calendars. One evidence-based study does directly address this issue, but it is still in a preliminary stage of research and reporting.[9]

Methodology

The lack of evidence-based hypotheses in the literature necessitates an exploratory approach to the present study. Thus focus groups were deemed the most appropriate research methodology. While neither the focus group participants nor the findings they yield can be considered representative of the general population of judges, focus groups are particularly useful when the goal is to generate information on attitudes, opinions, personal experiences and suggestions concerning topics about which limited information exists.

Accordingly, focus groups and interviews were conducted among judges in California and New York, two states at the forefront of testing new problem-solving court models. In selecting participants, attempts were made to recruit judges familiar with problem-solving practice. In nearly all cases, eligibility was restricted to judges with experience serving in a problem-solving court and with simultaneous or subsequent experience serving in a general calendar assignment. These judges, it was felt, would be most able to speak to the key research issues, perhaps drawing on their own personal experience in attempting to apply problem-solving practices in general calendar assignments. The research team worked with the California Administrative Office of the Courts and the New York State Office of Court Drug Treatment Programs to identify and invite judges familiar with the issues of interest.

Four focus groups (two each in California and New York) were conducted in August and September 2003. Twenty-nine judges—16 from California and 13 from New York—participated in the focus groups. In addition, individual interviews (in person and via telephone) were conducted with six other judges; thus, a total of 35 judges participated in the research. These judges were diverse in terms of their location (e.g., urban versus rural, and geographic region within California or New York), current assignments and, as the table below demonstrates, current and prior problem-solving court assignments. Since adult drug courts represent the majority of problem-solving courts nationwide and in these two states, it is not surprising that most participants have drug court experience. Nevertheless, judges with experience in other problem-solving courts are also represented, and several had been assigned to multiple types of problem-solving courts.

The focus groups followed a semi-structured protocol designed to give participants considerable latitude to raise issues while addressing three general topic areas: 1) core principles and practices of problem-solving courts that differ from conventional courts,[10] 2) the extent to which these principles and practices might be applied within conventional courts and 3) strategies to disseminate problem solving more widely throughout the court system. All focus groups averaged two hours in length (individual interviews averaged one hour) and were moderated by the authors. Participants were not paid but were provided lunch and travel reimbursement. The focus groups were audio-recorded and transcribed. All participants were assured that no comments would be personally attributed to them.

Emergent Findings and Themes

The dialogue in all focus groups was surprisingly consistent—there were few substantive differences across states or focus groups—and a number of clear themes emerged. Discussion focused principally on what judges could do to practice problem solving in conventional courts; the role of attorneys and other players received considerably less attention. Most judges, while describing themselves as naturally inclined towards a collaborative, problem-solving orientation, agreed that their own problem-solving court experience enhanced the frequency and effectiveness of their subsequent use of problem-solving principles and practices in conventional courts.

At the outset, some judges raised fundamental objections to the idea of applying problem-solving practices outside the specialized problem-solving court setting. They argued that the first relevant question was not could principles and practices be applied more broadly but should they. Two reasons why they ought not be applied were offered. First, problem-solving courts were created in part because the prior ad hoc administration of problem solving on general calendars was "haphazard" and "nonuniform." Now that specialized problem-solving courts are established, focus group participants raised the concern that encouraging problem-solving practice in conventional courts would result in a return to poor, inconsistent practice, and possibly siphon off the resources available to the specialized courts. Second, practicing problem solving might ethically or legally compromise the judge and the court process. Some perceived certain elements of problem solving—particularly its non-adversarial, team approach—as incompatible with conventional legal processes. However, these were minority views, which were generally disputed by other focus group participants. Most advocated its broader application, at least under certain circumstances and to the extent feasible.

Discussion was often spontaneous and moved rather abruptly from topic to topic, as is expected from a loosely structured protocol, but additional findings and themes are organized around the three key research questions.

1. Which problem-solving principles and practices are more easily applied in conventional courts and which are less easily applied?

In all focus groups, the initial response was to cite barriers that might prevent or limit judges from practicing problem solving in conventional courts. However, with further probing, suggestions for overcoming barriers emerged. Five principles and practices emerged as easiest and/or most appropriate to apply on general court calendars.[11]

Problem-Solving Orientation of the Judge

Focus group participants generally agreed that the proactive role of the judge in problem-solving courts could be applied to other cases and calendars in various ways—asking more questions, seeking more information about each case and exploring a greater range of possible solutions:

> *Where I otherwise may have just taken the proposed orders of probation from the probation department [and] signed them ... I will now ask the questions, did you look into X, Y and Z, did you look into this treatment option, have they had treatment before, and have they been examined for any mental health [issues]. I will ask those questions where I wouldn't have before.*

The information gained may lead judges to craft highly individualized, unconventional court orders—one judge gave the example of mandating an offender to visit the morgue and write an essay on what he saw.

The proactive, problem-solving orientation was deemed widely helpful outside of the problem-solving court setting, particularly in negotiation situations. Judges mentioned Matrimonial Court, Family Court or other civil assignments as particularly appropriate venues. One judge claimed to have become known, after leaving a problem-solving court, for "thinking outside the box" in civil negotiations.

Direct Interaction with the Defendant/Litigant

Direct interaction with the defendant/litigant was deemed a prerequisite for effective behavior modification, enabling the judge to motivate defendants to make progress in treatment, bringing to light the most crucial needs of parties in civil cases and laying the groundwork for positive solutions. Judges regarded this as one of the easiest practices to apply in conventional courts, perhaps because it requires no additional resources. While some expressed concern that, in criminal cases, defense attorneys would not allow such interactions for fear clients would incriminate themselves, several judges reported that they routinely address defendants directly, with few objections from the defense bar. Explained one judge:

> *I have never had an attorney say to me, "Judge, I won't let you ask him any questions." I may ask questions they don't like and then they say, "I am directing my client not to answer that"and they don't answer it. It helps us get through a lot of paperwork and a lot of malarkey.*

Several judges drew attention to specific aspects of their interaction with defendants that were deemed to have value both inside and outside the problem-solving court context—treating defendants with respect, showing compassion, having faith in defendants' ability to improve and seeing them as potential law-abiding citizens.

Ongoing Judicial Supervision

Requiring defendants, particularly probationers, to report back to court for treatment updates and judicial interaction was identified as one of the least controversial and most effective practices that could be applied in conventional criminal courts:

> *I used to give probation terms and wait for them to violate probation, and then we would file a petition and they would come back to court. Now I set review dates so that they have to come back in and prove to me that they have done something. And [I*

> *do that] because I know that that's what makes the drug court work, that they have to come back and tell me what is going on.*

Recognizing that caseloads are too heavy for probation officers to supervise cases effectively, another judge introduced return court appearances to ensure direct judicial supervision and accountability.

> *I have started telling people that they are ordered back and I will have them come back once a month. And I intend to use sort of a drug court model. I don't have all the resources of a drug court, I don't have the testing and I can't get probation to really supervise them. But I think the issue of judicial supervision and accountability . . . makes a difference.*

Judges in all focus groups, however, expressed concern about the limited time available to devote to supervision in conventional courts. Time limitations may force judges to select only a subset of cases for supervision. And the lack of clinical staff means that judges often cannot obtain the thorough treatment reports that could better inform their interactions with defendants. Nonetheless, many judges acknowledged that they had instituted enhanced supervision in their conventional court with at least some cases.

Integration of Social Services

Many judges reported that service coordination was a valuable tool in any court—especially for litigants with addiction, mental illness or vocational/educational needs. However, referring parties to treatment or other services was seen as more difficult in conventional courts, because they lack the additional staff/case management resources typically available in specialized problem-solving courts. Nonetheless, several judges from both

California and New York added that their problem-solving court experience increased the frequency with which they set treatment and other conditions (e.g., obtain high school diploma or GED, attend drug treatment or other program) as part of probation pleas. Explained one judge: "When you are in the [problem-solving] court you tend to come out looking at probation as a treatment plan."

Team-Based, Non-Adversarial Approach

Judges discussed the extent to which they could adopt a team-based, non-adversarial approach in general court calendars. While there was less consensus and greater skepticism about this than other practices, judges identified opportunities to adopt such an approach, particularly in juvenile or family law settings, where rules often explicitly foster a problem-solving approach—seeking the "best interests of the child."

Most focus group participants believed the judge plays a critical role in determining the extent to which an individual courtroom can and will adopt a non-adversarial approach. However, most also stressed that others—particularly attorneys—can enable or derail that approach, and gaining the trust and participation of attorneys greatly facilitates judges' ability to practice problem solving. It was generally agreed that the players tend not to act as a team until they develop trust, and that takes time. For example, one judge attributed the defense bar's willingness to let him talk directly to defendants to a "reputation" that inspires trust: "They know I am not going to slam [defendants] into jail . . . [so] they allow their clients to talk to me."

Most problem-solving courts hold regular case management meetings of court partners during which they address any recent developments or difficulties with specific cases (e.g., relapses, problems at an assigned program, questions about additional treatment needs, etc.). Some but not all judges felt that this practice was essential to functioning as a team, and could be adopted, albeit on a limited basis, in a conventional court. One judge reported that he had successfully introduced a team approach on his family court calendar:

> *I started with reviews, a kid who I know was in really rough shape. . . . They come back into court and then in chambers would be all of the service providers, probation officers, the mental health person, the staff worker. Occasionally, we bring the parents in, sometimes we bring a whole crew in and try to problem solve as a group. . . . It has been a real positive experience.*

As suggested above, focus group discussion extended to particular types of cases and calendars most ripe for problem-solving solutions. Appropriate case types were characterized in part as those in which a problem that can be resolved by court intervention and where lack of services contributed to the defendant's criminal behavior. Problems identified as appropriate included drug addiction, domestic violence, mental illness, DUI—all issues for which specialized problem-solving courts have been created. Criminal cases involving younger defendants were also cited. One judge summarized by noting that appropriate (criminal) case types are those "where the level of punishment required is diminished by the need to solve the underlying problem and so you'd rather solve the problem than punish the behavior."

Crimes of serious violence were virtually the only matters that a significant number of judges suggested as inappropriate for problem solving; yet it was also observed that violent offenses are staples of some problem-solving courts (primarily domestic violence but sometimes mental health courts as well). In fact, some judges conceded that if violence were tied to an underlying problem such as substance abuse, a problem-solving response might be appropriate.

Judges also identified specific stages in the criminal justice process—most notably bail and sentencing—as points at which problem solving was both appropriate and easy to implement. Although judges in several groups extended that to include plea negotiations, at least one judge objected on the grounds that plea bargaining is "a negotiation for what kind of punishment . . . they are going to receive, which is not a [problem-solving] court model and is probably inappropriate." Criminal trials were also generally seen as inappropriate for problem solving.

In addition to criminal matters, other court calendars were also discussed extensively. Juvenile delinquency and dependency courts were widely cited as appropriate venues for problem solving, particularly for practices such as addressing the problems that contribute to recidivism, using a team-based approach and interacting directly with all parties. Judges in both California and New York noted that the rules governing juvenile court explicitly encourage these practices: "There is already a rule [in California] that says it shall be non-adversarial to the maximum extent possible. There is already a rule in place that says the well-being of the child ... takes precedence over any issue."

In the California focus groups, family court—like juvenile court—was perceived as inherently more problem oriented, and as allowing greater flexibility and discretion than other courts. Judges in California also cited the Substance Abuse and Crime Prevention Act (commonly known as Proposition 36). Courts, which administer court-mandated treatment programs for a wide range of drug possession offenders, were viewed as particularly appropriate for problem-solving approaches.[12]

Finally, probation—not a court calendar, but a court-imposed sentence—was widely regarded as an excellent vehicle for problem solving. Setting probation conditions, monitoring compliance and responding to violations were all activities in which judges reported using problem-solving techniques. However, because probation departments are often overburdened and underfunded, judges in both states emphasized that judicial follow-up would often be required to ensure that defendants were in fact linked to programs and services, and that other probation conditions were met.[13]

2. What barriers might judges face when attempting to practice problem solving in conventional courts? How might those barriers be overcome?

Focus group participants discussed a number of barriers that they believed could seriously impede the ability to practice problem solving more widely. Limited time and resources and conflicting ideas about the judicial role received the most attention. Other barriers cited included: (1) attorney unwillingness or lack of education about the problem-solving approach, (2) legal and constitutional constraints on what can or should be done in a conventional court and (3) public safety concerns with regard to violent defendants. These latter issues, however, appeared to concern fewer judges and arose specifically during discussions of conventional adult criminal courts, not juvenile, family law or civil calendars.

Time and Resources

Limited resources were unquestionably the most significant barrier to practicing problem solving in conventional courts, according to focus group participants. Judges emphasized the limited time for providing individualized attention to each case, direct interaction with defendants and ongoing judicial supervision. They also cited institutional pressures to "move cases along." Explained one judge:

> *When you leave treatment court . . . you don't have time for the individualized attention. . . . You don't have access to the*

> *wide array of services. You are under a great deal of pressure to move cases. . . . The concern is not what are you doing for the defendant, but what are you doing about reducing your caseload, and you don't have the same kind of pressure in drug courts or [other] problem-solving courts. . . . It is just kind of frustrating, because you know that [problem solving] works.*

Across all focus groups, judges expressed particular concern about limited time and resources when the subject of return court appearances arose. While ongoing judicial supervision was cited as among the most readily applicable practices (see above), in practice multiple return dates create costs for a large number of personnel, not only the judge, and can incur resentment from other court staff, as one judge explained:

> *[Return appearances are] problematic, I think, especially in the budgetary crunch . . . and a judge is going to set it, it has to go back to his or her calendar. So then you start getting backlash from your staff. . . . You are the only judge that does it; nobody else does it. And then we have to break. . . . We break before noon, we have to break before five, our clerk's offices close down at three.*

While all judges agreed that limited resources posed a problem, they tended to be perceived as more critical by judges in higher-volume (generally urban) courts. Note too that domestic violence court judges from both states indicated that they faced high caseloads and pressure to move cases along rapidly within their specialized problem-solving courts. By contrast, drug and mental health court judges were far more apt to contrast the plentiful time available in their problem-solving court to the severely limited time available in other assignments.

Judges further lamented the lack of additional staff resources in conventional courts to link defendants to appropriate services and provide the court with detailed progress reports. Although probation departments have historically been asked to perform similar functions, judges reported that chronic underfunding has rendered probation far less effective than desired. Ideally, if treatment programs could provide detailed progress reports themselves, the need for court-based case management might be lessened. However, judges were generally critical of progress reports directly from the treatment programs. Several believed that without court staff demanding accountability, programs would not provide timely reports with a "sufficient depth of information about client progress" to inform judicial decision making.

Focus group participants were probed about how resource barriers might be overcome. Some judges initially seemed paralyzed by the limited resources in conventional courts and could see no way to overcome them, one noting that "there are a lot of things that could be done, but only Don Quixote could do them." Ultimately, two broad sets of strategies emerged.

The first involved what judges themselves could do, in their own courts and with their current caseload. Among the suggestions was a "triage" approach, in which only the most appropriate cases would be selected for ongoing judicial monitoring: "you have to be able to decide what sort of cases you are going to concentrate on and be able to take that smaller number and give it the increased attention." Another suggestion was for judges to assume greater personal responsibility for calling treatment providers, demanding timely progress reports and exerting courtroom leadership to build trust and encourage attorneys and other parties to change their practices over time. Since building trust often depends on seeing the same parties regularly, this would appear particularly effective for judges in smaller jurisdictions, where rotation among key players might be less frequent.

A second set of recommendations focused on longer-term, more systemic (and costly) solutions. Among the suggestions was to make the resources of existing specialized problem-solving courts available to all courts, and to establish courtwide screening, assessment and case management systems as well as additional dedicated staff.

Judicial Role and Personality

Conflicting judicial philosophies were discussed extensively as a barrier to the wider dissemination of a problem-solving approach. The consensus among participants was that in any courthouse, some judges' conception of the judicial role is inconsistent with problem-solving practice. Judges contrasted a "traditional" judicial role ("deciding cases," not "solving problems") with a more problem-solving, collaborative judicial philosophy. One noted that many colleagues view problem-solving approaches as "social work" and thus inconsistent with the "proper judicial role" of "deciding cases."[14] With criminal cases, a philosophical preference for punishment over rehabilitation was also seen as a barrier:

> *I just get so frustrated at times working with colleagues who snicker and laugh and make fun of the collaborative approach, because they say, well, "punishment." ... I have had [presiding judges] who said, this is the purpose of why we have courts, [it] is to punish people.*

In both states, judges from more rural and politically conservative counties tended to report that many, perhaps even the majority, of their colleagues have a more traditional conception of the judicial role. By contrast, several judges from large urban jurisdictions suggested the predominant philosophy in their courts was more conducive to a problem-solving approach, making the primary challenge not one of changing judges' philosophies but of imparting specific knowledge about how problem solving could be employed in their courtrooms. Indeed, focus group participants repeatedly invoked their experience in a specialized problem-solving court as critical in helping them find productive ways to apply problem solving elsewhere. This in turn raises the question of how to ensure that more judges receive such court experience and how the relevant skills might be imparted to judges without experience in problem-solving courts.

Participants also debated how the judge's personality affects their ability to effectively apply a problem-solving approach. Are certain "innate" personality characteristics necessary to practice problem solving? The issue aroused considerable emotion, and no consensus, in all focus groups. Some judges were vehement that problem solving was inherent to their personality: "Most of us sitting at this table have a personality that no matter what assignment we are in, we are going to be creative problem solvers." A few specific personality traits—empathy, honesty and interpersonal communication skills—were cited. Some felt that, even with training or experience in problem-solving courts, colleagues without the right personality traits would be ineffective. However, others disagreed, with one observing, "There are some [problem-solving court judges] [whose] personality would be the total antithesis of what you would expect of a collaborative justice court." Another stated that judges must always "be who they are," but that they can still be effective so long as they talk to defendants like real people and have faith in their ability to succeed.

3. How might problem solving be disseminated among judges and judicial leaders throughout the court system?

Discussion in the focus groups focused extensively on the need to change the attitudes and practices of judges who may not be familiar with or receptive to opportunities to apply problem solving in general court calendars. This, according to participants, is critical to promoting broader use of problem solving throughout the court systems. Indeed, the topic was raised by judges in all focus groups—prior to it being raised by the moderators—and received at least as much attention as the other issues discussed above. As one judge noted, "One of the biggest challenges is convincing other judges to do this."

In general, the dialogue in all four focus groups was consistent, and several common themes emerged. Judges linked interest in problem solving not only to judicial role orientation but also to individual personality and temperament. Accordingly, general consensus emerged that widespread adoption of problem solving would be a long-term process and that some judges would simply be unwilling to adopt new practices and roles: "You are talking about evolving or changing the role of the judicial officer and the colleagues. . . . The judicial officers who [came in] 20 to 25 years ago as a general rule don't perceive the position that way."

However, some participants left the door open for judges to come around to new ideas, noting that problem solving is to some extent a "learned behavior"—and "exposure to the concept" is key to changing attitudes. While some participants affirmed that all judges would benefit from exposure to the problem-solving concept, many suggested that new judges would be most receptive and thus ought to be a principal focus of any efforts: "New judges tend to be won over" and "the key is the crop coming out . . . so you gradually over time change the concept or perception."

Several themes emerged from the conversation about problem-solving dissemination:

Education and Training

Judges emphasized the need for greater education and training of judges (and others) in the principles and practices of problem solving. Education was seen as the most appropriate and effective method available, with judicial colleges and new judge orientations cited as preferred venues for disseminating information. Many, though not all, judges expressed support for mandatory training: "If you make it voluntary, the people who want it come, and the people who don't, don't." One judge noted that new judge orientations have recently placed greater emphasis on the "art of being a judge" and teaching ethics and fairness, so a section on problem-solving justice might be especially appropriate.

While discussion focused on the education and training of bench judges, focus group participants also cited the need to educate and train others "across the board," including attorneys and presiding judges, in order to build broader understanding and support for problem solving.

Informal Exposure/Word of Mouth

In all focus groups, judges recommended a number of less formal means by which judges might be exposed to problem solving, including mentoring, brown bag lunches among judges to discuss relevant issues and exposing judges to the results of this new approach (e.g., sharing success stories). One judge felt that the mere presence of the drug court, and the resulting informal dissemination of information about how it worked, had in fact already generated a change of attitudes in the local judiciary. Specifically, it had resulted in a greater understanding of addiction and a greater acceptance of practices that could be used in other courtrooms, such as mandating defendants to treatment and giving them multiple chances after initial noncompliance. A common theme was that receptivity to problem solving is enhanced if judges "hear it from other judges"—rather than from administrators, attorneys or academics.

Assignment/Rotation

Assignment to specialized problem-solving courts also received considerable discussion in the focus groups, on the hypothesis that such experience would enable judges to develop new attitudes and skills that they would take with them to subsequent general calendar assignments.[15] Participants appeared to distinguish—though most often implicitly—the impact of such assignments on judges' attitudes from their impact on judges' skills. Participants were skeptical that problem-solving court assignments alone enhance judicial receptivity to problem solving. While a few noted that their own experiences had moved them from mild opposition or disinterest to enthusiastic support for problem solving, most reported that colleagues who began as strongly opposed to problem solving had been unmoved by their experience in a problem-solving court.

By contrast, there was general consensus that experience can have a lasting, positive impact on judges' skills as well as their ability to apply those skills in future assignments. Despite this, focus group participants were largely unenthusiastic about mandatory assignment to these courts. When judges were asked how to facilitate broader use of problem solving throughout the court system, mandatory assignment emerged unsolicited in one of the four groups, where it was received negatively by several judges. When probed on the issue, participants in the other focus groups all agreed that problem-solving court assignments ought to be voluntary. The lack of enthusiasm was due primarily to concern about the potentially deleterious impact of mandatory assignment (and frequent rotation) on the problem-solving courts themselves. Participants noted that the assigned judge might be hostile to the court's goals or methods, and that too frequent rotation might introduce discontinuity in the problem-solving court team and harm program participants. Similar concerns and themes are found in discussions of other specialized court contexts.[16]

Judicial Leadership

Judges in California emphasized the need for presiding judges and other judicial leaders to encourage broader use of problem solving throughout the court system. This need was a prominent theme in California but not in the New York focus groups, and was the only significant cross-state difference to emerge in the research.

Participants cited the need for leaders to provide "encouragement" and "institutional validation." Some articulated this in terms of sending positive messages granting judges "permission" to apply problem-solving court principles on general calendars:

> *And so to transfer some of these principles, there has to be permission from above. . . . There are people who are in authority for judges, that [have to say] it is okay to do this, it is not really crazy, you are not some kind of radical outlaw bandit. . . . In fact, it may actually be encouraged. That message needs to be given if you are going to be successful.*

> *Another way [to encourage broader applications] is for the presiding judges to accept that this is appropriate. . . . I am sure all of you have had people make fun of you for what you do . . . who absolutely disagree with what we do in our courts. . . . Until we can get rid of that pervasive opinion that exists within our system, I think we are going to have problems and you are not going to see these great concepts being passed on to other assignments.*

One judge suggested that leaders might help to promote problem solving by redefining opportunities for promotion and advancement to place less emphasis on traditional case flow management, holding trials, or publishing, and greater emphasis on solving problems:

> *If one were really honest, one would have to talk about opportunities for promotion and advancement. . . . I think one way [to promote problem solving] would be to get a very clear message from people who determine judges' career paths and promotions—administrators—that this kind of approach is as important as how many days on trial you had in the last year. Everybody wants to be looked upon favorably by people who evaluate their performance.*

Discussion was often vague in terms of which specific leaders were and were not sufficiently supportive of problem solving. While it focused primarily on presiding judges (at the county level), participants in both California focus groups cited the need for buy-in at all levels of the court system and from elected officials as well.

Discussion

Focus group participants did not anticipate that engaging in problem solving outside specialized courts would come easily. For some, the barriers seemed overwhelming:

> *There are a lot of things that could be done. But only Don Quixote could do them. Because you're tilting at windmills when a lot of people would be resistant to it and wouldn't cooperate. And it would cost a lot of money. And you would have to be indefatigable. And you could never, never give up. Maybe you'd get some things done. And you'd be quite tired by the end of the week. You'd have to sleep all weekend to start again on Monday. So that's my view. I'm not cynical at all. I'm an optimist.*

While this judge was more pessimistic than most, the list of barriers that emerged from the focus groups was long and daunting indeed. Chief among those were the limited judicial time and resources in conventional courts, the lack of additional staff to effectively manage treatment program coordination, and philosophical opposition or lack of education among colleagues both on the bench and in judicial leadership positions. At the same time, most judges believed there were opportunities to apply problem-solving principles and practices even within the constraints just identified. Practices such as adopting a problem-solving judicial orientation, engaging in direct interaction with defendants and other litigants, and conducting ongoing supervision of treatment cases were deemed feasible and appropriate in many conventional court contexts. Most participants believed that judges willing to practice problem solving in conventional court assignments can do so, if only on a limited basis and for cases most clearly in need of a creative, collaborative approach.

Participants proposed specific steps that might be taken in the short term to better inform their colleagues. Included among these was formal education (e.g., incorporating problem-solving courses in new judge orientation and judicial college, encouraging training for prosecutors and defenders) and various informal methods (e.g., problem-solving court judges might mentor general bench judges and those new to problem solving, judges might be encouraged to observe specialized problem-solving courts or attend a drug court graduation ceremony). Focus group participants, particularly those in California, also suggested positive steps judicial leaders might take, such as encouraging bench judges to practice problem solving when appropriate and to volunteer for assignments to specialized problem-solving courts.

Longer-term, more systemic changes to enhance or more effectively use limited resources were also suggested. These included the centralization of treatment coordination and compliance monitoring staff and resources within each courthouse, and the development of jurisdiction-wide directories of community-based service providers to inform all judges about available programs (e.g., for substance abusers, the mentally ill).

The focus group findings provide additional empirical support to many hypotheses and personal accounts found in the current literature, particularly with respect to the barriers of limited resources,[17] the need to promote a new view of the judicial role[18] and the importance of judicial leadership in advancing problem solving.[19] The findings also suggest next steps for future research. For example, while few interstate differences emerged in this study, both California and New York are at the forefront of the problem-solving court movement—experiences and policy challenges in these states are not necessarily representative of those faced by problem-solving court judges nationwide. Thus a national study might explore the experiences and perspectives of problem-solving court judges in other states.

An additional avenue of research might focus on general calendar judges. Focus group participants argued that promoting problem solving more broadly depends on the participation of judges without experience in specialized problem-solving courts. There appeared to be an assumption that many general bench judges are unreceptive to problem-solving principles and that even those who are receptive are uninformed, but the extent to which these perceptions are accurate remains an empirical question. A survey of judges without experience in specialized problem-solving courts could provide answers to key questions concerning general bench judges' knowledge, attitudes and practices related to problem solving. It could also assess judges' openness to change (e.g., willingness to attend trainings or accept a specialized problem-solving court assignment). Such research would provide court managers and others with a fuller understanding of the judicial landscape, helping to inform their decisions about how problem-solving practice might be most effectively promoted, and the extent to which it ought to be promoted in the first place.

Problem-solving courts are created through the cooperation of multiple agencies including probation, prosecutors, defense attorneys, law enforcement and treatment providers. Taking these courts to scale can be accomplished only with the commitment of all justice system partners. While the project explores strategies and techniques that the courts can employ to bring these innovative principles and practices into the mainstream, it should be recognized that the success of these strategies depends on support from practitioners throughout the criminal justice and treatment systems.

Chapter Ten

And the Survey Says . . . : State Court Judges and Problem-Solving Courts

AUBREY FOX

In 2001, the University of Maryland's Survey Research Center (in partnership with the Open Society Institute and the Center for Court Innovation) conducted phone interviews with over 500 judges, including 286 criminal court judges and 217 judges who preside over problem-solving courts. The 20 minute survey was designed to test several hypotheses that have been advanced by proponents of problem-solving courts: Are judges frustrated with the results that conventional case processing achieves? Are criminal court dockets cluttered with cases involving addiction, domestic violence and mental illness? Are judges interested in testing new approaches like the more aggressive use of judicial monitoring or the creation of new links to off-site treatment providers?

The results were provocative: while overwhelmingly satisfied with their jobs (and mostly unfamiliar with problem-solving courts), judges are nonetheless very interested in, and supportive of, problem-solving approaches in cases involving addiction, domestic violence and mental illness.

Survey Results

The results of the survey include:

The Open Society Institute provided funding for the survey described in this chapter. Points of view and opinions in this chapter do not necessarily represent the official position or policies of the Open Society Institute.

Significant support for an outcome-orientation for courts

Over 80 percent of the judges surveyed said they should be "extensively" or "moderately" involved in helping to reduce drug abuse among defendants, protecting domestic violence victims from continued violence and helping defendants who are mentally ill get into treatment.

Confidence in treatment as an effective sentencing option for a wide variety of offenses

Over 70 percent of the judges surveyed favored treatment over incarceration as a means of reducing recidivism among non-violent, drug-addicted defendants; close to 90 percent of the judges said that treatment for mentally ill defendants would "greatly" or "somewhat" reduce the likelihood of future offenses among this group.

Support for the active use of judicial authority

Ninety percent of the judges surveyed said they should be "extensively" or "moderately" involved in ensuring that substance-abusing defendants attend court-ordered treatment and defendants in domestic violence cases attend batterer intervention programs.

Willingness to engage with community groups

Over 60 percent of the judges said they should be "extensively" or "moderately" involved with community groups in working on neighborhood safety and quality-of-life concerns.

Commitment to building public confidence

Close to 95 percent of the judges said they should be "extensively" or "moderately" involved in building public confidence in the courts.

Satisfaction with problem-solving courts

Ninety-six percent of the problem-solving court judges reported being "very satisfied" (70 percent) or "satisfied" (26 percent) with their experiences presiding over a specialized court.

Preference for problem-solving courts over traditional case processing

Sixty-four percent of criminal court judges said that drug courts are more effective at reducing recidivism among addicted offenders than conventional criminal courts (only 11 percent favored criminal courts over drug courts). Forty-eight percent believed that domestic violence courts are better at reducing domestic violence than conventional criminal courts, while 22 percent favored criminal courts.

Interest in serving on a specialized problem-solving court

Although only 30 percent of criminal court judges reported being "very familiar" with problem-solving courts, two-thirds said they would be "very likely" (34 percent) or "somewhat likely" (33 percent) to accept an opportunity to preside over a problem-solving court.

What does all this add up to? While the judges surveyed expressed support for some of the basic elements of problem solving, they did not endorse problem solving per se. Many had never heard of problem-solving courts and even those who had heard of them expressed some confusion about the term. At the same time, the survey offers a snapshot of a surprisingly engaged and proactive judiciary willing to roll up their sleeves and get involved in addressing the kinds of problems that courts see on a daily basis.

The bottom line is that many judges and citizens support a problem-solving approach, even if they don't know what a "problem-solving court" is. Judges view the core components of problem-solving courts—the active use of judicial authority, a focus on achieving tangible outcomes like increased sobriety for addicts and a multi-disciplinary approach that brings non-lawyers into the courtroom—more favorably than might be expected given the value the judiciary typically has placed on continuity, stability and tradition.

Authors

Ann K. Bader

Ann K. Bader is deputy director of the Division of Grants and Program Development for the New York State Unified Court System. For the past 12 years she has implemented grant-funded court programs throughout New York.

Greg Berman

Greg Berman is the director of the Center for Court Innovation. He is currently working on a book about problem-solving justice to be published by The New Press. In addition, he has contributed articles to *Law and Policy, Court Manager, Justice System Journal, New York State Bar Journal, Judicature, U.S. Attorney Bulletin, Fordham Urban Law Review* and other publications.

Francine Byrne

Francine Byrne, is a senior research analyst with the Judicial Council of California, Administrative Office of the Courts. She conducts research on court-related programs including evaluations of drug courts, elder abuse courts and the impact of Court Appointed Special Advocates. In addition to her work on court programs, Ms. Byrne has authored papers on aging and substance abuse, and work training programs for the homeless.

Amanda Cissner

Amanda Cissner is a senior research associate at the Center for

Court Innovation. Ms. Cissner has served as the principal investigator on a process evaluation of the Brooklyn Youthful Offender Domestic Violence Court for adolescent perpetrators of relationship violence.

Donald J. Farole Jr.

Donald Farole is a senior research associate at the Center for Court Innovation. At the Center, he has authored, among other things, an evaluation of the Harlem Parole Reentry Court. He is currently involved in a national multi-site drug court evaluation funded by the National Institute of Justice. Prior to joining the Center, Dr. Farole was an assistant professor of political science at the University of North Carolina-Greensboro. He has published research on state appellate courts, including articles in *Law and Society Review* and a book, *Interest Groups and Judicial Federalism* (1998). Dr. Farole received his Ph.D. in 1996 from Indiana University.

John Feinblatt

John Feinblatt is the criminal justice coordinator of the City of New York. Prior to his appointment by New York City Mayor Michael Bloomberg, he was the founding director of the Center for Court Innovation. He has also served as director of the Midtown Community Court, deputy executive director of Victims Services (now Safe Horizon) and staff attorney at the Legal Aid Society.

Aubrey Fox

Aubrey Fox is the associate director of special projects at the Center for Court Innovation. Mr. Fox has contributed numerous articles to professional and policy journals. Prior to joining the Center, Mr. Fox received the Warren Weaver Fellowship, a one-year in-house residency with the Rockefeller Foundation.

He also served as a VISTA Volunteer in San Antonio, Texas, where he organized a traveling exhibition of photography and biography about the lives of 15 homeless people, and as a Coro Fellow in Leadership New York.

Dana Fox-Kralstein

Dana Fox-Kralstein is the associate director of research at the Center for Court Innovation. Ms. Kralstein studies family and juvenile drug courts, supervises researchers at two New York City community courts and is involved in a statewide cost-effectiveness evaluation.

Anne Gulick

Anne Gulick is a former associate planner at the Center for Court Innovation. She is currently enrolled in a Ph.D. program in literature at Duke University.

Melissa Labriola

Melissa Labriola is a senior research associate at the Center for Court Innovation. She is currently working on a random assignment study testing offender recidivism at the Bronx Misdemeanor Domestic Violence Court. She is also conducting an evaluation of the Queens Misdemeanor Treatment Court and of the Bronx Juvenile Accountability Court.

Michael Magnani

Michael Magnani is the director of the Division of Grants and Program Development for the New York State Unified Court System. He played an integral role in the creation of many of the state's problem-solving courts, including the Midtown Community Court and the Brooklyn Treatment Court. He also helped institute the nation's first dedicated felony domestic violence court, the Brooklyn Domestic Violence Court, as well as New York's first mental health court.

Nora Puffett

As a senior research associate at the Center for Court Innovation, Nora Puffett has been involved in studying domestic violence courts for the last four-and-a-half years.

Michael Rempel

Michael Rempel is director of research at the Center for Court Innovation. He is currently principal investigator of a random assignment experiment testing the impact of batterer programs and two types of court monitoring on the behavior of domestic violence offenders. He also recently co-authored the evaluation of Brooklyn's Felony Domestic Violence Court. He has previously published articles on contemporary social theory and the political sociology of advanced industrial societies and co-edited the volume *Citizen Politics in Post-Industrial Societies.*

Robert V. Wolf

Robert V. Wolf has been the director of communications at the Center for Court Innovation since 1999. In that capacity, he has written numerous white papers and articles about problem-solving courts, community prosecution and other topics related to criminal justice reform. Prior to joining the Center, he worked for the *Staten Island Advance* in various capacities, including reporter, columnist and editor.

Notes

Introduction

1. See Malcolm Gladwell interview at http://www.gladwell.com/books2.html#q_and_a (accessed July 20, 2004).

2. See C. West Huddleston III, Karen Freeman-Wilson and Donna L. Boone, *Painting the Current Picture: A National Report Card on Drug Courts and Other Problem Solving Court Programs in the United States* (Alexandria, VA: National Drug Court Institute, May 2004).

3. For more information on the results achieved by problem-solving courts to date, see Chapter Seven, "Just the Facts, Ma'am: What We Know and Don't Know About Problem-Solving Courts."

Chapter One: The Hardest Sell

1. David B. Rottman and Randall M. Hansen, *How Recent Court Users View the State Courts: Perceptions of Whites, African Americans, and Latinos* (Williamsburg, VA: National Center for State Courts), 3; available from http://www.ncsconline.org/WC/Publications/Res_AmtPTC_PerceptionsPub.pdf.

Chapter Two: The Future of Drug Courts

1. See *Drug Court Activity Update: December 15, 2003* (Washington, D.C.: Office of Justice Programs Drug Court Clearinghouse, 2003); available at http://www.american.edu/justice/publications/2003factsheet.pdf (accessed April 6, 2004), for a state-by-

state breakdown of drug courts in planning and in operation. The 1997 figure was obtained from *Cutting Crime: Drug Courts in Action* (Washington, D.C.: Drug Strategies, 1997); available at http://www.drugstrategies.org/acrobat/CuttingCrime97.pdf (accessed April 6, 2004).

2. See Lisbeth Schorr, *Common Purpose: Strengthening Families and Neighborhoods to Re-Build America* (New York: Anchor Books, 1997), 4.

3. "'The feds did not expect the states to take this expense on without the drug courts proving themselves first,' said Connie Payne, a state court official. 'Unfortunately, just as we're proving successful, the state is in the middle of a financial crisis.'" John Cheeves, "Drug Courts Are Facing a Crunch: State Is Strapped But Grants Are Ending," *Lexington Herald-Leader*, November 24, 2003.

4. A rich literature exists on drug courts. The National Criminal Justice Reference Service lists over 180 articles on the topic; see http://www.ncjrs.org/drug_courts/publications.html (accessed April 6, 2004). For a good discussion of drug courts' origins, see W. C. Terry (ed.), *The Early Drug Courts: Case Studies in Judicial Innovation* (Thousand Oaks, California: Sage Publications, 1999). Also see John Goldkamp, *Justice and Treatment Innovation: The Drug Court Movement* (Washington, D.C.: National Institute of Justice, 1995). Most of the literature on drug courts consists of evaluations of individual courts or descriptions of basic drug court principles.

5. Only a few pieces address drug court institutionalization issues, though the number is increasing of late. Those include Susan Tashiro, et. al., *Institutionalizing Drug Courts: A Focus Group Meeting Report* (Washington, D.C.: Bureau of Justice Assistance, 2000), available at http://www.ncjrs.org/html/bja/idc/ (accessed April 6, 2004); Jeffrey Tauber and C. West Huddleston, *Development and Implementation of Drug Court Systems*

(Alexandria, VA: National Drug Court Institute, May 1999), available at http://www.ndci.org/admin/docs/develop.doc (accessed April 6, 2004); Pamela Casey and David B. Rottman, *Expanding the Problem-Solving Approach: Developing a Coordinated, System-Wide Reponse for the Court System* (Williamsburg, VA: National Center for State Courts, August 25, 2003); and Fox and Berman, "Going to Scale: A Conversation About the Future of Drug Courts," *Court Review* (Fall 2002) (Also see Chapter Four.) Also, in October 2003, the National Association of Drug Court Professionals, the Congress of State Drug Courts and the National Program for Therapeutic Courts at William & Mary Law School co-sponsored a conference on "The Nationwide Implementation of the Drug Court Model," with the goal of "develop[ing] a strategic plan for nationwide implementation."

6. Becker and Harrell are both quoted in Fox and Berman, "Going to Scale," p. 11.

7. John Goldkamp, "The Impact of Drug Courts," *Criminology and Public Policy* Vol. 2, No. 2 (2003): 197-206.

8. See Table 6.24, *Sourcebook of Criminal Justice Statistics* (Washington, D.C.: Bureau of Justice Statistics, 2001), 495. With 800 prisoners per 100,000 residents under jurisdiction of state and federal correctional authorities on December 31, 2001, Louisiana had the highest rate of incarceration of all 50 states. The national average was 470.

9. Judith S. Kaye, "State of the Judiciary," March 23, 1998; available at http://www.nycourts.gov/admin/stateofjudiciary/stofjud8/stofjud98.htm.

10. "An Oklahoma City police officer for 20 years, Judge [Charles] Hill said he didn't want the Oklahoma County drug court when it was first assigned to him. Some of his former law enforcement colleagues dubbed it the 'Hug the Thug' program." Ed Godfrey, "Drug Court Scores Hit: Addiction Treated as Cause of Crime," *Daily Oklahoman*, July 5, 1999.

11. James Nolan, *Reinventing Justice: The American Drug Court Movement*, (Princeton, NJ: Princeton University Press, 2001).

12. For years, advocates have been dogged by concerns about the methodological quality of drug court research—though this debate has largely been confined to a small group of researchers and critics. For example, reports issued by the General Accounting Office questioned whether methodological shortcomings made it impossible to conclude anything about drug court effectiveness. Over the past two years, however, the research literature has been advanced by several major studies of the Portland and Las Vegas drug courts, the Pensacola and Kansas City drug courts, Ohio State drug courts, New York State drug courts and a random assignment study of the Baltimore City Drug Court. These studies highlight a number of positive findings; for example, New York drug courts reduced the new conviction rate by 29 percent over a three-year period (an unusually long evaluation period).

13. Thomas B. Fomby and Vasudha Rangaprasad, *DIVERT Court of Dallas County: Cost Benefit Analysis* (Dallas, TX: Department of Economics, Southern Methodist University, August 31, 2002), 2.

14. Harry Connick, "Connick Objects to How Drug Courts Operate," *The Times-Picayune*, August 20, 1999, B6.

15. Susan Finch, "High court rules in Connick's favor; DAs hold the keys to probation programs," *The Times-Picayune,* October 18, 2000, 2.

16. According to a Criminal Justice Police Council study: "To fully fund drug courts to meet the requirements of H.B. 1287 would require $1.5 million in additional funding." See Alma I. Martinez and Michael Eisenberg, *Initial Process and Outcome Evaluation of Drug Courts in Texas* (Austin, TX: Criminal Justice Policy Council, January 2003).

17. *Confronting the Cycle of Addiction and Recidivism: A Report to Chief Judge Judith S. Kaye by the New York State Commission on*

Drugs and the Courts (New York State Unified Court System, June 2000); available at http://www.nycourts.gov/reports/addictionrecidivism.shtml#11 (accessed April 8, 2004).

18. The Wyoming Health Department, for example, issued a comprehensive blueprint for building drug courts and improving treatment services throughout the state. The Health Department's recommendations, which were substantially adopted by the Wyoming legislature and funded with $50 million in tobacco settlement money, call for the creation of a statewide adult and juvenile drug-court system, investment in outpatient and residential treatment programs, incentives for establishing drug-free workplaces, and utilizing community coalitions to coordinating local efforts. See Wyoming Department of Health, Substance Abuse Division, *Reclaiming Wyoming: A Comprehensive Blueprint for Prevention, Early Intervention, and Treatment of Substance Abuse* (Cheyenne: Wyoming Department of Health, November 11, 2001).

19. Drug court funding in Utah is distributed through a committee composed of representatives of the court and the state's human services agency. By statute, 13 cents of every dollar allocated is distributed to general court operations and 87 cents to fund treatment programs.

20. Only first- and second-time offenders would have been eligible. Offenders who have been convicted of a violent felony within the last five years would have been ineligible, as would defendants currently facing a charge involving violence, drug trafficking or drunken driving.

21. Michael Rempel, et. al., *The New York State Adult Drug Court Evaluation: Policies, Participants and Impacts* (New York: Center for Court Innovation, October 2003); available at http://www.courtinnovation.org/pdf/drug_court_eval.pdf (accessed April 8, 2004).

22. Ibid.

23. See Fox and Berman, "Going to Scale."
24. Mark A. R. Kleiman. "Controlling Drug Use and Crime Among Drug-Involved Offenders: Testing, Sanctions, and Treatment," in P. B. Heymann and W. N. Brownsberger (eds), *Drug Addiction and Drug Policy: The Struggle to Control Dependence* (Cambridge: Harvard University Press, 2001); available at http://www.sppsr.ucla.edu/faculty/kleiman/harvard.PDF (accessed April 8, 2004).
25. This strategy was given a big boost in 2001 by a joint resolution by the Conference of Chief Judges and Conference of State Court Administrators, which called for "the broad integration over the next decade of the principles and methods employed in the problem-solving courts into the administration of justice."
26. Morris B. Hoffman, quoted in Douglas Marlowe, et. al., "A Sober Assessment of Drug Courts," *Federal Sentencing Reporter* Vol. 16, No. 1, October 2003.
27. Goldkamp, "The Impact of Drug Courts."
28. Jacqueline Soteropoulos, "Restored funding saves drug program: Drug Treatment Court and others will benefit from changes to the Pa. budget deal," *Philadelphia Inquirer*, January 3, 2004.
29. D. B. Marlowe et al., "The Judge is a Key Component of Drug Court," *National Drug Court Institute Review* (forthcoming).

Chapter Three: Institutionalizing Innovation

1. See Gregory P. Falkin et al., "Drug Treatment in the Criminal Justice System," *Federal Probation* Vol. 58, No. 31, 31 (1994), which describes the strains of the war on drugs on the various components of the criminal justice system.
2. See Ethan G. Kalett, "Twelve Steps, You're Out (of Prison): An Evaluation of 'Anonymous Programs' as Alternative Sentences," *Hastings Law Journal* Vol. 48, No. 129 (1996): 133-136, which discusses the overcrowding in jails and prisons caused by the war on

drugs.

3. See W. Clinton Terry III, "Prosecutors and the Evaluation of Dedicated Drug Treatment Courts," *Prosecutor* 31 (March-April 1997): 32, which refers to the impact on courts and prosecutors of increased drug caseloads and suggesting the consideration of drug courts to increase the speed of drug crime enforcement.

4. See Hon. Peggy Fulton Hora et al., "Therapeutic Jurisprudence and the Drug Treatment Court Movement: Revolutionizing the Criminal Justice System's Response to Drug Abuse and Crime in America," *Notre Dame Law Review* Vol. 74, (1999): 439, 459-62, which describes how drug arrests have outpaced other criminal arrests since 1980. See, generally, Colloquy, "The Drugging of the Courts: How Sick is the Patient and What is the Treatment?" *Judicature* 73 (1990): 314.

5. Chief Judge Judith Kaye, "Second Annual State of the Judiciary Address," February 8, 1999; available at http://www.courts.state.ny.us/admin/stateofjudiciary/stofjud9/State99.htm (last accessed July 24, 2004).

6. New York State Commission on Drugs and the Courts, *Confronting the Cycle of Addiction and Recidivism: A Report to Chief Judge Judith S. Kaye* (June 2000); available at http://www.nycourts.gov/reports/addictionrecidivism.shtml (last accessed July 24, 2004).

7. Ibid., 15.

8. Judith S. Kaye, "Making the Case for Hands-On Courts," *Newsweek*, October 11, 1999, 13.

9. Steve Belenko, "Research on Drug Courts: A Critical Review," *National Drug Court Institute Review* Vol. 1, No. 10, 43 (1998).

10. Ibid., 66.

11. Robert Fiske is the former U.S. Attorney for the Southern District of New York and a partner with the law firm of Davis Polk and Wardwell. The 10,000 estimate is based on the number of offenders who would have been eligible for treatment under

the Fiske plan in 1999. See New York State Commission on Drugs and the Courts, "Confronting the Cycle of Addiction and Recidivism," 4; see also Katherine E. Finkelstein, "New York to Offer Most Addicts Treatment Instead of Jail Terms," *New York Times*, June 23, 2000, A1, which mentions how New York will be the first state to offer all nonviolent drug offenders the option of treatment instead of jail and discussing the program.

12. New York State Commission on Drugs and the Courts, "Confronting the Cycle of Addiction and Recidivism," 11.

13. Ibid., 1, 12. A "snapshot" of the state prison system in February 2000 showed that 22,000 of the state's 71,000 inmates were imprisoned for a drug crime.

14. *The New York Financial Plan, Fiscal Yrs. 2000-2004* 38 (2000).

15. New York State Commission on Drugs and the Courts, "Confronting the Cycle of Addiction and Recidivism," 58.

16. *The New York Financial Plan*, 5.

17. *The New York Financial Plan*, 10.

18. *The New York Financial Plan*, 14.

19. Greg Berman and John Feinblatt, *Problem-Solving Courts: A Brief Primer*, 2000 (unpublished paper on file with authors); see also David Rottman and Pamela Casey, "Therapeutic Jurisprudence and the Emergence of Problem-Solving Courts," *National Institute of Justice Journal* (July 1999): 12, which argues that courts should be engaged in collaboration with local and state agencies to find opportunities to promote therapeutic outcomes for individuals (therapeutic jurisprudence).

20. See Berman and Feinblatt, *Problem-Solving Courts: A Brief Primer*, 9.

21. Ibid., 1-2.

22. See *Summary of Drug Court Activity by State and County* (Washington, D.C.: Office of Justice Programs, Drug Court Clearinghouse and Technical Assistance Project at American University, 2000), which states that 46 states have implemented

and four are planning drug courts; available at http://gurukul.ucc.american.edu/justice (last accessed July 24, 2004).

23. Ibid.

24. Belenko, "Research on Drug Courts: A Critical Review," 10.

25. Ibid., 29-30.

26. Ibid., 36.

27. Ibid., 37.

28. Ibid., 39-41 (indicating lower re-arrest rates for drug court participants compared to others in nine studies).

29. Ibid., 39.

30. Ibid., 41.

31. Ibid., 27.

32. Ibid., 34.

33. Ibid., 34.

34. New York State Commission on Drugs and the Courts, "Confronting the Cycle of Addiction and Recidivism," 26.

35. The $ 500 million annual figure is determined by subtracting the cost of program implementation from total projected benefits. Press Release, New York State Office of Court Administration, "Cost Versus Project Savings of New Court-Mandated Treatment Program," June 2000 (on file with authors).

36. Ibid.

37. New York State Commission on Drugs and the Courts, "Confronting the Cycle of Addiction and Recidivism," 121.

38. Susan K. Knipps and Greg Berman, "New York's Problem-Solving Courts Provide Meaningful Alternatives to Traditional Remedies," *New York State Bar Journal* Vol. 72, No. 5 (June 2000): 10.

39. Finkelstein, "New York to Offer Most Addicts Treatment."

40. See, generally, Greg Berman, "What is a Traditional Judge Anyway?: Problem-Solving in the State Courts," *Judicature* Vol.

84, No. 1 (2000).
41. Ibid., 7.
42. See Bennett H. Brummer, "Independent, Professional Judgment: The Essence of Freedom," *St. Thomas Law Review* Vol. 10 (1998): 607, 611.
43. "What Does It Mean To Be A Good Lawyer?: Prosecutors and Defenders in Problem-Solving Courts," John Feinblatt and Derek Denckla (eds.), *Judicature*, Vol. 84, No. 2 (2000).
44. New York State Commission on Drugs and the Courts, "Confronting the Cycle of Addiction and Recidivism," 15.
45. This is according to the New York State Department of Correctional Services. Ibid., 15.
46. Berman, "What is a Traditional Judge," 4.
47. The Kaye plan does not contemplate offering treatment to offenders whose current crime is a violent offense. New York State Commission on Drugs and the Courts, "Confronting the Cycle of Addiction and Recidivism," 4.
48. Center For Court Innovation and State Justice Institute, *Experiments in Technology: A Handbook for Court Administrators* (1997).
49. Morris B. Hoffman, "The Drug Court Scandal," *North Carolina Law Review* Vol. 78 (2000): 1437, 1533; see also Eric Cohen, "The Drug Court Revolution," *The Weekly Standard*, December 27, 1999, 5, which questions whether drug courts really work, and examines their impact on the judicial system.
50. See "What Does It Mean to be a Good Lawyer?" Feinblatt and Denckla (eds.).
51. Ibid.
52. Kaye, "Making the Case for Hands-On Courts."
53. See Lisbeth Schorr, *Common Purpose: Strengthening Families and Neighborhoods to Re-Build America* (New York: Anchor Books, 1997), which contends that Americans can create strong and effective public institutions to solve social problems, and gives

examples of welfare, education, and child protection reforms.

Chapter Seven: Just the Facts

1. Lawrence W. Sherman, "Thinking About Crime Prevention," in *Preventing Crime What Works, What Doesn't, What's Promising*, Lawrence W. Sherman et al. (eds.) (A report to the United States Congress, prepared for the National Institute of Justice, 1996), 2-1, 2-15.

2. Peter H. Rossi, "The Iron Law of Evaluation and Other Metallic Rules," *Research in Social Problems and Public Policy* (1987): 4.

3. See Robert Martinson, "What Works? Questions and Answers about Prison Reform," *Public Interest*, Vol. 35, No. 22 (1974).

4. Ibid., 25.

5. Ibid., 25.

6. Ibid., 24.

7. Sherman, "Thinking About Crime Prevention," 2-21 - 2-22.

8. Ibid., 2-21.

9. Ibid., 2.21 (discussing what is unknown about crime prevention programs).

10. For the purposes of this essay, "problem-solving courts" refers to drug courts, community courts, domestic violence courts, mental health courts, juvenile intervention courts and family treatment courts. Specialized court initiatives seek to focus the energies of judges, lawyers and administrators on solving difficult social, human, and legal problems.

11. Lawrence W. Sherman, "Conclusions: The Effectiveness of Local Crime Prevention Funding, in What Works," 10-1, 10-15 to 10-18.

12. See Ibid., 10-16 to 10-18 (noting that neither Congress nor state legislatures have funded evaluations of research programs).

13. Ibid., 10-20 to 10-21.

14. See, e.g., Center for Court Innovation, *Problem-Solving Courts*, at http://www.problem-solvingcourts.org, which notes that "over

the past decade, hundreds of experimental courts have sprung up across the country."

15. Ibid.

16. Steven Belenko, *Research on Drug Courts: A Critical Review 2001 Update 1* (New York: National Center on Addiction and Substance Abuse at Columbia University, 2001), available at http://www.casacolumbia.org/usr doc/researchondrug.pdf (last accessed March 15, 2003). Since this chapter was originally published in *Fordham Urban Law Journal*, the Center for Court Innovation and New York Unified Court System have published a major drug court study that was not included in Belenko's review. The executive summary of the study is Chapter Eight of this book.

17. Ibid.

18. Ibid., 9.

19. Ibid., 1.

20. Steven Belenko, "Research on Drug Courts: A Critical Review," *National Drug Court Institute Review* Vol. 2, No. 2 (1999): 26-27; available at http://www.npcresearch.com (last accessed March 15, 2003).

21. Ward S. Condelli and George DeLeon, "Fixed and Dynamic Predictors of Client Retention in Therapeutic Communities," *Journal of Substance Abuse Treatment* Vol. 10, No. 1 (1993): 11-16.

22. Sherry Holland, "Gateway Houses: Effectiveness of Treatment on Criminal Behavior," *International Journal of Addictions* Vol. 13 (1978): 369, 371-72, 374.

23. Belenko, "Research on Drug Courts," 26-37.

24. See Ibid., 37 (noting that criminal activity is reduced in the drug court programs).

25. Adele Harrell et al., *Findings from the Evaluation of the D.C. Superior Court Drug Intervention Program* (Washington, D.C.: Urban Institute, 1998), 53-62.

26. See Ibid., 47-67.

27. See Daniel S. Nagin and Greg Pogarsky, "Integrating Celerity Impulsivity and Extralegal Sanction Threats into a Model of General Deterrence: Theory and Evidence," *Criminology* Vol. 39, No. 1 (2000): 3; available at http://www.ssc.wisc.edu/econ/Durlauf/networkweb1/London/Criminology1-15-01.pdf (last accessed March 15, 2003).
28. Ibid.
29. Ibid., 24 (reporting that coefficients for probability and severity are negative and statistically significant).
30. Ibid., 25 (stating that the deterrent impact of extra legal consequences is at least as great as that for legal consequences).
31. Adele Harrell and John Roman, "Reducing Drug Use and Crime Among Offenders: The Impact of Graduated Sanctions," *Journal of Drug Issues*, Vol. 31, No. 1 (2001).
32. Belenko, "Research on Drug Courts," 33.
33. Ibid.
34. Michael W. Finigan, *An Outcome Program Evaluation of the Multnomah County S.T.O.P. Drug Diversion Program* (Alexandria, VA: Prepared by the State Justice Institute for the Multnomah County, Oregon, Department of Corrections, January 6, 1998), 6.
35. Ibid.
36. Ibid.
37. Reginald Fluellen and Jennifer Trone, *Do Drug Courts Save Jail and Prison Beds?* (New York: Vera Institute of Justice, 200), 1-2; available at http://www.vera.org/publication pdf/drugcourts.pdf (last accessed March 15, 2003).
38. See Ibid., 2.
39. Ibid., 4.
40. Ibid., 6.
41. Belenko, "Research on Drug Courts," 54-55.
42. Ibid., 55.
43. See Ibid., 56.
44. Adele Harrell and Alice Goodman, *Review of Specialized*

Family Drug Courts: Key Issues in Handling Child Abuse and Neglect Cases (Washington, D.C.: Urban Institute, 1999), available at http://www.urban.org/uploadedPDF/speclizd.pdf (last accessed March 15, 2003).

45. Ibid., 36. "Immediate outcomes [for children] include the duration and number of foster care episodes while the case is before the court and the final placement (parents, in kinship foster care, and in foster care). Longer-term outcomes for those placed with their parents include the percentage named in subsequent abuse or neglect petitions, and, for those in which parental rights were terminated, the percentage adopted. Immediate outcomes [for parents] include treatment graduation/failure, substance abuse and participation in aftercare following case termination, perceptions of fairness of court process, effects of process on treatment motivation and retention, and assessment of the relationship between FDC services and reductions in problems faced by parents."

46. Ibid., 36-37. "System impacts. For courts, these include; the duration of cases, the number of hearings; the demands for staff, courtroom space, and other resources; the net widening effects of encouraging early intervention; the potential efficiencies of combining multiple petitions for multiple children in a family in a single case; and the potential for linking of cases active in different courts or dockets. For other agencies, these include the impact on demand for staff and services, the requirements to change procedures, and the barriers to participation based on agency mandates or funders."

47. Ibid., 37.

48. Ibid.

49. John S. Goldkamp and Cheryl Iron-Guynn, Criminal and Justice Research Institute, *Emerging Judicial Strategies for the Mentally Ill in the Criminal Caseload: Mental Health Courts in Fort Lauderdale, Seattle, San Bernardino, and Anchorage* (Washington,

D.C.: Bureau of Justice Assistance, Office of Justice Programs, U.S. Department of Justice, 2000); available at http://www.ncjrs.org/pdffiles1/bja/182504.pdf (last accessed March 15, 2003).

50. Ibid.

51. See Eric Trupin et al., *Mental Health Court: Evaluation Report* (City of Seattle and Seattle Municipal Court, 2001); available at http://www.cityofseattle.net/courts/pdf/mhreport.pdf (last accessed March 15, 2003).

52. Superior Court of California, Santa Clara County, *Mental Health Court Progress Report* 7 (2001).

53. See generally Goldkamp and Iron-Guynn, "Emerging Judicial Strategies," 9-57 (discussing mental health courts in Fort Lauderdale, Seattle, San Bernardino and Anchorage).

54. See Michele Sviridoff et al., *Dispensing Justice Locally: The Implementation and Effects of the Midtown Community Court* (New York: Center for Court Innovation, 2000); available at http://www.courtinnovation.org/pdf/disp just loc.pdf (last accessed March 15, 2003).

55. See Michele Sviridoff et al., *Dispensing Justice Locally: The Impacts, Costs and Benefits of the Midtown Community Court*; available at http://www.ncsconline.org/WC/Publications/ResCtCommMidtownExecSumPub.pdf (last accessed March 15, 2003), 5.

56. Sviridoff, *Dispensing Justice Locally: The Implementation and Effects of the Midtown Community Court*, 2.

57. See Ibid., 7.

58. See Michele Sviridoff et al., *Dispensing Justice Locally: The Impacts, Costs and Benefits of the Midtown Community Court*, 5 (noting that these factors were considered when evaluating the Midtown Community Court).

59. See Michele Sviridoff et al., *Dispensing Justice Locally: The Implementation and Effects of the Midtown Community Court*, 1.

60. See Michele Sviridoff et al., *Dispensing Justice Locally: The Impacts, Costs and Benefits of the Midtown Community Court*, 2.
61. See Michele Sviridoff et al., *Dispensing Justice Locally: The Implementation and Effects of the Midtown Community Court*, 6.
62. Ibid.
63. Ibid., 7.
64. Ibid.
65. Ibid.
66. Ibid.
67. Ibid.
68. Ibid., 7-8.
69. Ibid.
70. Ibid., 8.
71. Ibid.
72. See Ibid.
73. Ibid., 6.
74. Ibid., 9.
75. Ibid., 6.
76. See Ibid.
77. Ibid.
78. See Michele Sviridoff et al., *Dispensing Justice Locally: The Impacts, Costs and Benefits of the Midtown Community Court*, 6-7.
79. Ibid., 10.
80. Ibid.
81. Greg Berman, *Red Hook Diary: Planning a Community Court* (New York: Center for Court Innovation, 2001); available at http://www.courtinnovation.org/pdf/redhook diary.pdf (last accessed March 15, 2003).
82. See Ibid. (noting the residents' need for judicial services); see also David C. Anderson, *In New York City, a "Community Court" and a New Legal Culture* (Washington, D.C.: National Institute of Justice, 1996), 5; available at http://www.ncjrs.org/pdffiles/commcrt.pdf (last accessed March 15, 2003).

83. Anderson, *In New York City*, 5; Berman, *Red Hook Diary*, 2.
84. Community Justice Exchange, *Community Survey: Brooklyn, New York*; available at http://www.communityjustice.org/frameset.asp?heading=bestPractices%5F1 (last accessed March 15, 2003).
85. John S. Goldkamp et al., Crime and Justice Research Institute, *Developing an Evaluation Plan for Community Courts: Assessing the Hartford Community Court Model* (Washington, D.C.: Bureau of Justice Assistance, Office of Justice Programs, U.S. Department of Justice, 2001).
86. Ibid., 9.
87. Ibid., 42.
88. See Kerry Healey et al., "Batterer Intervention: Program Approaches and Criminal Justice Strategies," *Issues & Practices Criminal Justice* (February 1998): xii; available at http://www.ncjrs.org/pdffiles/168638.pdf (last accessed March 15, 2003).
89. Ibid., 1.
90. Larry W. Bennett and Oliver J. Williams, *Controversies and Recent Studies of Batterer Intervention Program Effectiveness* (Harrisburg, PA: National Electronic Network on Violence Against Women, 2001); available at http://www.vawnet.org/VNL/library/general/AR bip.html (last accessed March 15, 2003).
91. Ibid. These findings concur with a 1999 BIP literature review authored by Robert C. Davis and Bruce G. Taylor, "Does Batter Treatment Reduce Violence? A Synthesis of the Literature," in *Women and Domestic Violence: An Interdisciplinary Approach*, Lynette Feder (ed.) (Binghamton, NY: Hawthorne Press, 1999), 69, 72, 82-83.
92. Bennett and Williams, *Controversies and Recent Studies*, 90.
93. Ibid.; see Rhea Almeida and Ken Dolan-Delvecchio, "Addressing Culture in Batterers Intervention: The Asian Indian Community as an Illustrative Example," *Violence Against Women*

Vol. 5 (1999): 654, 654 (discussing Somerset, New Jersey's Cultural Context Model for a batterers' intervention program).

94. Robert C. Davis et al., "Does Batterer Treatment Reduce Violence? A Randomized Experiment in Brooklyn - Executive Summary Included" *The NIJ Research Review* Vol. 1, No. 2 (2000).

95. Ibid.

96. Ibid.

97. Ibid.

98. Ibid.

99. Wayne L. Peterson and Stephen Thumberg, *Evaluation Report for the San Diego County Domestic Violence Courts* 26 (Alexandria, VA: State Justice Institute, 2000).

100. Ibid., 27.

101. Ibid.

102. Robert C. Davis et al., "Prosecuting Domestic Violence Cases with Reluctant Victims: Assessing Two Novel Approaches in Milwaukee, in Legal Interventions" in *Family Violence: Research Findings and Policy Implications* (Chicago: American Bar Association, 1998), 71; available at http://www.ncjrs.org/pdffiles/171666.pdf (last accessed March 15, 2003).

103. Ibid.

104. Ibid.

105. Ibid., 71-72.

106. Adele Harrell and Barbara E. Smith, "Effects of Restraining Orders on Domestic Violence Victims," in *Do Arrests and Restraining Orders Work?* Eve S. Buzawa and Carl G. Buzawa (eds.) (Thousand Oaks, CA: Sage Publishing, 1996), 214, 238-41.

107. Ibid., 214-15.

108. Ibid., 216.

109. Ibid., 231.

110. Ibid., 232-33.

111. Ibid., 240.

112. Ibid., 241.
113. Susan Keilitz et al., *Civil Protection Orders: The Benefits and Limitations for Victims of Domestic Violence* (Williamsburg, VA: National Center for State Courts (1997), 3.
114. Ibid.
115. Myrna Dawson and Ronit Dinovitzer, "Victim Cooperation and the Prosecution of Domestic Violence in a Specialized Court," *Justice Quarterly* Vol. 18 (2001): 593.
116. David A. Ford and Mary Jean Regoli, "Selected Findings and Implications Drawn From The Indianapolis Domestic Violence Prosecution Experiment, in Legal Interventions," 62.
117. Ibid.
118. Ibid., 63.
119. Ibid.
120. See Christopher D. Maxwell et al., "The Effects of Arrest on Intimate Partner Violence: New Evidence from the Spouse Assault Replication Program," *National Institute of Justice Research in Brief* (July 2001); available at http://www.ncjrs.org/pdffiles1/nij/188199.pdf (last accessed March 15, 2003).
121. See Lisa Newmark et al., *Specialized Felony Domestic Violence Courts: Lessons on Implementation and Impacts from the Kings County Experience* (Washington, D.C.: Urban Institute, 2001); available at http://www.urban.org/uploadedPDF/410381domviolcourts.pdf (last accessed March 15, 2003).
122. Ibid., 17-19.
123. Ibid., 19-20.
124. Ibid., 56, 60.
125. Ibid., 60.
126. Ibid.
127. Ibid.
128. National Institute of Justice, Current NIJ Grants, *Testing the Impact of Court Monitoring and Battering Intervention Programs at the Bronx Misdemeanor Domestic Violence Court* (Grantees Fund

for the City of New York and Center for Court Innovation, 2001); available at http://www.ojp.usdoj.gov/nij/vawprog/grnt 2001 09.html (last accessed March 15, 2003).

129. Ibid.

130. Ibid.

131. David B. Rottman, *On-Line Court Reform: Can Technology Boost Public Confidence in the Courts?*, Judgelink; available at http://judgelink.org/insights/1999/reform (last accessed March 15, 2003).

132. Ibid.

133. David B. Rottman and Randall M. Hansen, *How Recent Court Users View the State Courts: Perceptions of African-Americans, Latinos, and Whites* (Washington, D.C.: National Institute of Justice, 2001), 18.

134. Ibid., 13-14.

135. Center for Court Innovation, State Court Judges Survey, Executive Summary (2001) (unpublished survey, on file with the Center for Court Innovation).

136. Ibid.

137. Ibid.

138. Survey Research Center, University of Maryland, College Park, State Court Judges Project #1409 Crosstab 12 (2001) (unpublished report, on file with the Center for Court Innovation).

139. Ibid., 16.

140. Ibid., 8.

141. Sviridoff et al., *Dispensing Justice Locally: The Implementation and Effects of the Midtown Community Court*, 9.

142. Ibid.

143. Ibid.

144. Greg Berman and John Feinblatt, *Problem Solving Courts: A Brief Primer* (New York: Center for Court Innovation, 2001); available at http://www.courtinnovation.org/pdf/prob_solv_

courts.pdf (last accessed March 15, 2003).
145. Ibid., 136.
146. Ibid.
147. See Sviridoff et al., *Dispensing Justice Locally: The Implementation and Effects of the Midtown Community Court*, 3 (noting that some were doubtful that the project would have an effect on "business as usual").

Chapter Eight: Evaluating Drug Courts in New York

1. Quantitative findings were based on analyses of program participation data provided by the New York State Unified Court System and criminal history and recidivism data provided by the New York State Division of Criminal Justice Services. Drug court policy information was obtained from two surveys administered in April 2001 and July 2002; and from stakeholder interviews and court observations during site visits at nine of the eleven courts.
2. The post-program period begins on the graduation date for drug court graduates, the release date from jail or prison for drug court failures, and, for the comparison group on the release date or if there was no sentence of incarceration on the disposition date. Defendants were assumed to serve two-thirds of any jail sentence (a standard "good time" assumption) and the minimum prison sentence if there was a range.
3. In the first four years of the Brooklyn program, defendants were not routed to the drug court if arrested in two of five geographic arrest zones in Brooklyn; hence defendants arrested mainly in those zones could comprise the comparison group. In Rochester, in the early years of the program, certain arraignment judges did not refer cases to the drug court; hence defendants arraigned by one of those judges could comprise the comparison group.
4. Belenko (1998) estimates that drug courts nationwide have an

average one-year retention rate of 60 percent, which substantially exceeds retention rates outside of drug courts. Three-month retention rates range from just 30 percent to 60 percent across a nationwide sample of community-based treatment programs (Condelli and DeLeon 1993) and one-year retention rates range from 10-30 percent across a sample of therapeutic communities, a common residential treatment modality (Lewis and Ross 1994).

5. The impact of graduation status on post-program recidivism was significant in three of four courts tested. In Queens, the fourth court, there was a small sample of drug court failures available for the analysis, leading the effect to be non-significant; but the odds ratio of .311 suggests the possibility of a similarly powerful impact.

6. Many courts do experience delays placing certain categories of participants: (1) with co-occurring mental health disorders, (2) requiring residential treatment, and (3) experiencing a case processing delay between intake and formalization of drug court participant status. This last finding highlights the need for streamlined referral and intake processes designed to move cases rapidly through the system.

Chapter Nine: Applying Problem-Solving Principles in Mainstream Courts

1. In California, these projects are referred to as "collaborative justice courts," while in New York and other states they are referred to as "problem-solving courts." Throughout this report, we use the more prevalent "problem-solving" terminology.

2. Although it is premature to offer a definitive assessment of the newer problem-solving court models, a consensus has recently emerged that the evaluation literature now offers clear support for the effectiveness of adult drug courts in reducing offender recidivism. See, e.g., Adele Harrell, "Judging Drug Courts: Balancing the Evidence," *Criminology and Public Policy* 2 (2003):

207; John Goldkhamp, "The Impact of Drug Courts," *Criminology and Public Policy* 2 (2003): 197.

3. See Daniel Becker and Maura Corrigan, "Moving Problem Solving Courts into the Mainstream: A Report Card from the CCJ-COSCA Problem Solving Courts Committee," *Court Review* 39 (2002): 4.

4. E.g., Barbara Babb, "Fashioning an Interdisciplinary Framework for Court Reform in Family Law: A Blueprint to Construct a Unified Family Court," *Southern California Law Review* 71 (1998): 469; Phylis Skloot Bamberger, "Special Series: Problem Solving Courts and Therapeutic Jurisprudence: Specialized Courts: Not a Cure-All," *Fordham Urban Law Journal* (2003): 1091; Pamela Casey and David B. Rottman, "Therapeutic Jurisprudence in the Courts," *Behavioral Science and the Law* 18 (2000): 445; William Schma, "Judging for the New Millennium," *Court Review* 37 (2000): 4; David B. Wexler, "Robes and Rehabilitation: How Judges Can Help Offenders Make Good," *Court Review* 38 (2001): 18.

5. Therapeutic jurisprudence may generally be defined as a normative legal theory regarding the potential for law to contribute to therapeutic outcomes. Many of the scholars and practitioners associated with this school of thought support efforts to expand the healing capacity of judicial processes (for offenders, victims, communities and others), in addition to achieving appropriate legal outcomes.

6. See Shirley Abrahamson, "The Appeal of Therapeutic Jurisprudence," *Seattle Law Review* 24 (2000): 228; Steve Leben, "Thoughts on Some Potential Appellate and Trial Court Applications of Therapeutic Jurisprudence," *Seattle Law Review* 24 (2000): 467; David B. Wexler, "Just Some Juvenile Thinking about Delinquent Behavior: A Therapeutic Jurisprudence Approach to Relapse Prevention Planning and Youth Advisory Juries," *University of Missouri-Kansas City Law Review* 69 (2000):

93; David B. Wexler, "Therapeutic Jurisprudence and the Criminal Courts," *William and Mary Law Review* 35 (1993): 279.

7. E.g., Greg Berman, *The Hardest Sell?: Problem-Solving Justice and the Challenges of Statewide Implementation* (New York: Center for Court Innovation, 2004); Aubrey Fox and Robert Wolf, *The Future of Drug Courts: How States are Mainstreaming the Model* (New York: Center for Court Innovation, 2004); Aubrey Fox and Greg Berman, "Going To Scale: A Conversation About the Future of Drug Courts," *Court Review* 39 (2002): 4; John Feinblatt, Greg Berman and Aubrey Fox, "Institutionalizing Innovation: The New York Drug Court Story," *Fordham Urban Law Journal* 28 (2000): 277; Susan Tashiro, Victoria Cashman, and Barry Mahoney, with Ed Brekke, Caroline Cooper, Mary Durkin and Mack Jenkins, *Institutionalizing Drug Courts: A Focus Group Meeting Report* (Washington, D.C.: Justice Management Institute Report submitted to the US Department of Justice, Office of Justice Programs, 2002).

8. For a discussion in the therapeutic jurisprudence context, see David B. Rottman, "Does Effective Therapeutic Jurisprudence Require Specialized Courts (and Do Specialized Courts Imply Specialist Judges)?," *Court Review* 37 (2000): 22.

9. Pamela Casey and David B. Rottman, "Problem Solving Courts: Models, Commonalities, and Trends. The View from the United States," presented at Problem Solving Courts: An International Perspective, Psychology and Law International, Interdisciplinary Conference, Pre-Conference Workshop, Edinburgh, Scotland, July 8, 2003.

10. This part of the focus group protocol was designed primarily as a warm-up period. The findings are not presented here but are included in the complete project report.

11. Sanctions and rewards, although often identified as a unique and critical element of most problem-solving court models, did not emerge as a prominent topic in the focus groups.

12. In November 2000, California voters passed Proposition 36, the Substance Abuse and Crime Prevention Act (SACPA), an act mandating treatment in lieu of incarceration for non-violent drug offenders. As a result of the act, many counties established specialized drug court-like calendars. These specialized courts serve to centralize and streamline the processing of eligible cases and to monitor defendants agreeing to enter treatment. Each of California's 58 counties has its own specific list of eligible charges, case processing methods, and programmatic features. See Douglas Longshore, Elizabeth Evans, Darren Urada, Cheryl Teruya, Mary Hardy, Yin-Ing Hser, Michael Prendergast and Susan Ettner, *Evaluation of the Substance Abuse and Crime Prevention Act of 2002 Report: Implementation: July 1, 2001 to June 30, 2002* (UCLA: Report prepared for the Department of Alcohol and Drug Programs California Health and Human Services Agency, 2003).

13. For a similar discussion, see Bamberger, "Specialized Courts: Not a Cure-All," 1091.

14. For a discussion of judicial role orientation as it relates to problem solving, see Roger Hanson, "The Changing Role of a Judge and its Implications," *Court Review* 38 (2002): 10.

15. See Deborah Chase and Peggy Fulton Hora, "The Implications of Therapeutic Jurisprudence for Judicial Satisfaction," *Court Review* 37 (2002): 12.

16. See Stephanie Domitrovich, "Utilizing an Effective Economic Approach to Family Court: A Proposal for a Statutory Unified Family Court in Pennsylvania," *Duquesne Law Review* 37 (1998): 1; Jeffrey Stempel, "Two Cheers for Specialization," *Brooklyn Law Review* 61 (1995): 67; Rottman, "Does Effective Therapeutic Jurisprudence Require Specialized Courts?," 22.

17. See Bamberger, "Specialized Courts: Not a Cure-All," 1091; Tashiro et al., *Institutionalizing Drug Courts.*

18. See Casey and Rottman, "Problem Solving Courts: The View

from the United States"; Fox and Berman, *Going To Scale*, 4; Chase and Hora, "The Implications of Therapeutic Jurisprudence," 12.

19. Feinblatt, Berman and Fox, "Institutionalizing Innovation," 277.

Center for Court Innovation

The winner of an Innovations in American Government Award from the Ford Foundation and Harvard's John F. Kennedy School of Government, the Center for Court Innovation is a unique public-private partnership that promotes new thinking about how courts and criminal justice agencies can aid victims, change the behavior of offenders and strengthen communities.

In New York, the Center functions as the state court system's independent research and development arm, creating demonstration projects that test new approaches to problems that have resisted conventional solutions. The Center's problem-solving courts include the Red Hook Community Justice Center as well as drug courts, domestic violence courts, and mental health courts.

Nationally, the Center disseminates the lessons learned from its experiments in New York, helping practitioners across the country (and the world) launch their own problem-solving innovations. The Center contributes to the national conversation about justice through a variety of written products, including original research. The Center also provides hands-on technical assistance, criminal justice planners throughout the country. Current areas of interest include community justice, court technology, problem-solving principles and methods, drug courts, domestic violence courts, mental health courts, and research/evaluation.